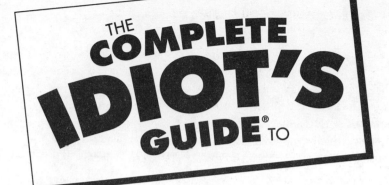

THE **COMPLETE IDIOT'S GUIDE** TO

Making Money with Rental Properties

Second Edition

by *Brian F. Edwards, Casey Edwards, and Susannah Craig-Edwards*

ALPHA

A member of Penguin Group (USA) Inc.

This book is dedicated to hard-working landlords everywhere.

ALPHA BOOKS

Published by the Penguin Group

Penguin Group (USA) Inc., 375 Hudson Street, New York, New York 10014, U.S.A.

Penguin Group (Canada), 10 Alcorn Avenue, Toronto, Ontario, Canada M4V 3B2 (a division of Pearson Penguin Canada Inc.)

Penguin Books Ltd, 80 Strand, London WC2R 0RL, England

Penguin Ireland, 25 St Stephen's Green, Dublin 2, Ireland (a division of Penguin Books Ltd)

Penguin Group (Australia), 250 Camberwell Road, Camberwell, Victoria 3124, Australia (a division of Pearson Australia Group Pty Ltd)

Penguin Books India Pvt Ltd, 11 Community Centre, Panchsheel Park, New Delhi - 110 017, India

Penguin Group (NZ), Cnr Airborne and Rosedale Roads, Albany, Auckland, New Zealand (a division of Pearson New Zealand Ltd)

Penguin Books (South Africa) (Pty) Ltd, 24 Sturdee Avenue, Rosebank, Johannesburg 2196, South Africa

Penguin Books Ltd, Registered Offices: 80 Strand, London WC2R 0RL, England

Publisher: *Marie Butler-Knight*
Product Manager: *Phil Kitchel*
Senior Managing Editor: *Jennifer Chisholm*
Acquisitions Editor: *Paul Dinas*
Development Editor: *Ginny Bess Munroe*
Production Editor: *Megan Douglass*

Copy Editor: *Jan Zoya*
Illustrator: *Shannon Wheeler*
Cover/Book Designer: *Trina Wurst*
Indexer: *Tonya Heard*
Layout: *Ayanna Lacey*
Proofreading: *John Etchison*

Contents at a Glance

Contents

Foreword

The number-one question most frequently asked on the popular landlording website, MrLandlord.com, by new and aspiring real-estate investors is, "What do I need to know to be successful?"

Look no further for your answer! Brian and Casey Edwards have provided within the following pages a clear road map for landlords new and old of all aspects of property management you'll need to build wealth with rental properties. These authors represent over 40 years of investing and management experience and their "real-world" advice is packed in the new edition of their best-selling book, *The Complete Guide to Making Money with Rental Properties, Second Edition.*

Twenty plus years ago, I too was asking the same question. My wife Dot and I had no previous real-estate investing experience and when we started we actually became landlords by "accident." Our first home came with a mortgage payment that was more than our newlywed budget could afford. Thanks to a tip from a friend, we discovered and purchased a second home (fixer-upper), with a smaller, more affordable mortgage payment. Deciding to hold on to our first house, we rented it out and our tenants, to our surprise, called us "landlords."

After we saw that we were able to buy a second home, a light bulb went on in my head and we earnestly sought out low-cost seminars and credible (but hard-to-find) books on real-estate investing and management that opened our eyes further to the possibility of building monthly cash flow and net worth with rental property. In the early '80s, we began buying single-family to small multifamily buildings. After renting out our first house to a couple who turned out to be great tenants, the next 50 rental units we purchased after that brought many challenges that we were totally unprepared for.

Along with our success, I have even been fortunate enough to develop the most widely visited website by rental owners, MrLandlord.com, written *The Landlord's Kit*, and I now am invited to speak throughout the world coaching other landlords on how to be successful.

As you devour the many nuggets of wealth in this book, you will see that owning real estate requires the kind of learning you did not get in school and a mindset that can only be imparted by other successful rental owners. You can't learn what you need to know about landlording from your co-worker at the job, or your relative who merely watches late-night television and thinks he is the family real-estate expert.

Despite our initial naïveté, my wife and I have been successful with rental property over the past 20 plus years. This is due in large part because of our determination to seek out the best resources of information available, as is the case with this book. Brian and Casey Edwards offer real-world advice. They do not give "get-rich-quick" mumbo jumbo. Instead they share from decades of professional hands-on experience and reveal what it takes to stay in control of your real-estate business from moving in rental residents to move-out, which is what you need to know if you are going to "last" in this business and move toward financial independence.

After learning that my friends Casey and Brian Edwards were updating their book, I was excited to review the manuscript. The latest edition is even more comprehensive than the first, and I was anxious to start offering this latest edition through the MrLandlord.com website. I even invited the authors to speak at my MrLandlord.com National Convention attended annually by hundreds of rental owners seeking instructions from the top landlording experts in the field. Casey and Brian are definitely in that category and whether you are a new or seasoned landlord, their book should definitely be in your library if you want to make money with rental property.

Jeffrey Taylor

Author of *The Landlord's Kit* and founder of MrLandlord.com

Introduction

Many people who consider owning rental investment property think that any idiot can make money with rental property. After all, what does a landlord really do but wait around for the rent money to come pouring in? These same people have no idea what a Profit and Loss statement is or the difference between a lease and a month-to-month rental agreement. They have no idea how to begin to analyze investment property returns, collect rents, or handle emergency calls in the middle of the night. And the first time the rental unit is destroyed or they lose an eviction case in court, costing them scads of money while preventing them from making any money with the property, they will probably come to the realization that perhaps *they* were the idiots.

The truth is that rental property can and will make you money. Rental-property ownership is a much more specialized real-estate profession than perhaps it was years ago. Today's rental-property investor is also a landlord who needs to understand basic investment concepts, recognize characteristics of good and bad investment property, and to be aware of property rights for both tenants and landlords as well as building, housing, and many other types of codes, in order to help ensure that the investment is a successful moneymaker.

This book, the second edition of *The Complete Idiot's Guide to Making Money with Rental Properties*, attempts to guide both new and seasoned rental-property investors through the experience of rental ownership. We attempt to shed some light on many common rental theories and concepts that affect property owners. We also define the most common terms used by landlords and property managers in regards to their profession. This book acts as a reference guide and a handbook of sorts that we hope can help you achieve successful returns on your rental-investment property. It is important to understand that laws and regulations regarding rental ownership are subject to change. It is beyond the scope of this book to list every state and local law that might apply. Always check your state and local laws before making decisions. This book represents the opinions of the authors and, even though the information herein has been carefully researched, it is not designed to give legal advice. The smart investor should always seek legal or other professional advice in regard to the ownership and operation of rental property.

Think investment property is for you? Well, if you're interested in finding a place to make money, real estate is a good, logical place to start looking. There are a few ways to achieve that goal with rental property, rental income, and reselling a property once its value has appreciated. There are several factors that will affect how much money you will make with a property regardless of your ownership intention. This book describes many of theses issues in depth, and will educate and hopefully lend you the confidence needed to invest in rental property and manage it effectively. This book mainly focuses on real-estate management, and income earned from rents, but also discusses how to analyze real-estate purchases and values in an area. As you build good management techniques, and learn to recognize the different aspects of property values, you will hopefully then increase your own net worth by applying what you've learned. *The Complete Idiot's Guide to Making Money with Rental Properties, Second Edition*, strives to help rental owners or investors make money with their real-estate investments. The secret to any successful investment is knowing when to buy and knowing when to sell. With real estate, good management can also determine success. It's our opinion that it's always the right time to buy investment property, but only you can tell when will be the right time to sell. We wish you the best of success with your rental property!

How This Book Is Organized

There are five parts in this book; each part focuses on a particular element of the rental industry.

Part 1, "So You Want to Be a Landlord," lists several different types of ownership concepts that investors must consider before acquiring property. This part also gives you a brief lesson about real estate and takes you on a ride to look at investment property.

Part 2, "Welcome to Landlording!" stresses the importance of treating the operation of investment property as a business. Here you will find valuable tips that can help you advertise and prepare rental units and screen and select tenants. This part also reviews rent control and discrimination regulations and law.

Part 3, "The Money Accounts," covers basic accounting techniques that help keep track of income while satisfying property expenses. This part also looks at rent collection techniques as well as methods for handling security deposits.

Part 4, "The Tenant-Landlord Relationship," covers techniques for handling disputes between a landlord, tenants, and authorities. Here we also review certain legal rights as they pertain to rental owners and tenants.

Part 5, "Protecting Your Investment," covers certain techniques that might help preserve and maximize your investment such as hiring property managers, maintaining the property, and joining a property owners' association.

A Little Something Else!

Don't forget to check out the appendixes, which contain rental management forms, state statute information, important contact information, and a list of some available management software, all of which you might find useful.

In addition to the numerous explanations and techniques offered in this book, several tips, tools, and facts are provided for the reader's enjoyment as well as some bits of information that a landlord might find useful. These tips are presented in the following sidebars:

Facts for Rent

This box contains facts and odd information about the rental industry meant to pique the reader's interest.

Landlord Lingo

Here we explain terminology commonly used in the rental industry.

Rental Red Light!

Here you'll find information of which rental owners should be aware.

Landlord's Toolbox

Here you'll find useful tools to help you with your landlording chores.

Edwards' Advice

These are tips and information that a landlord might find useful.

Acknowledgments

Without the patience, support, and knowledge of Happy Edwards, this book would not have been possible. Thanks, Mom! You're the greatest! Special thanks to John Edwards for providing us with cartoons. We also would like to thank Paul Dinas for his insight and motivation to release a new edition on this subject matter. Also we thank landlord organizations everywhere for the wealth of information they continue to provide to landlords. Special thanks to Karen Pio, Ken Purcaro, Tom Lawler, and Phyllis Miller for their continued efforts to protect landlord interest in Connecticut. And a special thanks to all of our clients or customers, a.k.a tenants, whom we have rented to over the many years that we have been in this business. Without them the knowledge we gained would not have been available to share. Thank you all!

Trademarks

All terms mentioned in this book that are known to be or are suspected of being trademarks or service marks have been appropriately capitalized. Alpha Books and Penguin Group (USA) Inc. cannot attest to the accuracy of this information. Use of a term in this book should not be regarded as affecting the validity of any trademark or service mark.

Part 1

So You Want to Be a Landlord

Do you want to be the next Trump or Helmsley? Does owning rental property seem like a profitable idea to you? Then it's time to diversify your investment portfolio and make some money from rental real estate. Maybe you already have dabbled in the stock market and/or started your own business, hoping to somehow make more money. Investing in real estate is the next logical step in becoming a true investor. After all, all the big shots own real estate!

Before you make any purchases, however, there are a few things you need to learn about real estate and landlording. You need to understand the different methods of owning and operating the property. You also need to be able to properly evaluate an investment property. Only then will you be a smart landlord who is making money with rental property!

What Is a Landlord?

In This Chapter

- A brief history of the landlord
- The pluses and minuses of owning rental property
- Owner-occupant and absentee landlords
- Owners versus property managers

According to the *American Heritage Dictionary*, a landlord is a "person who owns and rents land, buildings, or dwelling units." In short, a landlord is the owner of rented property. This means that unless you have people actually renting your property, you are not a landlord; you are simply a property owner. Sound strange? Think about it. A landlord is the person recognized by an occupant of a property as the owner of the property. Hence, no occupant means no landlord.

Being a landlord means many things, and the perception of a landlord as the one who gets the rent every month has created a negative stigma. But don't let that scare you from entering the world of rental-property investment. Rental property can be very profitable as an investment, and a certain satisfaction can be associated with supplying one of humankind's basic needs, housing.

A Brief History of the Landlord

Since the beginning of humankind, food, clothing, and shelter have been the primary needs for survival. The earliest landlord was probably a caveman who found a nice three-family cave with a view of a volcano. The first eviction probably had something to do with a club and a lot of hair pulling. Many of us would still agree with that today.

Landlord Lingo

Landlord, landlady, or landperson? The politically correct term should be, of course, **landperson.** The term landlady came into existence at the beginning of the nineteenth century when women were not a big part of the daily workforce. Many times, when a married couple lived in and owned rental property, the woman took care of the day-to-day activities at the property while her husband was at his job. The reputation of the landlady was usually one to be reckoned with because the "landlady" was no one to fool with.

The most recognized origins of the landlord-and-tenant relationship can be traced back to some political and military systems that became popular during the tenth and eleventh centuries, *seignorialism* and *feudalism.*

Being a *landlord* today is much different than it used to be. The power associated with being a landlord and controlling property and tenants is still perceived as inherited, even though in reality that is not true. A landlord today needs to be able to wear many different hats. Rental property is a business and needs to be treated as such. A landlord must be a businessperson and an investor who is skilled at locating property of value at a reasonable price; negotiating with lenders, tenants, contractors, and authorities; and working with contracts, office policies, tax issues, laws and legal issues, accounting techniques, construction, and maintenance. To be successful, a landlord must truly be a jack of many trades.

Rental Property: The Popular Investment Choice

When considering dabbling in financial markets, investors search out areas where rewarding returns seem evident before investing large sums of money. Obviously, the motive is to acquire wealth and expand financial growth. The questions investors must ask themselves are where, when, and how much to invest. Over the years, two prominent places that have always been favored by successful investors are the stock market and real estate.

Most investment guides instruct readers to diversify investments, the "don't get caught with all your eggs in one basket" concept, and we adamantly agree. Good investment strategy that includes diversification is a solid approach to investing money. However, one investment principal that is often not stressed enough is the fact that markets have the quirky characteristic of being cyclical in nature with periods of growth and decay. An investment that suffers a decline in value over a period of time may realize a much stronger period of growth later on. Of course there is no crystal ball to predict an investment's outcome, but careful research, hard work, patience, and a little luck can potentially produce a calculated risk that delivers profitable returns.

In the 1990s, the United States experienced a well-documented surge of growth in the stock and related markets. With the popularity of online trading, Wall Street witnessed a surge of new investors attempting to cash in on various stocks. In the same time, the real-estate market in many areas of the country witnessed a recession. Many investors were caught off guard by the sudden change in diminished property values and tried to sell, or, in many cases, were either foreclosed on or walked away from properties they owned.

Because the '80s brought an ultrasonic surge in real-estate prices, many investors got caught between the price they paid for their property and the new value created by the recession. Loss of jobs, a drop in the rental market, and the reduction of monthly rent, along with the reluctance of first-time renters to leave the nest or people doubling up in rental units, created a reduction of revenue. All of these factors created high monthly payments that forced many people into foreclosure.

The lenders were not able to resell the foreclosed properties to regain their losses so they discounted the loans and cut their losses by selling the properties at great discounts. The discounts were passed on to people who had loans, and this discounted amount was a gain on their 1040, creating more hardship to the originator of the note.

Once again the table has turned and, with the absence of a bullish stock market in recent years, investors have noticed the values of real estate increasing and are investing money in all types of rental property. Although real estate is not as liquid as stocks, meaning that it's not as simple to sell, the returns and property value appreciation in many cases are quite impressive. This, combined with increasing rents and interesting tax benefits, again make the real-estate market an attractive place for investors both savvy and novice to invest money.

What's the Plan?

Smart investors should devise a plan or set goals regarding what they hope to accomplish by investing. The usual goal is to make money. So the next obvious question is how. When you invest in rental property, there are a few potential ways in which to do so. The money could come from the rents that are charged or from the profit realized when the property is resold. In respect to these options, consideration should be given to how long you intend to own the property. Is this investment based purely on speculation? Or is a tax shelter all you hope to accomplish by owning the property?

Whatever your reason, a smart investor will consider each of the previous points carefully because, unlike the liquid nature of stocks, the investment may be difficult to unload unless your property's location is in high demand. Careful plan management coupled with wealth management will help you to make educated decisions, not impulse decisions regarding your investment. Typically, real estate will appreciate in value over time and rent income can prove to be quite impressive. A properly managed rental investment property truly can make you money while you sleep, if you let it!

The Pluses and Minuses of Owning Rental Property

Owning rental property can be a profitable and interesting investment opportunity. Housing is still one of humankind's essential needs for survival and is therefore an excellent investment. It's kind of an investment in life.

In urban centers during the Industrial Revolution of the nineteenth century, the need for housing grew significantly in the United States. People were moving into cities like never before, attracted to the prospect of finding work. Many buildings were built to accommodate the need for shelter and privacy. Although investors purchased many, a great deal more were purchased for the owners to also live in. The idea of many people who purchased rental property was to put all of the profit made back into the building during the years that were work-productive for the owners. This way, the owners could fall back on a property that was free of a mortgage and could enjoy their golden years. It was a good plan and it worked.

Today, many people buy investment property with the hope of someday reselling and making a profit on the return of sale. People also buy investment property to live in themselves, using the income either to live off of or to help pay for the house itself. Some people look at investment property as a career choice to provide a base income and support for their family. Others, unfortunately, seem to like the sense of power associated with owning rental property while taking advantage of all the other reasons mentioned. Owning your own home is still the American Dream but owning one that makes you money is the Sweet American Dream!

Facts for Rent

According to the United States Census Bureau in a report called the Property Owners and Managers Survey conducted in 1995, the most popular reason for acquiring rental property was income from rents. The second-most-popular reason for acquiring rental property varied by size of property ownership. For small-property owners, fewer than five units, use as a residence either when it was purchased or presently was just as common a reason as acquiring property for rental income. For medium- to large-property owners, the second-most-common reason was for long-term gain of capital.

Facts for Rent

According to the Property Owners and Managers Survey conducted in 1995 through the U.S. Census, the yearly median cost of operating multifamily rental property is $2,300 per unit for small properties and $3,300 per unit for large properties. According to this survey, the median percentage of rental income spent on maintenance ranged from a low of 13 percent for small properties to 17 percent for medium and large properties.

Advantages of Owning Other People's Homes

Money, money, money is the first thing people think of when they consider owning rental property. Most people can't believe that the owner of a rental property is doing anything but making money. It is reasonable to understand why people would feel this way. Put yourself in the shoes of a tenant for a minute. This person lives in a house that you own; it is his or her home but you still own it, and that takes money. The tenants never see real-estate tax bills or, in many cases, water and sewer bills. They probably will never pay for repairs to the building; therefore, they never know what these things actually cost and that it takes money. The tenant will probably never pay for management services such as secretarial work, advertising, or legal council in regards to the property—and that takes money.

Income generated from rent can be quite considerable if a property is bought and managed correctly. The object, of course, is to keep expenses down while servicing the tenants, keeping the apartments rented, and maintaining the building so that rent received is maximized. Sounds easy, huh? Well, if you're reading this book, you're probably not convinced. There are other reasons for owning rental property; for instance, you may want to attempt to increase your net worth or take advantage of certain tax incentives. There is a sense of achievement in the world associated with property ownership, but remember to keep that ego in check. Many people obviously cannot afford their own homes (most tenants, for example), and many may resent the fact that you own their home.

> **CAUTION**
>
> ### Rental Red Light! _____
>
> This may be the only job in the world that you can't just quit. The responsibility and liability associated with the property are yours for as long as you own it. So if someday you get up in the morning and decide rental ownership is not for you, the reality is that you're still responsible until you either sell or transfer the title to someone else or file for bankruptcy and lose the investment.

Disadvantages of Owning Other People's Homes

Work, work, work is the first thing anyone who either owns or owned a home, single or multi, will think of right after the money. Without question, property ownership is labor intensive unless it is a piece of raw land and no one cares whether the grass is cut. But in any situation in which you own a property where someone else lives or will live, you can bet on spending some time and effort maintaining and improving the property. The more apartment units you own or are responsible for, the more work you can count on. The more units you own or manage, the more responsibility and liability you have to make sure the rental units and property are safe for residents and visitors. Work, work, work!

What Kind of Landlord Will You Be?

There are a couple different types of landlords in this world. The two most notable names for describing rental owners are *owner occupant* and *absentee*. As you will see, the differences are quite evident in how the property is operated and in what the overall perception is from the community. Owner occupant means that the owner of the property not only owns the property but also lives there. An absentee landlord is one who owns the property for investment purposes only, who does not live there, and whose presence is considered absent from the property daily. Both types of rental owners suffer many of the same challenges and reap the same rewards. Why you want to own rental property will determine which you become.

The Owner-Occupant: Open 24 Hours

When the owner resides at the property, the property's condition usually benefits and appears to be better. A responsible property owner always picks up garbage or debris from the property when he or she sees it, but an owner who lives at the property will probably clean the property much more quickly and more routinely than one who does not live there. "In sight, in mind" is the basic concept here.

In the owner-occupant scenario, the land-person has constant knowledge of the day-to-day happenings at the property. If a tenant or someone at the property is creating a disturbance, the owner is more available to handle the problem than an absentee landlord would be. There is a huge benefit perceived by the community when an owner resides at the property. The chance for better property care combined with an ownership presence in the neighborhood helps to ensure stability for residents in the surrounding area.

Edwards' Advice

To prevent late-night emergency house calls, set up house rules in advance. (See Chapter 8 for tips on how and what to set up as rules.) Letting tenants know in advance when they can and cannot disturb you will help prevent future disputes.

Facts for Rent

In 1997, Harvard University issued a report titled "The State of the Nation's Housing," which stated that approximately one third of the 67 million property owners reside in multifamily structures.

The flip side to living with your tenants is that, as the landlord, you are always available. Or at least that's how the tenants will perceive your time. Let's say it's 11:30 P.M., and Tenant B upstairs notices in her apartment an uninvited creature, which she promptly removes. Tenant B suspects that the creature has friends and that this might be a job for you. Tenant B could wait until the next day to alert you, her landlord, to the possible rodent problem, but why wait when the landlord is only steps away?

As an owner-occupant landlord, be aware that you are on call 24 hours a day. To the tenant, it's more a matter of convenience than an intention to invade your privacy. Make tenants aware that landlords have a life after work hours, too!

Absentee but Not Forgotten

The absentee owner is a much more difficult scenario than the owner occupant. The absentee owner most likely will not be at the property as much as an owner who lives

Facts for Rent

Any person who sells or leases property for someone else must not only be licensed as a real-estate sales agent but also affiliated with a licensed real-estate broker. In other words, it is not enough to simply hold a sales license; an agent must also work for a broker.

there, and the daily maintenance of the property will suffer. The absentee owner is not as easily accessible to handle on-premises disturbances, which will annoy tenants and neighbors. Unless the absentee owner operates a management company, a management company may have to be hired to manage the daily activities of the property and to service the tenants. Unfortunately, the absentee owner has been the brunt of much criticism from many community organizations as the source of community problems when, in fact, society should be blamed as a whole.

Owner-Occupant vs. Absentee: Your Choice

It may sound like the owner-occupant situation is the best. As previously mentioned, however, under those circumstances, the owner is working and on call 24 hours a day. The owner-occupant is very accessible to the tenants, which can be good unless the tenants misuse this privilege. It also is extremely difficult to treat rental property as a business when it is also your home. The personal relationship that exists between the tenant and you when you share a home can be very stressful for you to live with if the rent is late or the tenant violates your rules. Living with that kind of discomfort every day is not for everyone. As an absentee landlord, the pressure of keeping home separate from work doesn't exist.

The owner-occupant trend has been very popular in the United States. Years ago, most rental property was owner-occupant by necessity of the owner. Today, however, the federal government has instituted programs that boost owner-occupant ownership of rental property. These programs usually instruct and offer assistance to new owners regarding how to manage and operate rental property. These programs are expected to help stabilize the decline of troubled neighborhoods.

Owners vs. Property Managers

Sometimes a rental owner will hire a property management company to manage the daily activities of the property. A management company is a specialized professional real-estate service that, for a fee, can do the following:

- Rent or lease apartments
- Negotiate major and minor repairs
- Collect and disburse monies

- ◆ Service tenants

- ◆ Keep accounting records

- ◆ Evict tenants

Basically, a property management company can do just about everything discussed in this book. It has been said that an owner who manages his or her own property has a fool for a client. It might be a good idea to use this type of service if you do not possess the skills or tools associated with operating rental property. If you work another job that does not leave you the time and energy to invest in the property, or if the property is at a distant location and you find it hard to manage from that distance, you may want to hire a management company. If you needed the services of a lawyer or doctor, you would hire one, and the same regard should be given to this type of service. The real-estate industry has many facets of expertise. Some companies deal with selling property, some develop, and some manage property.

Landlord Lingo

Superintendent does not mean property manager. A superintendent is someone you hire to work for you, either as an employee or as an independent contractor, to do minor repair in and around the property. A superintendent does not need to be licensed as long as he or she stays within the scope of minor repair. A superintendent should not be handling any money, renting apartments, or signing leases associated with your property. We will discuss the activities of the superintendent more in Chapter 19.

There is no special license requirement for buying and owning rental property, but there is a license requirement if you plan to manage property for anyone but yourself. Anyone who negotiates, charges, collects, and disburses the monies of others needs a license to do so. Therefore, before you hire a particular company for management services, make sure the company is licensed in accordance with the laws of the state in which the property is located. The license is generally called a real-estate brokers license to operate this kind of service. A broker is the licensee or holder of the state license. He or she might have employees called salespeople or leasing agents either selling or renting property, and these people also have to be licensed in accordance with state laws.

The fee for property management is generally based on a percentage of income plus expenses. Some property managers have a repairperson on staff to correct minor problems at the property and can pass this savings on to you.

You should try to hire the best you can. Ask around and network with local landlords to find out who has the best reputation and best fits your needs. The management company should be familiar with properties like yours and should have the manpower to oversee its daily operation. This company must be easily reached both by you and your tenants in the event of an emergency. The company should be familiar with laws that govern your property to help protect you from liability. Remember, however, that it is your property, and you will still be the bottom line if something goes wrong, not the property manager. The property manager will probably not enter your property every day, but if it is managed correctly, he or she may not have to.

Landlord Lingo

Whether you like it or not, most angry tenants, neighbors, and public officials have referred to landlords as **slumlords.** Don't be offended; to be a slumlord, you need a slum tenant. The truth is that the number of responsible landlords well outnumbers the irresponsible ones. A true slumlord is a person who buys a property, drains it of all potential rent, and then abandons it intentionally. After many years in this business, we have found this person to be almost nonexistent.

Ownership Theories

There are some differences of opinion about why and how to operate investment property. We touched on some of them earlier in this chapter, but it's worth repeating and defining them again. The practice of these theories will affect not only your investment but also the surrounding neighborhoods of your rental property.

One theory of operating rental property is to buy a property, rent it, and earn profits without ever putting any of the returns back into the property. This theory is called *short-term gain*, and it means to reap immediate rewards from profit from the property. This method used to be most common for small investors who were neither very handy around the property nor very good investors. The old idea was that you could purchase a rental building and never go there except to collect rents. Although the owner may have actually made quite a bit of money with the short-term method, often the effects were negative. Eventually the building will suffer from disrepair, property value will plummet, and the neighborhood will suffer.

The theory of long-term ownership is better for the owner, the tenants, and the surrounding area of the property. Money made from profits is still the bottom line, but instead of simply draining all the profits from the property, some of the rental profit, through the use of good escrow techniques, is used to constantly make capital improvements to the property. This, in effect, helps maintain the property, increases its value, and benefits the surrounding neighborhood.

Rookie Landlords

This book is obviously designed for the investor who is new to rental-property management, so we feel it is relevant to point out a few common concepts that new landlords tend to ignore when they first begin. We hope that by pointing these out you will consider each as you read through the rest of the book and during your daily management activities at the property, as they will assist you and your profit potential.

◆ Treat your rental property as a business and make decisions accordingly. Never let your actions get personal!

◆ Respect your tenants as customers and clients; you cannot survive in this business without them!

◆ Safety comes first with all maintenance aspects at your property. If you don't know how to fix something, hire someone who does!

◆ When you know everything you know nothing at all. Keep an open mind because education will be a key to your success.

If you can get a firm grasp on these concepts and keep them in your back pocket, you'll do well with your rental property and keep your sanity as well.

The Least You Need to Know

◆ There are advantages to owning rental property besides income from rents.

◆ Many responsibilities and liabilities are associated with rental ownership.

◆ An owner-occupant rental owner lives at the property that he or she rents, while an absentee owner of rental property does not live at the property he or she rents.

◆ Management companies supply the service of operating the rental property for a fee.

◆ Long-term ownership is a much healthier way of conducting a rental business than the short-term theory.

◆ Rookie landlords have a greater chance of success later on if they run their rental property as a professional business from the start.

Chapter 2

Real Estate 101

In This Chapter

- ◆ Learning the physical and economic characteristics of real-estate property
- ◆ Knowing the classifications of rental property and the property rights inherited with a property
- ◆ Preparing for liability while hoping it remains a sleeping giant
- ◆ Determining whether you want to own it alone or invest with a partner or as a corporation

It is time for you to learn a little something about real estate. If you were planning to open a bakery, you would want to learn something about baking, and before you go out and purchase a car, you must learn how to drive. So why not learn a little something about the real-estate business before making a sizable purchase like investment property?

There are different types of property and property ownership you should know about before becoming a landlord. Understanding these differences can help you in the long run. Don't worry, this chapter won't be graded. The grade will be determined by whether you can successfully operate investment property. And you've got the rest of your life to study for that.

The Many Characteristics of Real Estate

Real estate is made up of both physical and economic characteristics. As a landlord, you should be aware of these characteristics because understanding them will help you determine how the real-estate market in a specific area will perform. This information is important to you not only while investigating property for purchase but also for the life of your ownership. Understanding the local real-estate market will help you determine whether a property is rentable and at what price, as well as whether a property is saleable and at what price. This is all good stuff to know.

Let's Get Physical

Here are the main physical characteristics that determine real-estate property value:

◆ **Immobility.** Everything on top of land can be moved by actions of nature and people, but the geographic location of land will never change.

◆ **Lack of standardization.** No two pieces of land are exactly the same. Location, location, and location are the three big Ls of real estate and possibly its biggest characteristic. Even two pieces of land right next to each other will be different because of their locations. The lack of standardization is what affects value of real estate. Zoning restrictions and other encumbrances also add to the differences of real estate and affect the value of property.

◆ **Long life.** Land can have a life span of hundreds of years before a change is made in property lines or ownership.

◆ **Indestructibility.** Land is known to be durable and a relatively stable investment. Don't misunderstand: Value can be destroyed, but the land will still remain.

The Eco-Dynamics

When looking for real-estate property, take note of these economic distinctions:

◆ **Scarcity.** Land in very desirable areas will become scarce or very valuable. There is, of course, plenty of land available that can be purchased for low prices, but land in specific areas and for specific uses often is insufficient and does not meet demand.

◆ **Fixed investment.** Most improvements such as buildings cannot be easily moved, and it may take 20 or 30 years to repay the investment, so the investment is known to be long lasting. As an investor, you should try to determine how long a property's usefulness will last before purchasing or improving it.

♦ **Location.** Just as location plays a physical role, it also affects the economic aspects of land. Desirability, climate, and population shifts can increase the value of land in one location, while the value of similar land in other areas may decline.

♦ **Improvements.** Land has the capability to be modified or improved. Buildings, fences, and other things added to the land will directly impact its value.

Edwards' Advice

Recently, first-time investors Bob and Shirley (not their real names) found a great four-family home. The house was sound and in a nice area; the units needed little work and were fully rented. Anxious to invest, Bob and Shirley made up their minds right away and signed on the dotted line. Sound too good to be true? It was. In their haste to buy the property of their dreams, Bob and Shirley overlooked the location of the property. As we said, the house was in a nice area. So what's the problem? If Bob and Shirley had researched the area, they would have found out that the state had just voted to construct a new highway 63 feet in front of their property line! Learn from Bob and Shirley: location, location, location!

Most Common Types of Real Estate

There are different classifications for improved property: residential, commercial, industrial, farm, recreational, and government. *Improved property* simply means land that contains structures. Even though you may only be concerned with owning property that would meet one or two of these improved property classifications, you still should know what the other classifications represent:

♦ **Residential.** Residential property includes any type of structure designed for personal living. A wide range of properties are included in the residential categorization of property. In addition to single-family homes, there are apartments, town houses, row houses, condominiums, cooperatives, and mobile homes.

♦ **Commercial.** Commercial property represents any property designed for retail or wholesale services, financial services, office space, and shopping centers. Buildings with storefronts and apartment units are also considered commercial. Usually this type of property is acquired for investment purposes only.

Facts for Rent

Harvard University's 1997 report, "The State of the Nation's Housing," reported that the current housing inventory comprises 115 million units. Excluding land, the combined value of these residential structures makes up 35 percent of the nation's total tangible assets of $22.6 trillion. When land is included, the national housing stock is conservatively valued at nearly $10 trillion.

◆ **Industrial.** Industrial property is improved land intended to be used for manufacturing and warehousing of industrial and consumer products. Factories, warehouses, and utility companies are just some examples of industrial property.

◆ **Farm.** Farm property, sometimes referred to as rural property, is usually used for agricultural purposes. Farmland, ranches, orchards, and pastures all fall under this classification.

◆ **Recreation.** Recreational property is improved land used for leisure activities and vacations. Mountain- or ocean-side resorts, golf courses, and city parks are examples of recreational property. Many times, real-estate developers will set aside land solely to be used for recreational purposes.

◆ **Government.** Government surplus land is property used and owned by the government. Much of this type of land is designated as public areas. The government, through its many agencies, owns approximately one third of all the land in the United States.

Most Common Types of Rental Property

With the exception of government land currently being used in some governmental capacity, all the other types of property have the potential of being purchased for investment purposes. And sometimes the government has been known to sell land that is no longer needed. Many industrial properties are rented as warehouse space for big industrial companies, just as there are instances in which farms and recreational property have been purchased by investors for rental income.

However, the most common types of real estate that are bought as investment property are residential and commercial properties. These categories of real estate start to take on new definitions when considered as rental real estate. So I hope you're taking notes! The classifications technically remain the same; your local Uncle Sam figured out how to tax property differently based on the sizes and uses of properties.

Residential property is still classified as property designed for living in, but for it to be considered residential for tax purposes, there must be no more than four rental units in a building. So a five-family apartment house is still a residential property, but it is not taxed at a residential rate. Instead, this same five-family building is taxed

at a commercial rate because it is now considered commercial property. Confused? I'll bet you are! And we haven't even begun to talk about zoning and mixed-use areas. Don't worry about that, though; just try to remember that this change in the definition of residential property relates only to tax issues. Residential property is considered one to four units regardless of whether the owner resides at the property.

There are also differences between residential and commercial property when it comes to operating these types of rental properties. You're probably thinking, what's the difference? Property is property, right? The rules, my friend, the rules. There are rules that deal not only with how to use property but also how to manage it. The laundromat is handled much differently than the cottage at the lake. The law treats commercial property and residential property differently. Landlord and tenant responsibilities and liabilities will differ as will eviction procedures and office policies. We will explore these differences later in this book. Remember, though, that landlords don't make the rules; they just try to live by them.

The Bundle of Rights

Any professor who teaches real estate knows about the *bundle of rights*. The bundle of rights refers to the belief that when you purchase real estate, you also purchase certain individual rights that are inherited with the ownership and use of the land and/or property.

If you already own rental property, you might be wondering, "What rights?" It can be, and very often is, debated that property rights are fewer with each passing year. Regardless of personal opinion, the basic definition of real estate includes land, every interest and estate in land, and any permanent improvements on the land.

Real estate combines a physical element as well as the element of ownership. The land and everything permanently affixed to it are the physical portion. The ownership element refers to the nature, extent, amount, and quality of rights that a person or persons can possess in land. The basic concept of ownership is defined as the right to control, possess, enjoy, and dispose of property in a manner allowed by law. Some of the rights that relate to the physical aspects of the property may include mineral rights, air rights, and water rights. Other inherited rights of ownership are the rights to use, occupy, sell, and of course, rent.

Who Owns What?

You think you're ready to take the plunge into the world of owning investment property? Well, before you find yourself up to your neck in shark-infested waters, you need to carefully plan how you will own your investment. You might be thinking, "What do you mean *how?*" There have been many before you who have not considered the extent of the liability associated with rental property, who did not plan accordingly, and who lost not only the investment but also much more.

So you thought you would just buy a rental property the same way you and your spouse bought your personal home. It is important for you as a new investor to recognize the different types of ownership that exist because selecting one or the other may award certain benefits and protection. A landlord today has a lot of liability, and the assets of the landlord need to be protected. Careful planning is necessary before investing in any venture, especially rental property. The same care should be taken before owning rental property as before investing in the stock market or starting a business. As a smart investor, you need to try to structure a plan that will successfully protect your assets from harsh liabilities and expensive taxes.

What's All This Liability Stuff?

Along with the prestige of ownership comes the liability of ownership. Lawsuits are very popular in today's world, and a landlord must take the proper steps to insure and protect his or her investment. Remember that operating rental property is not just an investment but also a business. Accidents happen, and the results can be damaging. The old "slip and fall" or unfortunate discoveries of environmental hazards such as lead paint are just a couple examples of an owner's liability. It's impossible to guarantee that no such hazard will occur or to watch over your property 24 hours a day. It also is not healthy to live in constant fear of these or other possible dangers. Therefore, you should examine and consider the different types of ownership and see if one will allow you to operate your property with peace of mind.

Choosing the Right Type of Ownership

The three main forms of business ownership are sole proprietorship, partnership, and corporation. As you will see in a moment, there are similarities and differences in each. The requirements to start each vary from state to state. You should do your homework about each and should consult with a licensed attorney or financial planner who specializes in this area to determine which form of ownership is right for you. Here are some simplified definitions for ownership and some varieties of each:

- **Sole proprietorship** means that you bought it and you own it all by yourself. Sole proprietorship is the easiest form of business to start because you need only to obtain whatever licenses are required to operate the business. Licenses are not yet a requirement for owning rental property, and sole proprietor ownership is the most common among rental owners. As the sole owner of a business (or property) you will also be solely responsible and personably liable for the business (or property). Therefore, your personal assets will be attackable in the event of a lawsuit. Still, it is easier to own something without having to keep special records and make special filings as you would with other forms of ownership.

- **Partnership** means that you bought it with another person or persons, and each of you owns it. The Uniform Partnership Act defines a partnership as "an association of two or more persons to carry on as co-owners of a business for profit." This does not mean that the partners own equal shares or that the liability is equal (or the profits, for that matter). However, the basic concept is to share the responsibilities of ownership with another.

 Rental Red Light! _____

> If someone finds a reason to sue you and is successful in doing so, the courts might award the individual a settlement greater than the value of the equity you have in the property including the value of your insurance policy. Let's do some math on a rental property example:
>
> Fair market value: $300,000
>
> First mortgage: $200,000
>
> Insurance policy: $100,000
>
> You have a combined amount of money in the property that can be used to pay a judgment of $200,000. If the court awards the plaintiff $250,000, you will be $50,000 short. This most likely will have to come from your personal bank accounts or from the equity you have in something else unless you take the right steps to protect yourself from the very start.

◆ **Corporation** means that you didn't buy it and you don't own it, but a legal entity that you and others own does own it. Starting a corporation may be a complicated undertaking, yet it gives you better protection against liability than other forms of ownership. Incorporation also gives you a better chance of obtaining long-term financing. This is because you are not held responsible for the corporation, and your personal assets, including personal bank accounts, are not attackable if the corporation is sued. Some corporate real estate tycoons sell shares of their company through *Real Estate Investment Trust (REIT)*.

Landlord Lingo

A **Real Estate Investment Trust (REIT)** is another popular form of corporate ownership in investment real estate. REITs enable investors to invest in apartments or other types of investment property indirectly through the purchase of shares of companies that own and manage these properties. There are more that 200 publicly traded REITs for which statistics are available from the National Association of Real Estate Investment Trusts (www.nareit.com). Most of these companies are specialists, and those that deal with apartments either own or manage between 10,000 and 250,000 apartment units each.

The Limited Liability Company (LLC) is a very popular way in which to purchase and own rental property. An LLC is a combination of a corporation and a partnership. There are certain tax and legal advantages that make it a preferred choice of ownership. The LLC typically is taxed as a partnership, which means there is one level of taxation instead of the two that occur with close or "C" corporations. If the funds and operations arc kept separate from personal assets and activities, limited liability can be achieved for its members. Basically, this means that if the LLC gets sued in court and loses, only that property which the LLC owns can be taken to satisfy the debt, preventing other properties from being affected by the lawsuit. This is one advantage to keeping each property in a separate LLC.

The limited liability means that the members of the LLC are responsible only up to the amount of their own contribution. In other words, if you put a property in an LLC and keep your home and other assets separate, only that property is attackable if your LLC is sued. Some investors place each property they purchase in a separate LLC; this way, each investment is protected separately. LLCs sometimes have as many investors as possible (but there can be a limit to the number of shareholders—check with your state regulations). The idea here not only is to reduce the amount of liability for each member but also to make it difficult for a plaintiff to find all the other partners to serve in a legal action. The more partners the better, and the more legal representation will be available.

The Ghost

As previously mentioned, the main reason people consider creating LLCs is to try to protect personal assets from lawsuits. Of course, liability insurance is available for the very same reason, and, in fact, LLCs will purchase it as well. So why would you consider working with LLCs or worry about lawsuits if you're insured? Good question! The problem is that you can't always buy the insurance you need. It is our opinion that you don't need to utilize the LLC unless you can't insure for certain things and, in the rental property business, the two main concerns are lead paint and mold hazards. It is becoming increasingly difficult to purchase insurance that will protect you against the liability associated with these hazards whether they exist or not. If these types of risks potentially exist at your property, or if your property is subject to insurance rejection for other reasons, you may want to consider the LLC as a form of ownership.

Because there are drawbacks to using LLCs, this type of ownership may not be for everyone. First, the entire concept depends legally on whether personal assets and funds are kept separate from those of the LLC. Each LLC is a legal entity, which must be able to perform on its own. Each must have its own bank accounts, bills, employees, and tools. It must be able to make its own decisions with the guidance of its members. Separate accounting methods for multiple properties owned by individual LLCs might be the most difficult of the separation concept to accomplish. Because of this aspect some investors will group multiple properties in only a few LLCs to try to simplify management procedures. However, by doing so the properties are less protected than having each property owned by a separate LLC.

Other drawbacks include the requirement of professional services such as an attorney during eviction proceedings. Also, several states charge an annual tax for each LLC.

As you can see, there is a lot to the LLC. Following the rules of the LLC is important to prevent a court ruling that the LLC is bogus and holding you personally liable anyways. As with anything, you have to take the good with the bad. If you would like to know more about what it takes to set up and run a Limited Liability Company for your properties, then contact an attorney or the office of the Secretary of State.

Rental Red Light! _____

One of the biggest problems with using a Limited Liability Company is operating within the rules of the LLC. One such rule is that you must use an attorney to represent the LLC in any legal matter. This becomes a problem for a landlord who wants to evict a tenant without the help of a lawyer. This action is called doing an eviction "Pro-Se," meaning you are representing yourself. (See Chapter 17 for more on Pro-Se evictions.) An LLC is a legal entity that exists by its own name, not yours, and therefore needs the services of a licensed attorney.

You may be successful in doing the eviction yourself for the LLC, but if you get caught, opposing counsel can "pierce the corporate veil." This means you want the limited liability available from the LLC but will not work within the rules of the LLC. The immediate consequence may be nothing, but if you get sued later on over some other issue, opposing legal counsel could pick the LLC apart, leaving you high and dry!

The Least You Need to Know

◆ Real estate has many physical and economic characteristics that affect its value.

◆ Several different classifications define real estate by type.

◆ Before you invest in rental real estate, you should research the many different types of real-estate ownership available to you.

◆ With the help of professionals, careful research, and financial planning, you can help deter possible claims against you for liability and maybe help protect your personal assets as well.

Chapter 3

Checking Out the Neighborhood

In This Chapter

◆ Scoping out the territory before purchasing property

◆ Determining the biggest factors in buying rental property: price, location, and rental rates

◆ Researching distressed property

◆ Knowing what characterizes a good neighborhood

Just about every town in America has rental property. Take a ride through the town in which you live, and I'll bet you will find some. As you drive around, look for windows above storefronts for apartments; heck, the storefronts themselves are probably being rented. Count the number of mailboxes or electrical meters on a building; this sometimes indicates the presence of separate units.

Usually, a town will have a section in which most of its rental housing stock is located and is most evident. Typically, the downtown area or the more urbanized areas will contain apartments. But even in rural areas and in small country towns, there will be an apartment or two. Sometimes they are not easily recognizable. A basement apartment for the in-laws or a room over the garage for the college kid might not be so noticeable. However, it is impossible not to notice some rental property types; the large apartment complexes and big, multifamily homes seem to take on a look all their own. Of course, any property could be rented if an owner chooses. Single-family homes, mobile homes, condominiums, offices, retail stores, just about anything. Most of the property on Main Street, USA, is probably some form of rental property. The simple fact is that landlords are everywhere.

Where Should You Buy?

Anywhere you want to and can afford to. Determining where to buy should depend on what you want to buy and how much it costs. These are the questions you should ask yourself:

- How much do I want to invest?

- What kinds of property would I like to own?

- What kind of property can I handle?

Facts for Rent

The United States Census Bureau reported in 1997 that the United States had approximately 34 million renter-occupant units.

If you are interested in owning apartments or commercial space to rent, you need to locate an area where there is either a demand for apartments and commercial space or a potential for demand. Supply and demand, the very basics you learned about in your college economics class, have an impact on how successful your rental property will be. For most people, the price of a property and their ability to hold on to the property will determine where they can buy.

Obviously, when there is a high demand for housing and a short supply of housing, the housing will be more expensive to buy. The same holds true for commercial real estate as well. As an investor, you need to research the area and the property to help determine what you should pay for it. We will discuss how to use an income operating statement in Chapter 5 to help you evaluate the investment.

For now, you should consider the distance between where you live and the area in which you are considering buying. This is an important factor if you plan to own property that's a great distance from where you actually live or if you live very close.

Rental property ownership is a very demanding business, and a rental property requires constant care. If you plan to own property a great distance from where you live, it will be very difficult for you to care for your property unless you hire a management company or a handyman to oversee daily repair and other business affairs.

When you're a landlord, the emergency call in the middle of the night is inevitable. Whether the property is a great distance or just a few minutes away, the stress and anxiety associated with not being closer to the property can make the whole experience quite miserable.

On the other hand, if you live in very close proximity to the rental property, you also will become very accessible to tenant needs. This is good for the tenant but not so good for you. If and when the emergency call comes, you will have the peace of mind of being close, but when calls that are not emergencies come in at all hours, the situation will become annoying and stressful. A tenant will usually not make a long-distance call to simply complain about his or her rental unit unless it is a real emergency, but a local call is no big hardship for a tenant to make if he or she simply wants to complain. If you plan on being an absentee landlord who will run the property on your own, it might be smart to pick an area to own property that is close to where you live but still a toll call away.

Rental Red Light!

Vacation property that you might plan to enjoy yourself, such as a time-share or summer rental in areas that are seasonal (14 weeks), can realistically expect 7 to 14 weeks of actual rent received depending on demand for the area.

Edwards' Advice

Unless you are experienced with inspecting rental property, it might be wise for you to hire a private inspector to evaluate the property before you purchase it. Environmental concerns and structural hazards can prove quite costly.

A Sale Isn't Always a Bargain!

"Buy low and sell high" is the motto of the investor. No one ever wants to overpay for something he or she wants to own and neither do you. The local real-estate market will determine what property is selling for and what you can expect to pay for similar properties. In a hot real-estate market in which property is in high demand and supply is low, it may be difficult to find a bargain. Not impossible but certainly more difficult than finding bargains in areas where the demand is not as great. If you are interested in buying a two-family house in a specific, desirable area, you should affiliate yourself with a real-estate agency familiar with that area and take a look at the agency listings to see what two-family houses are available and for how much.

Edwards' Advice

Foreclosed property can be purchased either directly from a lending institution or at an auction. Special care should be taken when buying foreclosed property at auction. You might want to hire a lawyer or an agent to do a detailed title search of the property to be sure there are no liens, taxes due, or other encumbrances that could affect the ownership of the property.

Remember that just because someone is asking a certain price for a property, it doesn't mean the property is worth that price. Something is only worth what someone else is willing to pay for it. There are several ways to determine what people are paying for property in an area. You can pick up special publications such as the *Commercial Record*, a newspaper that lists actual sales and prices by the towns in which they occur. Town halls keep records of property transfers and prices for their respective areas. Real-estate agents can tell you what prices certain properties in the area have sold for. As you will see in Chapter 4, you should be aware of some special considerations before purchasing a rental property. These considerations will help you to determine if the investment is a bargain.

You should also beware of a property with a low price tag attached. The blue-light specials of this world should be researched and analyzed just as much as the higher-priced properties. Ask yourself why the property is so available, do a thorough inspection of the premises, and make sure you're not simply purchasing someone else's headache complete with costly environmental hazards and other such liabilities. We're not suggesting that you should not purchase this type of property; just be sure that you know what you're getting into beforehand. We believe that, whatever you purchase and at whatever price, you should first carefully analyze the property and make sure it fits your investment needs.

Locating Distressed Property

It is no big secret that the best deals are usually found in the wake of someone else's hardship. A distressed property is one that is either suffering or has suffered from some other underlying problem that is affecting the right of ownership. Although this is unfortunate, it does remain true that distressed property can sometimes be a real bargain.

Death, divorce, and destitution are the three Ds of finding distressed property. When the owner of a property is faced with some of these difficult life challenges, it can affect the owner's capability to still own the property and can force the sale of the property, possibly well below market cost. Over the last 10 years, environmental concerns such as lead paint and asbestos, which are commonly found in buildings built prior to 1978, have forced many property owners who could not afford to correct these problems to lose their property. In some areas, high taxes combined with the high cost of daily repair have created negative returns from a property. When this happens, a mortgage payment might not be able to be satisfied, forcing either the sale or foreclosure of a property.

Distressed property is not as difficult to find as it may sound. Property in great need of repair is a good indication that the property is experiencing problems. High grass, broken windows, and no sign of resident activity may indicate a property that has been abandoned. There are several ways to locate this type of property; you might find some while driving your car around town, or you can inquire about property at the town hall where there is a wealth of information handy for finding distressed property. You can find out who the owner of record is for the property at the town hall and can contact this individual directly to see if he or she wants to sell. Liens and foreclosure activity are a matter of public record available at the town hall. Many towns keep a list of empty or abandoned housing in the town area.

Legal ads in a newspaper will inform the public of estate and property auctions in the area where the paper circulates. Your lawyer or accountant might have a client who needs to liquidate a property due to financial troubles. You can contact local banks and ask to speak with someone in charge of the real estate owned (REO) department.

A bank will have a list of property that has been foreclosed on by that bank. You can also contact mortgage companies for lists of property; some of these companies will also have foreclosed property available. This is sometimes the best way to locate and buy distressed property because the bank or mortgage company that wants to get rid of property may be willing to take back the paper on the loan with little money down just to quickly sell it. Contact the state in which you want to own property for a list of licensed banks and financial lenders in that state.

> **CAUTION**
>
> **Rental Red Light!**
>
> The idea behind obtaining foreclosed property is to take advantage of reduced prices. This is not always possible, however, because sometimes the cost of recovery added to the value of the mortgage might be higher than the fair market value of the property.

CAUTION

Rental Red Light! _____

If you're dealing with a bank or a lending institution about a distressed property, the trick is to recoup their loss to them in return for a very low interest rate and a long term of fixed years with little to no money down. Would you pay 10 times the value for a property? The answer is yes if you had nothing to start with, if the terms were right, and if you could make money without putting any money down while owning it in an LLC without a personal signature. This may sound too good to be true, but when you deal with distressed property, many possibilities are available. Remember that a lender is a lender, not a property manager. The lender is probably not having much success operating the property.

Also, many lenders will turn the property over to a VP in the office, someone who will now be working nights and weekends and will really want to dump the property and assist you in making a deal. If you find a property you like, make a cash offer; don't be afraid to offer a low price. You can always go up in price, but you can never come down. If you buy it right and refinance it right away for 100 percent of whatever you paid, you're ahead of the game. This is called "buying a property with mirrors."

Signs of a Good Neighborhood

How do you spot a good neighborhood? Do you open your eyes and look for the obvious or is there something more to it? Perhaps the following indicators can help:

- People appear well groomed.
- Dark alleys are without shady places of employment.
- No rats.
- Drugs are sold in pharmacies only.
- The schools don't have broken windows.
- The animals have four feet, not two.

The truth is that neighborhoods are all different, and beauty is in the eye of the beholder. What might seem like a bad neighborhood to one person may seem good to another.

The classic definition of a bad neighborhood is one with a high crime rate, deteriorated buildings, and declining property values. On a more personal note, an impoverished neighborhood should not necessarily be considered a bad neighborhood.

Unfortunately, this attitude usually is held by society's upper class simply because a neighborhood may not appear the way these people feel it should. Deteriorated buildings and declining property values may be associated with poorer neighborhoods simply due to lack of revenue in the area. But it's the people who live in that area who will determine whether it's a good place to live. The best definition of a bad neighborhood is one that has lost its spirit and can't seem to get it back. Don't be misled: Money can be made in these types of neighborhoods with rental property.

Nonetheless, while shopping for investment property, certain indicators will help you determine the value of not only a neighborhood's property but also the spirit of its people:

- **For-sale and for-rent signs.** If you see several for-sale signs in an area, it may indicate a stagnate market where property is not selling. The same may be true for rental units. If large quantities of people in an area are trying to sell and move out of the area, perhaps some other problems exist and will affect your success with owning rental property in the same area. When there is an over-supply of housing and rental space, prices will have to be reduced to entice new investors, and rents will be low to appeal to new renters. If you are planning on purchasing property to resell for a profit, this type of area may not be the best suited for your purposes.

- **Vacancy rate.** Supply and demand will directly affect a neighborhood. High vacancy rates mean that no one wants to live there. This may be because of a multitude of reasons, but the bottom line is that vacancies will cost you money as a rental owner and will make operating the property effectively very difficult. You can check classified ads in local newspapers to see how many rental units are being advertised for rent, or you can check with the local town hall for vacancy statistics.

- **Taxes.** Local property taxes affect a neighborhood in many ways. High property taxes make it difficult for rental owners to turn a profit on their investment while maintaining the physical appearance of the property—especially when demand for such a property is low. The result is very often an unattractive property in the area. On the other hand, lower taxes help put money back into property while increasing the owners' profit.

- **Employment.** Look for industry and job opportunities in an area. Jobs mean employment and wages. The better the types of employment, the higher the wages and the greater the need for housing. Remember, the higher the demand, the higher the market rent will be, and, hopefully, the higher the return on your investment. Unemployed areas as well as areas in which income is heavily subsidized by the government are usually more depressed economically and more deeply ridden with societal problems.

- **Crime.** Check with the local police department about police activity and crime rates in the area. High crime rates naturally have a negative affect on getting good renters to live there. Most people prefer to live in a safe community with low crime. (Many police departments will keep records of crime activity by property locations.)

- **Housing and rehabilitation projects.** Look for new housing starts in the area. This indicates a demand for housing and healthy market activity. Rehab projects of older building stock, specifically by new investors, also indicates a healthy real-estate market and a good rental market.

Landlord Lingo

Many areas have implemented what is known as a **neighborhood revitalization zone (NRZ).** By definition, these zones comprise the people who live or own businesses in the area and enable them to make decisions that will determine the future of the neighborhood regarding its plan of development.

- **Revitalization.** *Revitalization* efforts usually indicate that an area has suffered or is suffering from some economic and social problems. Revitalization organizations have popped up all over the country, usually in specific urbanized areas, to try to solve problems that they feel affect the area. The revitalization areas have been perceived as a good community development.

- **Schools.** School reputation is a big factor that new residents, whether owners or renters, will consider before moving to an area. People want the best for their children, and a quality education in a safe school is always a priority.

- **Public services.** New residents often are attracted to an area based on the quality of services such as garbage pickup, snow removal, the quality of the town infrastructure, and the condition of roads and sidewalks. The more quality services for their tax dollar, the happier they will be.

- **Parks and recreation.** New residents are attracted to areas with plenty of parks and recreational activities for children and adults.

The trick to locating a good neighborhood in which to purchase investment property is to find as many of these indicators as you can in an area and still be able to afford a property. Finding all these things in an area will seem like looking for nirvana. You should get to know an area before you purchase property in it. Make a list of what you feel are the good points in a neighborhood. Hopefully they will outnumber the bad ones, will help you in your decision of whether to purchase the property, and perhaps will even help you rent it. A great neighborhood is not a sure bet that money can be made with the property. Your success with a property will depend largely on what the property costs to purchase and manage.

The Least You Need to Know

- ◆ Rental property is everywhere; all you need to do is look around to find some.

- ◆ Price and affordability are determining factors for where to purchase, as is your living proximity to the property.

- ◆ Tracking the market for real-estate sales and rental rates in a given area will help you determine whether an area is desirable and whether the investment is profitable.

- ◆ Distressed property can sometimes be purchased at a real bargain.

- ◆ Good and bad neighborhoods can be perceived as such due to many different factors.

- ◆ The existence of good neighborhoods will not ensure whether a rental property is a good investment or not.

Chapter 4

Getting Ready to Buy

In This Chapter

- ◆ Factors to consider when buying rental property
- ◆ Estimating potential property expenses
- ◆ Inspecting the building and grounds

You have decided that rental property is a good investment because you know it's making money while you sleep. You have dreamt about that five-family building down the street that can be bought for a song, and if you hold on to it and collect rent while the property's value appreciates, you'll make all kinds of money. Sweet dreams, but beware of a nightmare on Elm Street!

A lot of investors have had sleepless nights because they didn't research the property correctly before marching blindly into a closing. Rental-property ownership can be profitable, but the amount of return from the property depends heavily on the actual purchase price of the property. The location and type of property you consider buying will affect the price it can be bought for, and, of course, the trick to buying something right is to buy it for as low a price as possible. Read through this chapter to learn what factors determine good and bad investments, and then turn to Chapter 5 for an example of a five-family building and how the numbers look on paper.

When Is the Right Time to Buy?

It is always the right time to buy! If you have researched the property values and rental values of the area, and have devised a good investment plan to follow, then jump right in. New investors should guard against procrastination and not hesitate on potential good deals or they might risk losing out on nice returns on their money. The best suggestion we can offer is to not be overly cautious regarding your ability to manage the property. Don't let cautiousness win out over other factors. A little self-esteem, a lot of elbow grease, and this book under your arm can help you go a long way in this business.

What Do You Want to Buy?

As a would-be investor, the first thing you should do before buying a property is decide what kind of property you are interested in buying. Will it be a two-family, three-family, four-, or more? Perhaps you have your heart set on a single-family home to use as a vacation rental down by the shore or a cabin up in the woods. Will the building have commercial or other mixed uses? Whatever it is, you need to decide what to look for so that the property type will be easier to locate and research. You can always change your mind if you want!

The next thing you should decide is the property's physical location. Real-estate markets are local by nature. A five-family house in one area can cost much less in another area even if the areas are close in proximity. Obviously, it is a good idea to purchase property in areas where the demand for such types of property is high. When there is a shortage of housing in an area, rents will probably be higher. Purchase prices will also usually be higher in thcsc types of areas, but you never know—there might be a deal out there somewhere. In areas where demand is low, prices will be much lower and so will rents. It's important to note that just because rents might be higher in some areas, it doesn't necessarily mean that those properties will make a profit. If a property can be purchased at or below market cost, or if the deal is structured correctly and the property is managed carefully and conservatively, then a property has a chance to make money no matter where it is.

> **Rental Red Light!**
>
> One-, two-, three-, and four-family properties are usually considered residential and are taxed accordingly. Five-family and up or any property with retail or office space is usually taxed at a commercial rate.

This Place Is Beautiful!

You have found the perfect property. It meets all the criteria that mean anything and everything to you. However, some reasons for purchasing a particular property may not be the right ones in the long haul. Remember that this is a business investment, not an investment in your ego!

Let's take a closer look at some popular reasons and why these reasons are not the best:

◆ **It's the right color.** The color of a house is not an important factor as an investment. Don't judge an investment by its color, even if you always wanted to own a white house with green shutters, and this is the one.

CAUTION

Rental Red Light!

When studying to become a real-estate agent, the first thing you learn is that the real-estate market is a local market. The three most important things about a piece of real estate are its location, location, and location. Unlike stock-market prices, which are not affected quite as easily, real-estate prices can vary quite a bit from state to state, town to town, and street to street.

◆ **Its location reminds you of your youth.** Memory lane should be driven down in your mind, not in the creases of your wallet. Don't buy a house just because your best friend in high school used to live in it or some such similar nonsense.

◆ **It's what your spouse once wanted.** You once visited the house with your wife, and she said that someday she would love to own a house just like this one. Your spouse's emotional opinion is important but not a prerequisite for purchase.

◆ **There is a swimming pool in the backyard.** Unless the property will benefit from a swimming pool, such as in a vacation area or where the climate is hot, you don't need it. A swimming pool is costly to maintain, and the liability associated with it is high.

◆ **It has beautiful, massive grounds.** To own land and become a land baron is a nice dream, but large yards with fancy landscaping can be extremely labor intensive and expensive to upkeep.

◆ **It's a true antique according to the historical society.** The *historical society*, sometimes referred to by seasoned landlords as the "hysterical society," has rules that govern how a property is to look and be used. Understand that if you purchase property in a historical zone, you might be taking on partners that you may not appreciate in time.

◆ **Your mother's friend told you it would make you lots of money.** Your mother's best friend might mean well, but be sure that he or she has a professional knowledge of real-estate investment. Remember that the mentality of the general public is that all landlords make money; after all, look at the rent they collect.

◆ **Your cousin's daughter lives at the property.** If there is a relative living at the property, you can say goodbye to that relationship. It won't be long before that side of the family stops talking to you.

Landlord Lingo

A **historical society** is a committee of individuals who are concerned with preserving the historical integrity of a specific area. Since the 1960s, organizations concerned with historic preservation have tried to rehabilitate and revitalize urban neighborhoods and business districts, with much success. There are national and state historical registers of property all over the United States. Contact the local town hall for more information regarding historical districts and local societies.

◆ **The price is right.** You know this to be true because you have been watching the for-sale ads in the paper, and you feel you have become quite good at determining the value of property. Do your homework but include the actual prices listed in land records at the town hall. These are the prices that properties are actually selling for in that area. Also, you should speak to your local banker and try to get a feel for what he or she thinks the value is; after all, the banker is going to be placing first mortgages on properties in the area and will not want to make a bad investment.

Let's Get Serious About Rental Property Ownership!

Now that we have explored some of the wrong reasons for purchasing property, let's look at some of the right ones:

◆ You are making too much money at your regular job, and your accountant thinks you need to be taking advantage of the IRS depreciation factors made available through property ownership.

- You are planning for retirement and would like to someday sell a property for a profit and add to the nest egg.

- You would like to set up a property account to act as a savings account for your children's college tuition.

- You simply want to earn some extra income.

- You want to set up a portfolio of properties to create a net worth that is attractive to lenders so that you can invest in a business venture and borrow more money than you could based on your current income.

- Research indicates that real-estate market values are increasing, and you would like to cash in on the appreciation made available by holding on to a sound investment.

- The business you are in does not provide a steady base income that is comfortable to you.

- If you purchase the building that your business is located in, it might help reduce the overall cost of operating the business and enhance your profits.

- You're diversifying your investment portfolio by owning real estate.

- You want to make money!

The one common denominator of all these reasons is money. We feel that unless you or your organization has some special motive for owning investment property, the only reason to purchase rental property should be income oriented. Remember that by purchasing rental property, you are truly entering into a business, and everyone knows you should never mix business with pleasure!

Expenses? What Expenses?

Yes, many expenses are incurred in operating property, especially when it's rental property. You'll need to determine these expenses before purchasing a property. The expense categories of the operating statement are important because they break down the various costs associated with the property. These costs are probably not much more than good estimates, and you should always portray these educated guesses to be kind of high. This is not a perfect world, nor is this form an exact science, and you are always better off preparing for the less-than-perfect situations. It is also important to note that many of these expenses can be offset if it is determined in the rental agreements with prospective tenants that the tenant pays for certain things like utilities or maintenance. Here's a breakdown of expenses:

- **Taxes** are the amount of money you will pay to the municipality in which the property is located. This amount is based on an assessed value of the property times a mill rate, and it is usually paid in two installments, six months apart (for more details, see Chapter 12).

- **Insurance** is a necessary expense on a property. In the event that either the property is damaged or someone is injured on it and a claim is issued, an insurance company will pay the loss of the claim up to the amount insured. You should contact an insurance agent for quotes associated with the specific type and location of building. It is important to note that multiple insurance policies might be required for the property such as *fire insurance* and *liability insurance* policies (for more details, see Chapter 14).

Landlord Lingo

Landlords must be aware of a couple different types of insurance. **Fire insurance** is a must for any owner of property. Fire insurance protects the owner against the loss of the investment value up to the amount insured. **Liability insurance** is similar to fire insurance except that it protects the owner against any claims of liability that may result at the property. There is also renters insurance, which we'll discuss in Chapter 14.

- **Electric** is the amount of money you will pay to illuminate the common areas of the building, such as hallways or stairways, and the outside grounds. Many times, apartments are rented to include utilities. This is a cost to the owner and must be estimated accordingly. This cost can be obtained from the seller's Schedule E of the 1040, or you can call the electric company with the owner's permission to get this information.

- **Heat** is another utility that sometimes an owner will supply to a tenant as part of the rent. Again, careful estimates must be made when placing a value on this expense. This information is also available on a Schedule E, or you can call the company that supplies energy to the building for the cost of the last season.

- **Hot water** is another possible cost for supplying a utility to the tenant. Hopefully, the tenants don't take long showers, or they might send your investment to the shower.

- **Water,** unless stated otherwise, is the owner's responsibility for the entire building. The area's water company will have information regarding water usage and cost.

◆ **Sewer,** unless there is a septic system on the property, is an expense you will probably have to pay (the cost associated with using the city sewer facilities). The cost of sewer usage can be a flat fee, or it can be based on water usage. This information can be obtained from either the service provider or the seller's 1040.

◆ **Gas and/or propane** is an expense if you plan to supply utilities. This source of energy is very common and is used for heating hot water and for cooking. Either the 1040 or the service provider can be used for heating estimates.

◆ **Oil** is another source of energy used in some buildings but not all.

◆ **Wood,** for you Abe Lincolns out there, can be used for heating. However, I highly recommend not using this type of heat in apartment dwellings. The cost? Who can put a price on calloused hands and sweat?

◆ **Snow** is an expense in areas that are likely to have it, because removal of snow will be necessary. Unless stated otherwise in the agreement, snow removal is the owner's responsibility. It is common in commercial leasing to pass this cost on to the occupant. When the plowed area is shared by many, the cost is divided.

 **Facts for Rent** _____

It is common in many older types of housing stock for the tenant to pay for the source of heat. This is because the buildings were usually designed that way, and most property owners would prefer not to pay this expense. Some landlords, however, prefer the added feature of paying the heating expense as a lure to attract tenants and fill vacancies. The landlord will try to adjust the rent to offset the expense. This works fine as long as the tenant doesn't misuse the heat in the apartment. In some instances, a landlord will regulate the heat from a controlled location to better protect against large heating expenses.

◆ **Elevators** can be an additional expense. If the building you are considering has one, the cost of servicing it could be yours.

◆ **Maintenance** is the cost of maintaining the building and property. One way to determine the maintenance cost of a property is to use a percentage such as 5 percent of gross income. The rule of thumb for most appraisers is to subtract the cost of vacancy from the gross income before using a percentage of gross income to arrive at a maintenance cost. The logic is that you will not experience maintenance on a vacant unit. The reality, however, is that there is a great deal of maintenance when preparing a vacant unit for rent. (For more details, see the income operating statement in Chapter 5, in which we use 5 percent of our gross income of $33,300.)

◆ **Vacancy** is the cost associated with the loss of money from your yearly gross rental due to a unit not being occupied. To think that you will not have a vacant unit from time to time is not realistic. You might never experience vacancy, but you should still plan accordingly. For the purpose of the income statement in Chapter 5, we are basing vacancy on having each unit be vacant one month during the year, a total of $2,775. You will have to research your area to find the figure that relates to that area. Many town planners, another department in the town hall, keep statistics on vacancy for the area. You might also be able to get this information from a local rental agency, which might even be able to assist you in renting.

◆ **Nonpayment** is the cost associated with the loss of money due to an occupant not paying the rent. From time to time, this unfortunate circumstance will occur, and you will need to factor in this loss. We are using a rate of 50 percent of vacancy in the Chapter 5 example.

◆ **Management** can be a cost if you seek assistance from someone else to oversee the day-to-day operation of the property. You should contact a management company in the area and find out what its fees are. Remember that the management service might include maintenance to the property, and you will need to separate the cost and include it in your maintenance figure.

◆ **Supplies** are materials needed to operate the property such as construction or maintenance supplies.

◆ **Rubbish** is a cost when the owner must remove it. If the town in which the property is located supplies rubbish removal, then the cost is included in the tax column. If, however, the town does not have removal services, then the property may require a dumpster. You should contact a garbage-removal service in the area for prices.

◆ **Advertisement** is the cost associated with advertising the property for rent. If you have a vacancy, then you most likely will incur some advertising expenses. The traditional for-rent sign may not satisfy the vacancy, and you will be forced to advertise in a local newspaper. Contact the area newspapers for advertising prices.

◆ **Legal** is a cost associated with obtaining the services of a lawyer, usually during an eviction or civil action.

Facts for Rent

Some owners have learned how to do evictions Pro-Se, or without the services of a lawyer, to help eliminate this cost. (See Chapter 17 for more information on evictions.) For now, you should still factor in legal as an expense. Plus, you might need a lawyer's expertise in some other business associated with the property. Contact a lawyer in the area to see what the cost is for eviction work. Sheriffs' or Marshals' fees, process servers' fees, and court filing fees should also be included in this category of expenses.

♦ **Accounting** is the cost related to the services you may require to help keep track of all the money you will make or to have an accountant fill out the Schedule E of your 1040 tax return.

♦ **Landscaping** is the cost associated with keeping the grounds of the property well groomed.

Rental Red Light!

Companies that perform inspections normally charge a flat fee for this type of service.

♦ **Other** is any other expense that may be associated with ownership of the property such as occupancy permits or rental permits required in some areas.

The Walk-Through: Inspecting Property

Before you purchase a property, it is important for you to walk through it and inspect it. Make sure the property meets the requirements that are important to this kind of investment. Check both the physical and the mechanical aspects of the property to be sure everything is in satisfactory condition. Certified inspection services that do inspections of property are also available for hire. These inspectors are usually quite thorough and are very good at explaining any problems they find as well as offering good advice as to how to fix them. If you hire an inspector, remember to get a copy of the written report and don't be afraid to ask questions. After all, they are the experts, and you are paying for their time!

It is a good idea before you inspect to make a list of the physical and mechanical features of the property. You should always start in the basement or mechanical room of the property and work your way up. Look for water damage, rotting materials, or environmental hazards. Locating such defects before purchasing may help in negotiating the price and relieving future headaches. Be sure to make a checklist of the following:

- Heating system

- Electrical service boxes

- Electrical wires

- Foundation

- Pipes

- Paint

- Fixtures

- Water

- Insulation

- Roof

The inspection is important. Make sure that the property is everything you hoped it would be before purchasing so that there are few surprises with your new investment.

Putting new knowledge to the test is always a challenge. With investments, smart landlords always turn potential expenses and income into real numbers.

The Least You Need to Know

- Don't purchase a rental property for sentimental reasons; examine your reasons for purchasing a particular rental property very carefully.

- Decide what type of property (one-family, two-family, three-family, or more) to buy before looking.

- Detail all possible expenses before purchasing, to help determine a good or bad investment.

- Inspect the building and grounds before purchase so that you know exactly what to expect.

Profit Potential or Money Pit?

In This Chapter

- ◆ Adding up the numbers to determine a good or bad investment
- ◆ Researching the history of a property
- ◆ The fourth approach to appraisal: The Profit or Loss approach
- ◆ A few other quick appraisal techniques

This is it! You've found the best rental property on the block, and you've got to have it. The asking price seems a little steep, but it might make a lot of money. The asking price cannot be changed, but will you make money? Maybe. Yikes! If thoughts such as these have entered your mind when considering a purchase, step back from your excitement and take a deep breath. Excellent … now we can proceed.

Before you whip out your checkbook, do your homework. That rental investment just might be a great deal, but the only way to be sure is to break it down. Deconstructing all the numbers—the purchase price, expenses, income, and mortgage payments—will reveal the truth. And only the truth will set you free!

You Found a Property You Like

Many people have entered into the world of real estate without doing their homework or without the knowledge needed to properly evaluate the venture being entered into. First it has to meet all of your personal requirements, like making money; then it has to prove to you that it will make money.

To examine a property being purchased for profit, you first must figure out whether it will make any money. You need a formula based on cash flow, not appreciation (increase of value over time) or depreciation (as it relates to a tax return). Later we will show how appreciation and depreciation will affect the numbers. The formula is simple:

> Gross Sales – Gross Expenses = Profit (or Loss)

The formula is so simple that you are probably thinking, "Go figure." Well, most people don't take the time to figure, don't know how to figure, or can't configure the figures. Remember that figures don't lie but liars figure. Now start figuring! We will now show you how to figure what you need to figure. Whew!

Performance or Not

The income operating statement, or *Profit or Loss statement* as we like to call it, is possibly the best tool you can use in determining whether to buy a particular property. As you will see in the following example, the income operating statement explains the various costs of operating the building so that you can make an educated decision on whether or not to purchase.

By examining the numerous costs and affixing prices to each, you will find out the gross expenses as well as incomes generated by operating the property. In effect, this method tracks the performance of an income-producing property. This method also helps you to decide what price you can afford to spend for a property and expect to break even with after expenses. This number—in other words, the result of your Profit or Loss statement—is important because you would not want to overspend and eventually lose money on an investment.

Now let's start exploring a Profit or Loss statement. We will begin by examining a five-family building, although the same formula can be used for any

Landlord Lingo

A *Profit or Loss statement* is an important tool used by appraisers and other real-estate professionals who are interested in determining value of property used for income purposes. Real-estate investors and landlords would be wise to add this tool to their box.

building containing rental units. To better simplify, numbers have been rounded off to the nearest dollar.

```
          THE PROFORMA OPERATING STATEMENT

Location    33 High St            Unit Size & Value
Type of property 5 Family Res.     3 Bed Room   $700.00
Price   $225,000.00                2 Bed Room   $575.00
Lot Size   37,500 sq. ft.          1 Bed Room   $500.00
Sq. Ft. of Building  5,000         1 Bed Room   $500.00
Zoning    Residential              1 Bed Room   $500.00
Age of property  1875                           $
Construction  Wood Frame           Total        $2775.00
No. of units     5
                               Total X 12 Equals Gross
Gross Income $33,300.00         Income   $33,300.00
Gross Expense $17,221.00
Gross Debt Service Yrly $16079.00 Down Payment $51,400.00
Gain or Loss Yearly    0
Divide by 12 Equals Monthly    Plus or Minus

Gross Expenses                  Comments
Taxes   $3,300.00
Insurance  $900.00
Electric   $180.00
Heat     Owner Pays Gas
Hot Water Owner Pays Gas
Water  $1,500.00
Sewer  $750.00
Gas    $3,063.00
Oil    None
Propane  None
Wood  None
Snow  $250.00
Elevator  None
Maintenance  $1,665.00
Vacancy  $2,775.00
Non-Payment  $1,388.00
Management  None
Supplies  In Maintenance
Rubbish  None                   Town Pick Up
Advertising  $750.00
Legal  $600.00
Accounting  $100.00
Landscaping  None
Other  None

Proposed Financing
Mortgage $173600 Rate of %8 No.Years 25 Mo.Payment$1339.90
Mortgage $_____ Rate of %__No.Years___ Mo. Payment_____


Mortgage $_____ Rate of $__No.Years___ Mo. Payment_____
Total    $173600.00                        $1339.90
Monthly Payment X 12 Equals Gross Debt Service.

Gross Income - Gross Expenses = Equals Gain or Loss - Debt
Service

Gross Income  $33,300.00      Yearly
Minus Gross Expense  $17,221.00      Yearly equals the
Total $16,079.00   Yearly Divided by 12 months equals
 $1,340.00    per month. This is the maximum you can allow
toward debt service and still break even monthly or yearly.
```

This example shows a Profit or Loss statement for a five-family building. Numbers have been rounded off to the nearest dollar.

Breaking Down the Operating Statement

Here is a line-by-line breakdown of the operating statement:

♦ **Location** refers to the property's actual address (in this example, 33 High Street).

♦ **Type of property** is a brief description of the property such as a two- or three-unit residential or commercial property. (33 High St. is a five-family house.)

♦ **Price** refers to what the building is being considered bought for. (In the example, the price is $225,000.)

♦ **Lot size** is the actual size of the land area on which the building is situated. (In the example, 37,500 square feet.)

♦ **Square footage of building** determines the size of the structure. To determine square footage, multiply the length by the width of the livable floor space of the building. (In the example, the square footage of the property is 5,000 feet.)

Facts for Rent

The first zoning ordinance in the United States was issued in New York City in 1916.

♦ **Zoning** is the permitted use for property located in the area in which this property exists. Zones can be any assortment of type such as residential, commercial, industrial, or any variation of these types. The zone is important to know because it can affect the way a property is used or how the properties in the same area can be used.

♦ **Age of property** is the actual date the land was improved upon or built on (in this example, 1875). Sometimes two ages are listed on the assessor's card. One is the actual date that the property was built, and the other is called "the effective age of the property." This means that it has been determined during the revaluation of the property that its physical appearance is comparable to another house built at another date. For instance, there could be an effective age of 1947 for a property that was built in 1875.

♦ **Construction** means simply what the building is made of (for example, wood, brick, steel, straw, and so on).

♦ **Number of units** refers to how many rentable units of space are in the building. (In the example, the unit has five apartments.)

- **Unit size and value** is the size of each rentable unit of space, designated by number of bedrooms or office spaces and so on, and the monthly rent associated with each space. The example has one three-bedroom apartment renting at $700 per month, one two-bedroom apartment renting at $575 per month, and three one-bedroom apartments renting at $500 each per month.

Facts for Rent

Revaluation is the process by which a town will analyze every property in the town for tax purposes. Over the course of ownership, the property will either deteriorate or be subject to physical improvements, which will affect value. The assessor or a company hired by the town will assign a value to every property in that town and then tax a certain percentage of that value. The percentages may differ in different areas. Call the assessor's office in the town in which the property is located to find out when the next revaluation is and what percentage of value is taxed. Knowing this will help you to determine what to expect in future tax payments.

- **Gross income** is the total monthly forecast of rent to be collected, multiplied by 12 months. In the example, the rent is $2,775 per month or $33,300 per year.

- **Gross expense** is the total of all monthly expenses associated with the property, multiplied by 12 months to get a yearly forecast. (In the example, we have taken the liberty of filling out a total of $17,221 in expenses.)

- **Gross debt service** is the yearly amount you will spend on mortgage payments associated with the purchase price of the building. (More on this later in this chapter.)

Edwards' Advice

The building department is another great place to dig up information about a property. The building inspector's office in the town hall sometimes keeps files on properties in that town. In those files will be copies of permits that may have been taken on a property as well as notices of past or present building-code violations.

- **Gain or loss** is how you can expect the property to perform in a year. In other words, it is your profit or loss for the year. This will be determined after we are done with the rest of the form.

Where to Get This Information

To get some of the information you will need for proper analysis, the first thing you need to do is visit the town hall in the town where the property is located. The town hall, or County Building, is usually divided into several departments. Most of the descriptive information about the property in question can be found in the assessor's office on what is called a field card or an assessor's card, which is on file for tax purposes and usually is available to the public. The field card will list the owner of record, the volume and page to reference in the clerk's office about the property, a description of the property (land and building), and a breakdown of the value. Some towns include one or more of the previous selling prices for the property. Many town offices have computers that will give you the information you seek about a property with the flick of a finger.

Edwards' Advice

To determine fair market rental value of a rental unit, you should seek assistance from a local newspaper in the marketplace used to advertise in the specific area. You can also check with other owners in the area to see what they are getting for rent. A smart landlord will always watch the local rental market to make sure his or her rents are in line with current prices. Joining a local property-owners association will help you with this type of research.

The clerk's office will have more information about the property. Town records usually are kept in a vault in the clerk's office. These records will give you a legal description of the property and will list any liens or encumbrances associated with the property. Some towns are split into counties and have one county office where the cards are available. Call the town where the property is located to find out what method the town uses and where the records are located. Some towns may even have records available on the web. Be sure to examine tax conveyance forms usually kept on file in a town clerks office. These forms will describe all the actual sales that happened in the town.

Beyond the Town Hall

The other descriptive factors, such as estimating actual costs of expenses, will require more research. To ascertain a correct value or price for the property, you can have the property appraised by a certified appraiser or seek the help of a qualified real-estate broker in the area who is familiar with like properties. Some assessor offices will keep a record of transfers of like properties so that you can see what similar properties in the area have sold for and when. Newspapers will list the asking prices for property, but it is more important to know what properties are actually selling for.

Other costs associated with the property, such as expenses, can be researched a couple different ways. You can ask the seller for a copy of his or her Schedule E, which is attached to the 1040 tax return, to see what he or she represented as expenses, or you can research and arrive at your own numbers. We recommend you do both. It is always best to affix estimates that are a little higher than exact numbers to help prepare for the worst-case scenarios. But beware not to increase amounts beyond reasonable, because you do want to get them as close to real as possible. Remember that the purpose of the Profit and Loss statement is to determine how much money you will need to put down to break even with the investment when you purchase the property. By achieving this information you can then determine if the investment will be good or bad.

> ### Landlord's Toolbox
>
> The Schedule E is another great tool to use when considering a property to purchase. The previous owner will have listed all the expenses from the property on the Schedule E of his or her 1040 tax return, although most of the expenses listed will probably be inflated to try to lessen the tax burden of the owner. The owner will probably be willing to clarify the Schedule E for you.

How Much Will You Pay?

Remember the formula? Gross income minus expenses equals monies left for debt service, profit, or loss. The Profit or Loss statement will help answer the following questions:

- ◆ How much of a first mortgage can you afford to take before it affects the investment profit and becomes a loss?

- ◆ How much money should you put down as a down payment to purchase the property in order to break even, have a profit, or experience a loss?

The price in the example is $225,000. The seller feels that the price is fair, and the broker thinks the price is comparable to like properties in the area. Your banker has had the property appraised, and the appraiser has determined that the fair market value is $225,000. The banker also has a program for which you might qualify that would enable you to purchase this property with 10 percent down, or $22,500. All this sounds pretty good to you. But is it really a good deal? Let's take a closer look and apply the Profit or Loss statement.

Determining Mortgage Payments

There is $33,300 in gross income for the year and $17,221 per year in expenses. If you subtract the expenses from the income, it leaves $16,079 that can be used for debt service in one year. If you divide this number by 12, it will equal $1,340, which reflects the monthly amount available for debt service or your mortgage payment. Remember, however, that the $16,079 also reflects what is available for profit.

The next step is to determine how much money you can borrow with the $1,340 available for debt service, based on the rate of interest your lender is asking and the terms available to you through your lender. For the purpose of this income statement, we will use a rate of 8 percent and a term of 25 years.

Using a Mortgage Table

To continue, you will need to obtain an amortization table. A comprehensive amortization or mortgage table schedule can be obtained from a local bank, purchased from a stationary store, or found on the Internet. A comprehensive amortization table is a book or table that tells you what the monthly payment will be on money borrowed based on the rate of interest and the term of years for which it is borrowed.

The next step is simple. Go to the next page in this book that represents the rate of 8 percent, find the 25-year column, and see what the $1,340 will buy for you in a loan:

$1,340 at 8 percent for 25 years

$100,000 at 8 percent for 25 years will cost $771.82 a month.

$70,000 at 8 percent for 25 years will cost $540.28 a month.

$3,000 at 8 percent for 25 years will cost $23.16 a month.

$600 at 8 percent for 25 years will cost $4.64 a month.

$1,339.90 in monthly payments equals $173,600 in borrowed money.

Is It a Good Investment?

The price of the property is $225,000, and the amount you can borrow is $173,600. If you subtract the amount you can borrow from the asking price, it leaves $51,400. This is the amount you would have to put down to purchase this property to make no money and have no loss on the investment.

If you put down more money, however, you will increase your chance for profit by reducing the debt service. If you put down less money, you will experience a loss. Remember that the banker said that this is a good property, and the bank offers a program that would require a 10 percent down payment, or $22,500. If you go into this investment based on the $22,500, you will lose money.

Amortization of a Loan — Monthly payment per $1,000 (Principal & Interest only)					
Interest Rate —%	10 years	15 years	20 years	25 years	30 years
4.50	10.36	7.65	6.33	5.56	5.07
4.75	10.49	7.78	6.46	5.70	5.22
5.00	10.61	7.91	6.60	5.85	5.37
5.25	10.73	8.04	6.74	5.99	5.52
5.50	10.85	8.17	6.88	6.14	5.68
5.75	10.98	8.30	7.02	6.29	5.84
6.00	11.10	8.44	7.16	6.44	6.00
6.25	11.23	8.57	7.31	6.60	6.16
6.50	11.35	8.71	7.46	6.75	6.32
6.75	11.48	8.85	7.60	6.91	6.49
7.00	11.61	8.99	7.75	7.07	6.65
7.25	11.74	9.13	7.90	7.23	6.82
7.50	11.87	9.27	8.06	7.39	6.99
7.75	12.00	9.41	8.21	7.55	7.16
8.00	12.13	9.56	8.36	7.72	7.34
8.25	12.27	9.70	8.52	7.88	7.51
8.50	12.40	9.85	8.68	8.05	7.69
8.75	12.53	9.99	8.84	8.22	7.87
9.00	12.67	10.14	9.00	8.39	8.05
9.25	12.80	10.29	9.16	8.56	8.23
9.50	12.94	10.44	9.32	8.73	8.41
9.75	13.08	10.59	9.49	8.91	8.59
10.00	13.22	10.75	9.65	9.09	8.78
10.25	13.35	10.90	9.82	9.26	8.96
10.50	13.49	11.05	9.98	9.44	9.15
10.75	13.63	11.21	10.15	9.62	9.33
11.00	13.78	11.37	10.32	9.80	9.52
11.25	13.92	11.52	10.49	9.98	9.71
11.50	14.06	11.68	10.66	10.16	9.90
11.75	14.20	11.84	10.84	10.35	10.09
12.00	14.35	12.00	11.01	10.53	10.29
12.25	14.49	12.16	11.19	10.72	10.48
12.50	14.64	12.33	11.36	10.90	10.67
12.75	14.78	12.49	11.54	11.09	10.87
13.00	14.93	12.65	11.72	11.28	11.06
13.25	15.08	12.82	11.89	11.47	11.26
13.50	15.23	12.98	12.07	11.66	11.45

Example:
Mortgage Amount $100,000— Mortgage Term 30 Years— Interest Rate 8.5%
100 x $7.69 = $769.00 monthly principal & interest

This is a mortgage table, also known as an amortization schedule, using the figures and details of our five-family example.

The Bottom Line

The bottom line in our sample investment is that the property does not work well as an investment property as far as cash flow in accordance with debt service while being purchased at that price and with those expenses. If you can alter any of those factors for the better, it will enhance the attraction of that investment. In other words, if you can increase the rents or reduce the expenses, you might reduce the amount of money needed to put down in order to break even with the property.

There are, of course, some other aspects to review while analyzing this property and determining whether this property is a good investment or a poor one.

For instance, the $51,400 that would have to be used as a down payment for the property to break even might be sitting in a bank collecting an interest rate of 4 percent, or $2,056 a year. If you remove this money from the bank, you will lose this interest payment, which is a safe return on your money. Not good!

On the other hand, if the property in the area where this one is located is appreciating at a rate of 20 percent per year, it will go up in value $45,000 the first year alone. Very good!

Rental Red Light! _____

Depreciation is another factor you should consider about an investment. The amount of depreciation on the building part of the property will be subtracted from your taxable income and will reduce the amount of taxes you pay. On the other hand, the depreciation is subtracted from your "basis" on the property, or the price you paid for it plus the cost of improvements. It is added back on when you sell the property less the improvements, making the amount taxable upon sale greater.

If your depreciation for one year is $20,000 and you are in a 20 percent tax bracket, your gain will be $4,000 in tax savings. Many people sell property to others based upon this method of arithmetic.

Figures don't lie, but you want this property to make sense based upon its performance, not yours. The numbers should depict how well the property can dance for you, and not how well you dance, Fred Astaire.

If you sell this property in one year, you might recognize a profit of $45,000, but it will be less the capital-gains tax payable to the IRS. I'll bet you forgot all about Uncle Sam. Well, you can be sure he didn't forget about you! However, a profit is always a profit, and you shouldn't be so greedy anyway.

Gross Rent and Gross Income Multiplier

Another way to determine the value of rental property is by calculating the Gross Rent Multiplier (GRM) or Gross Income Multiplier (GIM) for similar buildings in that area. The GRM is an investor's tool, which relates sales price to the income that the property produces. Typically, the formula for GRM is used for one- to four-family properties, while the GIM formula is often used for any property with more than 5 units, commercial or industrial type properties. GRM calculations will use gross monthly income, while GIM will consider gross annual income. The equations for each are as follows:

Sales Price ÷ Gross Rent = Gross Rent Multiplier

Sales Price ÷ Gross Income = Gross Income Multiplier

In order for this technique to be useful to an investor, you must first be familiar with the area that the property is located in and have researched comparable sales or like properties. You will need at least three or four other actual similar property-sales data to determine what a reasonable multiplier can be for the area, before using it to identify the price that other similar properties in the same area should be selling for. Once the GRM or GIM has been determined, you can then view a property for sale and quickly determine if the property is overpriced or not overpriced for the area. Following is the equation to determine this:

Gross Rent × GRM = Estimated Market Value

Cap Rates

Very similar to the GRM and GIM methods of appraisal that investors often look to are *Capitalization Rates* when investigating the purchase of income-producing properties. Investors often wish to try to predetermine what the rate of return is on an investment of capital in a particular property. The rate of return is called a Cap Rate. The capitalization method requires that the investor know the net income, and it is calculated as follows:

Net Income ÷ Sale Price = Cap Rate

As with the Gross Rent and Income Multiplier method, market data is necessary for using Cap Rates. If one can prove that similar properties sold also produce a certain Cap Rate for the area, then that rate can be applied to other buildings in the area.

The previous formula for Cap Rates has variations, each of which are important when dealing with investment property. These variations are as follows:

Income ÷ Rate = Value

Value × Rate = Income

The relationship between each of the numbers can help you as an investor to make certain estimates about what to expect from the property. It is important to note that GRMs, GIMs, and Cap Rates are not perfect sciences and are only good estimates at best. Although these techniques can prove useful for quick calculations and number crunching, they are not substitutes for considering the true net income that a property produces. Remember, deadbeat tenants do exist from time to time, especially in a poorly conditioned property, so don't follow the numbers too closely.

The Least You Need to Know

♦ A Profit or Loss statement helps you determine whether the income on the property is worth the mortgage.

♦ Doing thorough research of the history and past income of the property before purchase helps to protect you against a bad investment.

♦ A breakdown of the mortgage payments and costs will show profit and loss before you put the money down.

♦ Altering the factors of debt, expenses, and purchase price increases the property's investment potential.

♦ Gross Rent, Income Multipliers, and Cap Rates are tools that investors can use to estimate sale prices on income properties.

Part 2

Welcome to Landlording!

You did it! You took the first step into a larger investment world. You bought an investment property, but now to make any money with it, you have to prepare it for rent, determine rental values, make improvements, advertise, and initiate certain policies to help you screen out bad tenants and pick good ones. Your education has just begun, so keep an open mind!

Chapter 6

Welcome to the World of Real Estate

In This Chapter

♦ Getting started with the basics: bank accounts, office setup, and general business practices

♦ Making a clean transition with inherited tenants

♦ Preparing vacant units for new tenants

♦ Knowing what to repair and what attributes will increase value to the property to attract the best tenants

Congratulations on your new investment acquisition. Your emotions are probably running pretty high; after all, buying real estate is a pretty hefty expense and can be quite an unnerving experience. All your hopes and dreams of success combined with fears of failure and ideas on how to manage your investment property so that it will turn a maximum profit are a lot to think about.

After your celebration is over, take a deep breath, count to 10, and start treating your new investment as a business. The sooner you do this, the better off you will be. If the property you purchased is already occupied with tenants, then you are now a landlord. If you don't have any tenants yet, don't worry. You'll get some. There is a lot to this business of rental ownership. Good communication skills will have to be developed, and certain steps will have to be followed from the beginning to better ensure good results. One thing you should be glad to know is that you already have taken an important step by obtaining a copy of *The Complete Idiot's Guide to Making Money with Rental Properties, Second Edition*. The rest will be easy.

First Things First!

The first thing you should do as a new owner of a future rental property is to set up a bank account with which to operate the property. This account, preferably a checking account, should list the property name and address you will use for mailing purposes (such as rental payments received from tenants). This account should be separate from your personal accounts. Some landlords will open a separate account for each rental property they own. However you decide to set up the account, be sure to itemize all checks and deposits carefully for bookkeeping purposes. If you have a computer, you can set up the account using a third-party financial software package. With some programs, you can set up escrow accounts in the check register to save money for future expenses, and you can get detailed property reports showing inflows and outflows.

> **Edwards' Advice**
>
> Pick a name for your business, one that can be used for your property account. The only thing that matters about the account is that you must be able to deposit rent and write checks on the account. The name you choose should be easy to remember so that your tenants will always know whom to make their rent checks out to. We suggest using the street name and address of the property. Remember that if LLCs are being used, each will have a separate account and name.

The next and most important step is to set up escrow accounts and to determine the amount of money you need to save for future bills related to the property. An escrow account is an account into which money is placed every month for expense purposes only. The idea here is to have money generated by the property readily available for expenses when those bills are due.

Escrow is, without a doubt, one of the most important steps in operating property. Whether you use a separate account or a dummy account in your computer, divide each category that needs to be paid out (taxes, sewer, etc.) or that you might need funds for, such as potential repairs. If you don't separate your accounts, your funds will blend together, causing mismanagement of funds that will only cost you in the end.

There are long-term and short-term escrow accounts:

◆ **Long-term escrow** is money you will save for future expenses such as replacing a roof or heating system.

◆ **Short-term escrow** is money saved for expenses that will come due every three to six months while you own the property. Bills such as water, sewer, and property taxes will be paid out of this type of escrow account.

Categories that typically require money to be escrowed are as follows: taxes, heat, snow removal, water, sewer, maintenance, supplies, legal, accounting, and landscaping. Only expenses that are paid monthly will not require an escrow, such as electric or insurance bills. Other expenses unique to your property may also require money to be escrowed. We will discuss using property escrow accounts in Chapter 12.

Understanding the concept of creating and using escrow accounts is vital for the proper management of rental property. If this concept is ignored, eventually mismanagement of money will occur, resulting in the old cliché of Robbing Peter to Pay Paul in order to satisfy bills or simply not having the funds necessary to pay them at all.

Being a Landlord is a Job, Not a Hobby

As previously mentioned, owning rental property is a business. If you want a hobby, you should consider collecting stamps. A do-it-yourself landlord can expect to work some late hours. The emergency phone calls at three o'clock in the morning do happen. Hopefully, it won't happen too often, and you will not have to sleep with one eye open.

Any job worth doing is worth doing right, and being a landlord is no exception. You should equip yourself with the basic tools needed to accomplish the tasks required. A computer with an accounting program so that you can work off a check ledger is a must. You will also need skills to do some basic repair or at least have the names of reliable people who can do plumbing, electrical, or carpentry repair as

Edwards' Advice

One possible landlord motto is "The buck stops here." You will find that the buck does stop at you because in the final analysis, you are the person who will take full responsibility for the actions of the people who are representing you and your property.

It is important that you make sure all work is done correctly and within the law.

needed. You will need someone to cut the grass and remove the snow, collect the rents, lease the units, and handle the occasional complaints. And don't forget the professional services you will need, such as a lawyer for the eventual legal issues, and an accountant who will guide you at tax time and help you count all that money you have made.

When you're a landlord, your mentality has to be one that insists on getting the job at hand accomplished. You are the owner of your building and the owner of your business; there is no one for you to pass the buck to. If repairs and other work don't get done around your property, there is no one to blame but yourself.

Help Wanted: Office Skills Required

Office procedures are discussed in Chapter 21. However, a smart landlord should consider certain office prerequisites that will help make the landlording experience a good one.

Using Telephones

A smart landlord will develop good telephone skills. Telephones are a necessary evil for landlords. You will find that much of the business is handled through the use of telephones. People will be calling about that nice apartment you're renting, tenants will be calling to complain about that lousy apartment you rented them, and you will be calling your shrink. It's an excellent idea to put together an address book of contacts and phone numbers used in your daily operation. List vendors and contractors whom you use in the area. Utility companies, police, fire, and other local authorities should be listed in the book. Public agencies such as social services and the housing authority for your area also should be listed. Most important of all, though, make a list of your tenants' phone numbers so you can contact them regarding repairs, emergencies, or their late rent, which I'm sure is in the mail. Such a list must be updated regularly since tenants' phone numbers are subject to change rather frequently. A great place to list tenant phone numbers is on the Monthly Late List form in this book (see Appendix A).

Using Business Cards

Go out and order yourself some business cards. You're operating a business, right? Then start acting like you are. Business cards can serve an important purpose for landlords. Business cards associate professionalism and credibility to you and the property you operate. Plus, there are several uses that you do-it-yourselfers out there will find handy:

♦ Business cards are an excellent form of advertising for your rentals. Hanging them on bulletin boards in the area might help rent an apartment.

♦ Pass the cards out to your tenants as a reference for when they need to contact you. This will bring peace of mind to your tenants by creating a perception of a professional landlord.

♦ Pass them out to area vendors whom you will be using. Some suppliers refuse to sell to the general public but will sell to you if they believe you are a legitimate business.

♦ Pass your cards out to other landlords. A wealth of information about rental rates, bad tenants, inexpensive vendors, and property sales can be obtained from these contacts.

For more on setting up office procedures, see Chapter 21.

Edwards' Advice

Whether you operate your property from an office or out of your kitchen at home, invest in a good telephone and answering machine. Make sure the phone is comfortable; phones shaped like a football might be easy to throw and catch, but they're hard to hear through. And make sure the answering machine is easy to use. It should be one that lists the time and date of the call and that can access and save messages from another telephone away from home, even if it is shaped like a football.

Another option is signing up for voicemail through your local telephone company. Voicemail is more expensive in the long run because it will raise your monthly phone bill about $5 to $7, but it can also be more efficient. Accessing and saving messages from anywhere is easy. If you have a home office and live with one or more people, you can set up different voice "mailboxes" so that personal and business messages can be differentiated. When a tenant calls to tell you that the ceiling is leaking while your 12-year-old daughter is on the phone—again—you will still get the message if and when she ever gets off the phone.

Inherited Tenants

So you bought a property completely furnished with tenants. This is good as long as they are paying rent and are not destructive. Inheriting these tenants might make it easier to operate the property because rent is hopefully being paid without costly vacancies. By inheriting tenants, you have immediate occupancy without suffering the expense of advertising. On the other hand, these people were not selected by you, are not accustomed to your procedures, and probably are not paying the rental rate you want to achieve. They are not using your rental agreement or lease and may be protected by the one they do have. To get your business on track and to better ensure that things like rent collection continue to flow smoothly, you need to institute certain policies and take time to meet with your new tenants. You should make sure to obtain copies of all lease agreements prior to closing from the seller even if they are expired. If rent is currently not being paid, you should try to get the seller to evict them before purchase so that you can start with a clean slate, otherwise legal fees and a lengthy eviction process could ruin plans of a quick start of making money at the property.

Deposits

At the time of closing on your property, you should account for any deposits that tenants may have placed with the past owner. The total amount of the deposits should be transferred as well as any fees the tenants had paid for special services at the property for the month you take control, such as storage and parking fees. You will have to ask specifically about any security deposits or last month's rent that may have been collected by the previous owner. With all that's happening at the closing, it's easy for these items to slip by. You should check with the owner about the deposits before the closing; if he or she no longer has them, it might affect the purchase price, if you catch my drift. Typically, attorneys at a closing will use a balance sheet called a *RESPA* sheet, which will determine adjustment costs that the buyer or seller is responsible to pay at closing.

Landlord Lingo

RESPA stands for the Real Estate Settlement Protection Act that governs how money is to be escrowed and disbursed at a closing. RESPA is a consumer-protection statute that requires certain disclosure for buyers that will spell out costs of settlement. The Department of Housing and Urban Development (HUD) enforces RESPA.

If the seller filled up the oil tank before the transfer, for example, you as the buyer will have to pay the owner back for the full tank. Deposits will sometimes get washed into one of these balance sheets and may not appear to be there, but they are. Some attorneys will roll the security deposits into the RESPA sheet at the closing so that it will look like you will need less money to purchase the property. This is not a wise move because now you will need to escrow for the security deposits after the closing.

You will have to reimburse them to a deposit account. You will also want any interest that had accrued on security deposits, because tenants are entitled to have the interest, and you will be responsible for giving it to them. (We will discuss interest on security deposits in Chapter 11.) Ask lots of questions before and at the time of closing to be sure that you completely understand where the deposits are, how much the amounts are, and who is responsible for them.

Rental Red Light!

Some states dictate the amount of interest you must pay on security deposits each year, and this amount is different from year to year. Be sure that you know what rate of interest must be paid and be sure to get it in full at the time of closing.

A deposit is an amount of money that the tenant will expect to see returned at some point if certain conditions are met. This is not your money, nor was it the past owner's money. If the past owner has negligently spent the money, you will be forced to either subsidize the deposits yourself or bring legal action against the past owner if he or she doesn't pay them back. Deposit laws differ in every state; we will discuss deposits in more detail in Chapter 10.

If the deposits you receive are not enough, there isn't a whole lot you can do about it. Chasing the tenant to pay more money to the security deposit is likely to cause World War III. Don't bother worrying about it and don't waste your time arguing about it with the tenant. It will only create a bad tone for an already unsteady relationship. Take comfort in knowing that changes are occurring and that soon these tenants will be either following your terms or no longer living there.

Edwards' Advice

Get acquainted with your tenants; find out who they are and what their tendencies are. This doesn't mean you should take them bowling, just that you should be friendly and observant. You should always make an effort to act like you care about their concerns at the property, but be sure not to get too involved with your tenants. The business relationship should be protected at all times. You're in this business to make money, not necessarily friends. Just imagine how difficult it will be to evict your new pal when he doesn't pay the rent. Business with friends and family is always a dangerous proposition.

Getting to Know You

The next thing to do is introduce yourself to current tenants as the new owner or manager of the property. You can send a letter or, even better, take a letter to them with a personal visit. Good communication right from the beginning is essential in developing strong business relationships with your tenants. Chances are, the tenants have probably already heard the news about the building being sold and would appreciate being able to put a face to their new landlord. The tenants will want to know who you are. Are you a monster or are you friendly? Do you drive a Ferrari or a pickup truck? Are you strict or a pushover? Take the opportunity to meet with tenants individually and let them draw their own conclusions.

You should let them know in your letter that the building they live in has indeed been transferred to you. Give the tenants your name, address, and telephone numbers so that they can contact you when they need to. The letter should explain your procedures for rental payment and maintenance. Put their minds at ease about their security deposits if they had them, and let them know that they should expect to hear from you soon about signing a rental agreement or lease if they didn't already have one.

Gather Information

Although the previous landlord may have supplied you with information about the occupants, you will need to gather information about your newly acquired tenants. You should want to know who you have living in your building. In your letter to the tenants, you should supply a form for the tenant to fill out (with a self-addressed, stamped envelope so that it can be returned) asking for information about the tenant. You want the tenants' full names, addresses, and telephone numbers. How many people live in the apartment? What are their names? Whom should you contact in an emergency? And so on. This information will act much like an application would for tenants you select yourself. Give the tenants a couple of weeks to return this form.

Some of these tenants may not return the form, and others may not want to reveal themselves to you, as if they have a mysterious identity to protect and you are the FBI wanting to watch their every move. If you run into trouble such as this, before you try to tap their phones, simply try to explain that it's in their best interest to provide the information you need. Tell them that you will take every reasonable precaution to protect their privacy. Take the time to carefully explain the information form in person and try to get as much info as you can.

If you're lucky enough to have bought property from an owner who kept good records and credit checks on his or her tenants, this will make getting info even easier. Still, send a form to all tenants even if the previous landlord's records are complete. Tenants' situations (such as who and how many are living in the residence) may have changed since first moving in under the previous owner.

Your Contract vs. Theirs

Before buying the property, you should have found out what kinds of tenancies were being used by the previous owner. Were the tenants on a month-to-month agreement? Or was there a lease for a specific term, such as life? Ask the tenants if they have a copy of a lease or rental agreement; if they do have one, make a copy for yourself. If there is an agreement in writing, you will be bound by it for the term of the contract. Whatever kind of agreement the previous owner had with the tenants will govern your relationship with the tenants for a period of time.

If there isn't a lease for a specific period of time, you should still give the tenants some time to make a decision. How much time depends on the terms of the agreement they had. Unless the tenants have a lease, you should give everyone about 30 days to either accept your terms in the form of a new rental agreement/lease or move out. You should prepare a new lease or agreement and give it to the tenants 30 days before the old lease expires so that it will go into effect on the day the other expires. We will explore leases and rental agreements in Chapter 8. If the tenant still does not respect your wishes and refuses to cooperate and accept your terms, you will be faced with starting eviction procedures. We will discuss the different types of evictions in Chapter 17.

Edwards' Advice

At the closing, the old owner will hand you a pile of keys for your new building. You should try to sort these keys by determining what locks they are for and labeling them appropriately. Take them with you on your visit and try each one to make sure it works. Be sure to get rid of the ones that don't seem to unlock anything. Make sure you have keys for every lock in the building. If you find that a tenant has changed the lock on a unit, ask him or her for a duplicate or make a duplicate for yourself and return the original right away. If a tenant is reluctant to give you a key, explain that you must have one in case of emergency; otherwise, the tenant could be held responsible for damages that result from an emergency factor in his or her unit.

Playing by the Rules

Your rules at the property most likely will be covered primarily in your lease or rental agreement, and we will discuss many common types of rules in Chapter 7. However, when you obtain a property and inherit tenants, you will have to explain to them that you plan to manage the property your way, that they will be subject to certain rules at the property, and that you hope for their cooperation. Sudden changes can be a big shock for some people. If you try to initiate a "no pets" policy at the property and a tenant already has a dog, you might be in for a real fight. In this instance, it might be in your best interest to allow this pet while not allowing new tenants to have them. Be gentle but firm when instituting your new policies on pre-existing tenants; they're probably not used to a smart landlord like you. Let them know that you're not a pushover and that you mean business, and it will be easier to deal with them again later.

Rent

By now, you should have some idea of what the market rent for the area is, but you should still find out what the last owner was charging. Then you should find out how much the inherited tenants have been paying for rent. You might be surprised to find the amounts to be quite different. The last owner might not have had a copy of this book and might not have been very good at managing the property. That's probably why you got such a great deal on the building in the first place. Regardless, you will be the one who will have to clean up the mess left by the last owner. Tenants who either are behind in their rent or are not paying at all will have to be dealt with. If they cannot make arrangements to pay off the balance owed, they will have to either move on their own or be evicted. Remember to be friendly but firm. After all, this is a business you're in to make money; just like the guy who owns the grocery store on the corner, you expect to be paid for your product and service.

If you find that the rental amounts being paid are well under market rent levels for the area, you should make the tenants aware of an increase by giving them some notice, at least 30 days, before applying the increase. Although some may squawk, most tenants, even if they are unhappy with the change, will probably pay a fair market increase and not want to move. This is especially true if the increment raised is not staggering and they witness new improvements to the building.

Landlord's Toolbox

Here is an important tip for helping to determine the rental values of an area. Check out the website www.hud.gov, The Housing and Urban Development's home on the Internet. Under the Multifamily Housing link there is information regarding Fair Market Rent Surveys for practically every county in the USA. These surveys are updated every year and are used as a barometer for determining the value of Section 8 subsidy payments. Besides the FMR surveys, there is a wealth of information that rental investors may find useful on that website.

Apartment Preparation

If the building you purchased has empty units in it, you will need to get them ready for renters as quickly as possible. The kind of property you have will determine how you should go about preparing it. Big apartment complexes may require a team of laborers or a fully equipped property management company to prepare the units for rent. Do-it-yourself landlords who will be handling apartment make-ready on their own will have to devise techniques that they can utilize to quickly prepare the units. Vacant apartments translate to a loss of revenue, so it is imperative to get the units ready as quickly as you can.

Apartment make-ready can be very time-consuming depending on the apartment's condition and how much you want to improve the apartment before renting it. When dealing with residential apartments, it is a good rule of thumb to only offer a unit that you yourself would be willing to live in. This means decent, safe, sanitary standards of housing. You will set the standard by which the property will be regarded. The condition of the unit you present to prospective tenants will reflect the amount of care and regard you have for the property you are trying to rent. A unit that you are willing to rent in poor condition indicates to prospective tenants that you are not a conscientious landlord who is really all that concerned about the condition of the property or the safety of its residents.

Edwards' Advice

If you have a new building, it will be in your best interests to keep it looking as such for as long as you can. New interior paint, carpeting, and cleaning may be the only immediate maintenance necessary for quickly renting the unit. However, older housing stock might require some extra improvements to make it a better place to live as well as to reduce the time it remains vacant. A unit in poor condition may still be rented, but the same unit in fair or good condition will probably achieve a higher rent value depending on the area and demand.

Older buildings are harder to make ready than newer ones because of the deterioration of old age, poor maintenance, and years of heavy wear and tear. Products that were once considered a standard for construction and maintenance—such as lead paint and asbestos, which no longer are used and are now considered a hazard when found in a property—can be quite difficult and costly to remove if required. You should check with local health departments about what is required in your area regarding environmental concerns. It is always much easier to remove lead paint and other hazards from an empty unit, and not under the scrutiny of a health department after an order for removal is issued. Under these circumstances you might want to take the position that an ounce of precaution is worth a pound of repair.

Whether your building is new or old, don't waste your time bothering to fix something that will simply fall apart again because it wasn't fixed correctly. There is a right way and a wrong way to do everything when it comes to repair. It pays to fix something correctly the first time or to replace whatever is in disrepair with new products.

> **Facts for Rent** _____
>
> As a smart landlord, you will learn that you need to keep an open mind and a will to learn to be successful. If you're not particularly handy in the world of construction, you will find that many stores that sell the products you need for repair also have brochures or salespeople who can assist you in doing the job correctly. The days of fixing things with chewing gum and shoestring are pretty much over, and we don't believe that The Home Depot carries these products anyway.

Before you start installing Jacuzzis and swimming pools to make your property the best on the street, you need to make sure that the street your property is on supports such improvements. In other words, find out what the optimum market rent for the area is and whether the lavish improvements will warrant a higher rent. Remember that you're also looking for a return on your investment. Making expensive, unnecessary improvements may cost you more money than current rental rates may support.

Once again, you have to understand that renting property is a business and that decisions need to be business oriented. If there is a hole in a wall, should you replace the whole piece of sheetrock or just patch it? If the bathroom sink is leaking, should you rip it out and replace it or can it be fixed? Of course, assessing the apartment's condition will help determine what manner of action you should proceed with. One word of advice, though: Any time the damage or repair can affect the safety of current or potential occupants, such as substandard electrical or other defective mechanical features, there's no decision to make—fix it and fix it right! Always remember to put safety first!

Cosmetic surgery for your apartment building, however, might be a good idea. If new exterior siding, paint, and brass mailboxes will give the building a clean and decent appearance, it might also attract better tenants. If that new sheetrock and sink will enhance the unit so that it will have a shorter vacancy and demand more money for rent while enhancing the overall value of the property, then it's probably a good idea to make the improvements.

Bring the Property up to Code

As a landlord, if you're not already aware of special codes of standard regarding buildings, you soon will be. Several different codes might affect property in any given area. Every state has a building code that dictates the minimum standard to which all buildings must adhere. In many areas, there also will be a housing code, a fire code, and a health code that set standards for property. If a property is found not to be in compliance with proper codes for that area, notice of violations and expensive fines can be sent to the owner. Keep in mind with older properties that some building conditions will be grandfathered in and be allowed to remain in spite of existing or new codes. However, opening Pandora's box is never a good idea in regard to code enforcement. It is important to note that fire codes do not grandfather and all properties must adhere to present fire codes.

Edwards' Advice

The housing code should not conflict with the building code or other codes. Some towns will create a housing code that is more stringent than the state code; if this affects you, you will need to contact the state chief inspector's office to determine which code you should use and to settle the issue with the town.

The building code normally deals with the construction, electrical, and mechanical aspects of the property. A building code is a written piece of legislation that dictates how a building is to be constructed with regard to living area and number of occupants. It describes acceptable methods and techniques for construction, electrical, and other mechanical installation. A town official known as the building inspector or building commissioner will usually make sure that the code is adhered to when a building is being constructed. In most areas, a certificate of occupancy will be issued to the owner upon satisfactory completion of a project as per the building code regulations from the building inspector. This certificate means that the building has been inspected, meets the proper standards, and is safe to legally occupy.

The housing code in most areas deals with safety and sanitary aspects of the property. This is also a written code usually administered only at a local level. A housing code inspector will sometimes be hired to carry out the duty of making sure buildings in the area remain in compliance with this code. This code can cover a wide range of aspects for which it will set standards from garbage removal and building aesthetics to more safety-oriented issues such as electrical and heating apparatuses.

The fire code is about as common as the building code across the country. The fire code is concerned with safety issues and fire prevention for buildings. Most towns have a fire marshal on staff to make sure safety requirements are met for properties in the area. Smoke detectors, fire escapes, and means of egress in and out of a building are just some of the topics covered by this code.

The health code usually deals with health-related aspects such as environmental concerns and sanitary conditions. A health officer may be employed by a town to make sure specific conditions are maintained at properties in the town to protect against illness and infestations.

Other codes that may or may not exist in your area (but you should still be aware of them just in case) include resident codes, blight codes, maintenance codes, and historical codes. It is important for you to try to keep your property up to code at all times to ensure the safety of occupants and to protect yourself from violations and fines. A property that is up to code will give you piece of mind and some protection from liability concerns.

Edwards' Advice

Befriend your local fire marshal; he or she can be a valuable contact. Once a year, notify your tenants that you and the fire marshal will be making an inspection of the property and will be inspecting each unit for smoke detectors. This is a great opportunity to get a glimpse of your rental unit to see what its condition is and how well the tenant is treating it. Look for potential hazards such as extension cords, bare wires, paper piled next to heat sources, or anything that could threaten the safety of occupants and your investment. Some fire marshals will have a form for you and the tenant to sign proving that the smoke detectors were in good working condition at the time of inspection. This form also will explain to the tenant the penalty for tampering with a smoke detector. Just make sure you are pleasant during the inspection and have brought with you several new batteries.

Hire Out or Do-It-Yourself

You're probably wondering, with all these codes, what you can and can't do as a property owner without getting into trouble. The simple fact is that you can't do anything that requires a license in your state such as plumbing, electrical, or structural construction. To ensure the safety of occupants, only qualified service people should do repairs that could result in a condition that could harm the occupant. In many states, single-family, owner-occupied owners can do repairs of all nature unless otherwise prohibited by law. Check with your local building official to find out what you can and cannot do.

For the most part, there are plenty of repairs you can still do yourself without a license such as painting and patching holes in sheetrock or changing washers in faucets. There will be locks to change, carpet and tile to install, windowpanes to replace, and grass to cut. Don't worry about not having anything to do. When you're a landlord, there is never a dull moment. Keep in mind, though, that if you fix something and it harms someone, you will be liable and could suffer considerable losses and maybe even imprisonment. When in doubt, always check with your local building official to see if you are allowed to make such a repair.

The Least You Need to Know

- ◆ Set up a checking account from which to operate your property.

- ◆ Make sure security deposits and rental payments are transferred to you from the old owner.

- ◆ Introduce yourself to your new tenants and gather some basic information about them.

- ◆ Familiarize yourself with local codes of standards for buildings in the area.

- ◆ If you are smart about how you prepare the unit and property for rent, you can save money and achieve optimum performance from the rental property.

Chapter 7

Apartment for Rent: Handling Vacancies

In This Chapter

♦ Determining rental value before advertising

♦ Using the right advertising techniques

♦ Screening prospective tenants with a thorough rental application and credit check

♦ Avoiding discrimination

FOR RENT: Charming two-bedroom, furnished apartment with a view, close to shopping and bus line. Contact Joe Landlord for more details.

When you own rental property, it is imperative that you rent vacant units as quickly as possible to quickly generate revenue from the property. This money is necessary to pay encumbrances on the property such as taxes and insurance. No one is going to pay you to own empty buildings even though that would be nice. Cash flow comes from actively pursuing tenants who will fill vacancies and pay you a market rent. Therefore, smart landlords have to understand how to advertise empty units, show vacancies, and carefully screen potential tenants to make sure they are getting the best tenant and rental rate they can.

Determining Rental Value

In Chapter 4, we revealed a couple ways to help you determine what market rents are for an area. Today's landlord must also be an economist. You will have to keep an eye on the economy, paying close attention to the price of other consumer items as well as the rate of inflation. Typically, the perceived rents in an area are too low. The costs associated with operating the property, maintenance, and remodeling will normally surpass what a property is actually making in monthly return from rent. The rental value assigned to your units must cover certain expenses and still maintain a positive cash flow.

Newspaper ads listing apartments for rent in the local area are one of the easiest ways to get a feel for what other landlords are expecting to get paid in the same area. Many of these classified ads list the number of bedrooms, the rental price, and a contact phone number. If the price is not listed, don't be shy; there's nothing to prevent you from calling the contact number to inquire about the ad. By comparing rental amounts of similar apartments for rent, you can determine what amount others expect to get for vacancies similar to yours.

Remember that every piece of real estate is different. Even though the number of bedrooms or other amenities might be the same as in another rental unit, there will still be some differences that might affect the rate of rent you could collect. The location, age, and condition of the units will differ and alter the rental rate. You have to evaluate your rental property's strong points and exploit them. Ask yourself the following:

♦ What does my property offer tenants that other properties do not?

♦ What is the unit worth?

♦ Is it in a good neighborhood?

♦ Are there ample parking spaces, private entrances, security, or laundry facilities?

Edwards' Advice

Location can have different meanings to different people. One person's best location might be someone else's worst. Be careful not to prejudge a location based on what you find attractive, because you might be surprised to find out what someone else likes.

Desirable locations such as waterfront property or an area complete with nice views normally get higher rents than properties without these luxuries. Convenience to shopping, nearby highways, and proximity to employment or schools may attract higher rents. Newer units attract higher rents than older ones. Good condition of the unit and appliances also warrants a higher rent.

Another great way to stay current with market rental rates is to network with other landlords in the area by joining a local property owner organization. Some landlords like to brag about how much they receive for their units, while others complain about how low the rents are. Either way, a wealth of information will be available if you listen. See Chapter 22 for more on joining landlord organizations.

Edwards' Advice

Contact the housing authority in your area for more information regarding market rental rates. Usually, the local housing authority is in charge of the distribution of Section 8 rental subsidies for low-income tenants for that area. These rental subsidies are supposed to reflect the market rental rate for the area. Therefore, the housing authority needs to know this amount to be able to continue to supply funds for housing.

Another important item to consider researching at this stage is security deposits. Find out what amount other landlords are asking for as a security deposit. How much you ask for will affect how many prospects you get and how many good prospects you can expect will refer about your rental. Expensive security deposits can dissuade tenants from even investigating a unit for rent. Some states have laws that limit how much security can be charged. We will review security deposits in more detail in Chapter 11.

Advertise Your Property

Newspapers, fliers, and word-of-mouth advertising are some of the most popular and reliable ways to advertise rental units. You might want to use one or more of these advertising media, but first you should decide what kind of market population you're trying to reach with the advertising and which medium will be best suited. For instance, if you own rental property near a college, you most likely will be attempting to find decent students to rent from you. A college newspaper or bulletin board might be the ideal way to reach potential renters. Different geographical areas attract different populations of renters.

Although it's always a good idea to try to improve the class of people who rent from you, it's also a good idea to try to get people with a similar nature to rent from you, especially if they are responsible. It's important to identify your area and market rent so you don't waste time and money advertising the wrong way. Here are some specific advertising sources you should explore to determine which form of advertising would be best for you:

◆ **Word of mouth** is one of the best forms of advertising, especially when you're hunting for someone similar to the people already renting from you. You might want to put the word out to other tenants renting from you that you have a vacancy available.

◆ **Rental agencies** can be used to successfully advertise and rent your unit. Leasing agents typically are real-estate sales agents who specialize in leasing rental units. Rental agencies usually charge a fee based on a percentage of the rent being asked if and when the agent finds someone ready, willing, and able to rent the unit. In many instances, the commission paid for this service will come from the new tenant.

◆ **Local newspapers or gazettes** will advertise your rental in the surrounding area for a fee. Usually, you place an ad in the classified section of the paper for a selected period of time. Newspapers charge different prices for different size ads. The price is based on the number of letters or words used in the ad. This advertising is limited to the circulation of the local paper, but that may be all the advertising you need to find a tenant already familiar with the area.

Facts for Rent

Real-estate agencies sometimes offer a rental service even if the agency specializes in real-estate sales. Usually these agencies don't make much money from performing this kind of service. For that reason, advertising may be limited to the window of the office. Many times, a sales agency looks for rentals to accommodate new buyers and sellers who might need a rental temporarily while they wait for the deal to close on their new home.

◆ **City newspapers** are similar to local newspapers except that the price for advertising often is more expensive because the circulation is usually wider.

◆ **Flyers** are a good way to advertise your rental in areas around big institutions such as colleges or hospitals from which you hope to recruit tenants. Flyers require a little more active role in advertising because you have to print and place them. To place them in establishments such as retail stores and restaurants, you should ask the store management for permission. Colleges and other big institutions may require permission for postings.

◆ **For-rent signs** are possibly the best form of local advertising available to you. For-rent signs are inexpensive and easy to use. Simply place the for-rent sign in the window of the available rental unit. Make sure the sign is visible to

passersby; otherwise, it has no value. The color of the sign is also very important; a black and yellow sign is one of the most eye-catching, although black and
orange is also very popular. Be sure not to fill every window with rental signs
because it makes the building appear more vacant than necessary. A prospective
tenant may not want to live somewhere that other people don't appear to want
to live.

Edwards' Advice

Housing offices are available on many school campuses, military bases, and large
employers. These offices are designed to find housing for college, military, and company students, staff, and personnel. It is a good idea for a smart landlord to affiliate
him- or herself with these types of institutions to find good tenants. Usually there is not a
fee involved, but you must be sure to notify the housing office if you rent the unit so that
it can keep a good record of available rentals.

◆ **Rental guides and magazines** are available for advertising. Many different
rental guides might serve an area. Usually big rental complexes advertise in
these types of guides, which are available for free at different business establishments. Advertising in these guides can be rather expensive, especially for the
small-property owner of only a couple rental units. Sometimes there might be
a guide especially designed for smaller properties available in an area. These
rental guides won't be as expensive as some other guides. In areas with housing
shortages, advertising in rental guides might actually be free if the people
searching for the rentals pay for the guides. Look around establishments in
the area or contact your local landlord organization to find one.

◆ **Television and radio** are advertising media for sure. However, we have yet
to see a commercial for a two-bedroom apartment. The reason is the expense
involved with these forms of advertising. The cost of radio and television advertising most certainly surpasses what most rental properties could generate in
income to cover advertising.

◆ **The Internet** is a very popular way to advertise just about any product or
service. There are several websites in existence that offer advertising for a fee.
There are also sites that specialize in apartment rentals and sites that appear
much the same way as the classified section of a newspaper. Fees for advertising
with these types of sites may vary; some might only require that you become a
member of the site by paying a yearly fee. Of course, there's nothing to stop you
from developing your own web page and listing its address on business cards or

other rental advertising where you can list your own available rentals. Several software programs are available that can help you design your web page. The trick to online advertising is getting people to visit the site. By carefully indexing your site with web search engines you can better attract more site visitors.

Edwards' Advice

The World Wide Web is the newest medium of the advertising world. There are several Internet real-estate websites that list apartments for rent. Some of these sites are specifically designed for landlords such as www.edwardscompany.com. They offer content of interest to rental owners as well as listing rentals.

Edwards' Advice

Be careful of bait-and-switch in advertising. If you advertise an apartment for rent at a certain condition and price, make sure that it exists. It is illegal to lure people with false advertising. Don't get caught in this kind of trap; many property owners have been prosecuted for these types of practices.

Regardless of what type of advertising you choose to help rent your available unit, you should take care when describing your offered rental. Good advertising techniques require creativity, fact, and careful description. Is the rental on the north or south side of town? Is there a fireplace, porch, or balcony? The rental might be charming or quaint with big spacious rooms, or it might be small and efficient. You need to look at the unit carefully and depict the unit's best qualities for advertising purposes. Good advertising entices potential clients by painting a picture in their mind about the unit.

Truth is also a requirement for good advertising. Be careful not to depict the unit as something it is not. Don't say there's a private deck to the unit when in fact there is a deck but tenants share it. How you word your ad is very important. You need to be careful not to discriminate in advertising. Especially beware of language such as "on the good side of town" or "in an excellent, low-crime neighborhood." If the north side of town is a ghetto, you can't say the rental is not on that side of town. Such advertising can lead to trouble if someone takes offense. Advertising for "single Polka-dotted males only," "no children," or "no handicapped" is a clear violation of the Fair Housing Act, and it can lead to big trouble for landlords who aren't careful.

The Price

There are a few schools of thought when determining whether or not to advertise the rental with the price. On the one hand, you may not want to be bothered by anyone who reads the ad and can't afford it. On the other hand, withholding the rental cost from the ad gives you the opportunity to negotiate a price without it being pre-determined by an advertisement. Once the price is advertised in some type of public medium, it becomes fixed until changed publicly or the ad expires and it's no longer published. Using descriptive words in the ad like affordable or modern may have different affects on the reader. Also, if you have more than one apartment available, you may wish to show the range of value between them, for instance $500 to $850. Whichever method you decide to pursue, remember the basic negotiation concept that you can always come down on the price, but once you do, you can't go up. At least not initially!

Rental Applications

A rental application is a device that all smart landlords use in the process of finding suitable tenants for a rental. An application is simply a form that a prospective tenant must fill out; it lists pertinent information about the individual such as full name, current address, and monthly income. This information is essential for you to have to help determine whether this individual will qualify for renting the unit.

Rental Red Light!

Qualify the tenant by income standards before renting a unit. Rent should not exceed 30 percent of a tenant's gross income. This is currently the federal guideline for rental expenses. Although this percentage can be readjusted to suit a tenant's needs, it may not be in the tenant's best interests. If the tenant must pay more than 30 percent of gross income for rent, he or she is probably lacking some other important living expense such as food or leisure. The bottom line is probably an unhappy tenant who can cause problems for your bottom line. If a tenant must choose to pay either groceries or the full rent, you can bet the rent won't win.

Your application also should require information about where the tenants used to live (and for how long) and where they are employed (and for how long) so that you can better understand whether this person is regularly employed and/or moves around a lot. The application is part of a smart landlord's screening technique and will help you select only tenants capable of paying rent on a timely basis and keeping the unit in good condition. You are looking to rent the unit to someone who suits your expectations of a good tenant. You're typically looking for tenant longevity, which means the person will pay the rent but also stay in the unit for a long period of time and minimize tenant turnover.

On the application, ask for a rental-housing history (including evictions) and any criminal history. Also ask how many people will be living in the unit and who the closest relative is for contact purposes in the case of an emergency.

Facts for Rent

According the National Multi Housing Council, "More than half of apartment renters [in the United States] with incomes of less than half the area median—1.8 million in 1999—face severe housing cost burdens and pay more than 50 percent of their income for rent and utilities."

Rental Red Light!

Some state Fair Housing laws protect Section 8 tenants under source of income class and prohibit landlords from refusing to rent to or participate with the Section 8 program. Check with your state Fair Housing Department for information related to Section 8 in your area.

Social security and driver's license numbers also are extremely important information to obtain on the application. You need to make sure the people filling out the application are who they say they are. Therefore, two forms of identification are a necessity, and, if possible, you should make a copy of each. All this information could come in handy in the event that you rent the unit to this individual, and he or she eventually skips out and owes you money. This information could be used to track the tenant down and go after him or her in court for what is owed. (For an example of a rental application, see Appendix A.)

Source of Income

Source of income is an area of applicant qualification that has come under some scrutiny in recent years. The concern is that certain applicants who collect welfare subsidies may be refused apartments because they may not have a job. More and more judicial decisions are indicating that landlords must consider all types of welfare subsidies as lawful sources of income. Section 8 payments to food stamps must be calculated as income if an applicant can prove that he or she receives such subsidies.

Credit Checks

On every application, there should be a section requiring the prospective tenant to allow you to obtain his or her credit information with an explanation about the agency you use and a place for his or her signature. Every adult who wants to live in the unit should be checked separately. Use of credit-reporting agencies has become very popular for smart landlords. I know, it's another step in an already lengthy process, but it's one of the most important steps and is one every landlord should take. If you think you don't need to do this because you are a good judge of character, you should consider getting out of this business.

It is important for you to know whether the tenant has a good or poor history when it comes to paying bills on time. Rent is one of the tenant's biggest bills, and if the tenant has shown poor performance in paying smaller bills, it's probably a good indication that he or she won't pay the larger ones, either.

Many credit agencies also perform checks on a prospective tenant's criminal history. Normally, the check includes not only prosecutions but also arrests. This is important because you do not want to bring someone prone to illegal activity and police visits to your property.

Eviction history is also available to many credit agencies and can be listed on the report you receive. If a tenant has been evicted and an execution has been issued against the tenant, it will be listed on this report. Obviously, this is something else you would want to know about the individual. A good rental history is a plus for any prospective tenant who applies for your rental.

The credit report is a smart policy to adopt when screening tenants because it informs you about the tenant. You will have to join a credit-

Edwards' Advice

Many police departments keep a record of police activity at a property. Legislation in some states even holds the property owner responsible for repeated tenant violations, and authorities will seize the property. Don't put yourself in this situation; make it a policy to check all potential tenants' criminal histories.

Edwards' Advice

If a tenant is adamant about not paying for a credit check, the person probably does not have the money, knows that he or she doesn't have good credit, or has a criminal or eviction history and doesn't want to waste the money. Either way, you don't want this individual as a renter.

reporting agency in your area and will probably be charged an initial membership fee. Every report thereafter also costs a small fee; this fee, however, can be charged to the prospective tenant. These fees vary by company but usually run from $20 to $30. Some landlords charge a little extra for their time in processing the paperwork. Be sure to explain to the applicants that the fee is nonrefundable regardless of whether they are approved or not.

The credit report does not have to be done before showing the tenant the unit for rent. The credit check should only take place if the tenant is truly interested in renting the unit after having seen it. Some prospective tenants will attempt to submit their own copy of a credit check so that they don't have to pay for an additional check. You can take a look at it if they want you to, but you should not stray from your policy. Thank them for the report, but explain that you must have a copy from

Rental Red Light!

You may not discuss an individual's credit report with anyone except the person to whom the report belongs. It is against the law to discuss credit reports. Laws may differ by state, however, so you should check with the credit agency you use about laws of confidentiality in regard to the reports you receive.

the agency you do business with and that it is a policy. If a prospective tenant refuses to pay for either a new report or any credit check, you obviously have a right to refuse the person. If the individual claims not to have the money for a check at that time, let the person make arrangements to get the money and come back even though most do not.

Using detailed credit reports to screen tenants not only is a good way to find better tenants, it also protects your property from destructive tenants while maintaining a peaceful environment for your other good tenants. Sometimes you might have to make an exception on a prospective tenant; not everyone who comes to see your rental will be perfect. His or her credit might not be so good, or someone might not have paid some parking bills and gotten into some trouble. Even if you decide to rent the unit to this person, at least you will know whom you are selecting because of the information on the report. Smart tenants who are looking for a new place to live will welcome a strict screening procedure because it assures them that the owner has taken steps to weed out potential bad neighbors, making the unit a nicer place to live.

Reference Checks

Another good technique when screening tenants is to do a reference check on the prospective tenant. On your application, there should be a place for individuals to list present and previous addresses where they have lived. If they are currently renting or have rented in the last few years, they should list the current and previous landlords' names, addresses, and telephone numbers. By contacting their previous landlords, you can find out from people who already know them how they were as a tenant. Make sure that the people listed as prior landlords do, in fact, own property where they are said to. Sometimes a bad tenant might lie on the application (I know, it's hard to believe) and, instead of giving actual past landlords' names, give the names of friends who act as though they were the individual's last landlord. If you are concerned that this situation might be happening to

Edwards' Advice

Reference checks from previous landlords are better than those from current landlords. Unfortunately, dishonest landlords who are suffering with a problem tenant might give a tenant a good reference just to try to get rid of the person. A previous landlord who already has dealt with the tenant and is no longer being affected by this person will be more honest in an evaluation.

you, call the assessor's office where the property is said to be located and ask the assessor who is listed as the owner of record.

You should also check the prospective tenant's work references. Call the employer listed on the application and make sure that the prospective tenant does in fact work there, for how long, and what his or her wages are. Most company managers do not mind answering a few short questions about the individual, but remember to be polite and thank them for their time.

If a prospective tenant is collecting a subsidy such as Section 8, you should call the governing agency for such subsidies to make sure the individual is indeed collecting the subsidy and how much is being received. Also make sure that this individual isn't already locked into a rental agreement with another rental owner, which would prevent him or her from renting your unit without the other owner's permission.

Facts for Rent _____

According to the 2000 U.S. Census Bureau tabulations, New York City still ranks as having the highest percentage of renters, with 68 percent out of a total population of nearly 9 million people. Long Beach and San Diego, California, rank second and third with 52 and 45 percent, respectively. In comparison, Chicago ranks a bit lower on the scale of percentage of renters (35 percent) but ranks third in cities with the highest amount of apartment units. The ranking of apartment units includes both vacant and nonvacant units in five-family properties or larger.

Some rental agencies send a questionnaire to past landlords regarding the tenant for references. If you decide to use a rental agency to rent your unit, make sure to ask how they reference tenants. A questionnaire, although useful when filled out, may not get filled out very quickly if at all by past landlords, and the mail time to send it back and forth may be too time-consuming to quickly rent your unit.

Photographs and Check Sheets

It's always good to have pictures of a vacant unit before a tenant takes occupancy so that you have proof that the unit was in good condition when the tenant moved in. This comes in handy if you ever wind up in court battling a tenant over the condition of the unit. It's a great idea to take pictures of the unit with the tenant there, maybe even a couple of shots with the tenant in the picture. Of course, many people might wonder why you were doing that, as if you were anticipating future problems and perhaps making the new tenant a little skittish. If you do plan to take pictures while the tenant is there, just explain that it's a policy you use to keep a record of unit condition.

Digital cameras have become popular toys for Moms and Dads to share baby Kyle's first photos through an online album or for Uncle Joe to show off his latest trip to the world's largest ball of twine. All fun and games aside, the use of a digital camera in the management business has proven extremely valuable. Before and after photos of an apartment can act as excellent documentation. In fact, having a photo printout of the apartment attached to the lease at the time the applicant signs can certainly show the tenant that you mean business and are thorough about your documentation. It may seem intimidating now, but wait until someday when you're in court discussing housing code perceptions that the tenant is claiming always existed because he or she has forgotten how nice the apartment was when he or she moved in.

The digital photos are easy to store on your computer, and be sure to make a copy on CD or floppy disk to attach to the tenant's file as well. Print photos are fine but tend to become cluttered and drop from overstuffed files. A disk can be neatly taped to a folder and easily found when needed. Always date and label your digital photos, and be sure to take clear pictures of various apartment areas including smoke detectors. While digital cameras range in price and components, most basic models will do the job. Video is an option with some models but not necessary for filming apartments, since most housing courts will not accommodate you with a DVD or PC to play movies.

It is a good idea to develop a unit check sheet that you can share with the new tenant. The check sheet is a form that lists all the different aspects of the unit, walls, ceiling, bath fixtures, windows, and so on. You should walk through the unit with the new tenant and examine it from top to bottom. Next to each item you should check whether that aspect is in excellent, fair, or poor condition. When the sheet is completed, both you and the tenant should sign the form and keep a copy. This will prove that, at the time the tenant took occupancy, you both agreed about the unit's condition. (For a unit condition checklist, see Appendix A.)

Showing the Apartment

Before you show prospective tenants the rental unit, you should first have them fill out the application and then qualify them to make sure that they can afford the unit. If you make an effort to show a unit to someone before qualifying him or her, you are potentially wasting your time. Even if the person appears to be great and falls in love with the unit, if he or she can't afford it, he or she will never pay for it. By filling out the application, you accomplish two very important things before showing the unit:

◆ You find out what amounts are listed for income earned, enabling you to see whether people qualify for the unit.

◆ You have a better idea of whom you're showing the rental to, including a name, address, and telephone number for security measures.

The second reason mentioned is very important in today's world. You don't know who these people are, and you're showing this unit, possibly by yourself, to complete strangers. In recent years, people have been attacked and robbed by individuals to whom they were showing vacant units. Protect yourself and others who might work for you by making every potential tenant fill out an application before showing a unit. Other safety measures can also be implemented, such as keeping a time log for showing vacant units and making sure no one shows a unit alone.

Facts for Rent _____

There are special agencies that send people disguised as prospective tenants, called checkers, who will apply for a rental unit just to make sure you are not discriminating. If you offer someone a cup of coffee, make sure you offer it to everyone; otherwise, you run the risk of discrimination allegations.

When you take someone to see the vacant unit, make sure that the unit is clean and well lit so that the individual can inspect it carefully and get a good impression. Let the individuals walk freely around the unit and be ready to answer their questions completely. If the unit is occupied already, you should notify the existing tenant of your intentions to show the unit before actually bringing a stranger into his or her home. Set up reasonable times during the day and workweek that will enable you to show the apartment in the tenant's absence. It's better to try to show the unit in the tenant's absence so that you avoid possible input from existing tenants who are more than willing to point out every little thing that's wrong with the unit. Also take care while showing the unit not to make false material representations or promises to make certain improvements in the apartment. These kinds of comments could come back to haunt you later on.

Don't leave the person alone in an occupied unit and make sure no one touches any of the existing tenant's belongings. If you must show a unit while the existing tenant is home, make sure to be polite and keep the visit nice while you show the unit as quickly as possible.

Make sure your standards for showing the rental unit are constant with every applicant. Don't get into trouble with discrimination laws by not showing certain applicants certain units. Make sure to give all applicants as much time as they need to look the unit over and be ready to answer every applicant's questions about the unit with the same regard you would anyone else. You cannot discriminate against religion, creed, color, race, or origin in this country, and there are several other factors you must not discriminate against, too. We will discuss fair housing in more detail in Chapter 8.

Approvals and Denials

So you have a new potential tenant standing in front of you. The person has filled out an application and has seen and wants the unit. You have obtained a credit report, completed the reference checks, and everything checks out. None of the other applicants have checked out as good, and the choice is easy. Great! Let the person know that he or she got it and make arrangements for signing a rental agreement and taking occupancy.

In some instances, however, you might have a situation in which you have received several applications and many of them have checked out. The only fair way to handle the situation is by the order in which you received completed applications.

> **Edwards' Advice**
>
> In some cases in which you receive a lot of interest in a unit, you should tell applicants before they apply that you have a first-come, first-served policy. If the first applicant checks out to be a good tenant, you have to go with that first tenant. This makes turning away other good prospects much easier.

Denying applicants can be a little trickier than approving people. If you deny someone a unit, you have to give that person a good reason and an explanation as to why he or she was denied. Once again, you must be careful of elements of discrimination. A smart landlord should be able to spot reasons for possibly denying someone a rental unit during the application phase. Short of finding a direct lie on the application, the denial will probably be the result of something negative on the credit report. If so, there is a legal responsibility to the tenant to notify him or her as to the reason for denial.

A denial form should be used to explain to the tenant why he or she was denied and what credit agency, complete with address and phone number, you used in regard to the application. Most credit agencies will supply you with a form to use when you deny someone based on the credit report. This information must be given to the denied applicant so that he or she can investigate any discrepancies found on the report.

Most credit agencies allow people who have been denied on the basis of their report from the credit company to receive a free report. You must not give the denied applicant a copy of the report; he or she must receive one directly from the credit agency.

You can discuss the credit report with the denied applicant but not with anyone else. This includes the owner of a property you are leasing for someone else. Credit information is privileged, confidential information, and it is illegal to violate that confidentiality. Check with your credit agency about the do's and don'ts of credit reports.

The Least You Need to Know

♦ Take time to carefully evaluate your rental unit and the area around it before affixing a rental value.

♦ Investigate the advertising techniques available in your area and use the ones that best suit your needs.

♦ A rental application is an excellent tool for a landlord to use in the screening process.

♦ Credit checks are an all-important, necessary step in the screening procedure, and they can help to prevent future problem tenants.

♦ Be careful not to discriminate against people during the screening procedure.

A New Lease on Tenant Life

In This Chapter

◆ Deciding what works best for you: rental agreements, leases, or oral agreements

◆ Determining standard and special clauses to include in your agreements

◆ Knowing the eligibility of who can enter a tenant contract

◆ Staying alert to nontenant residents, a.k.a. roommates

◆ Protecting against sublets and lease assignments

Before you rent an apartment to someone and become that person's land-lord, you need to make some decisions about the kind of tenancy you will admit at your property. You also need to determine how long the tenancy will last and how you will govern that tenancy. The three biggest questions asked by new rental property owners are:

1. Should I use a month-to-month rental agreement?

2. Should I use a lease?

3. What's the difference?

In this chapter, we will answer question number three and will give you enough insight so that you can determine the answers to questions one and two on your own.

Rental Agreement vs. Lease

Rental agreements and leases are very similar in nature and are sometimes hard to tell apart. Each is a contract used for renting property to a tenant. Both list the terms of the rental contract such as the amount of rent and deposits required, the number of people who will live at the rental unit, and the basic rules for tenants to follow. The main difference between the two rental contracts is the length of the tenancy associated with each. A rental agreement lasts only from one month to the next, while a lease usually is for a longer fixed term.

Which of the contract types you decide to use depends on what you are trying to accomplish with your property. If you are looking for longevity from tenants, you may want to use a lease; if you expect high tenant turnover, then a month-to-month rental agreement may be the right choice. Whichever you decide to use, keep in mind the benefits of having a written rental contract as opposed to an oral agreement.

The Rental Agreement

A written rental agreement contracts a tenancy for a rather short period of time. This form of agreement is known as a month-to-month tenancy, even though it is legal for a landlord to contract for a shorter period of time such as week-to-week. In a month-to-month agreement, the contract is automatically renewed each month unless either the tenant or the landlord terminates it by giving proper written notice, typically 30 days. As a landlord, you can also raise the rent or change conditions of the agreement as long as you give the tenant proper written notice. There are a couple reasons why many landlords prefer this type of rental contract:

> **Rental Red Light!**
>
> In some states, laws allow for rental agreements to be terminated without giving a reason. Notice of termination must be given to tenants, but how many days required in advance differs from state to state. Some states even require that landlords deliver written notices via certified mail or other means of official delivery.

- A rental agreement enables you to raise the rent more frequently unless rent is controlled by local ordinance.

- A rental agreement enables you to get rid of problem tenants more quickly.

◆ Termination of a month-to-month agreement does not allow the tenant to create a defense based on code violations unless the landlord is also seeking rent arrears.

This type of rental contract is common among landlords in areas where there is a tight rental market in which rents are escalating and tenants are easy to find. The rental agreement gives a landlord certain flexibility within the terms of the tenancy. If you feel that the rental market in your area is on the upswing and values are rising, you may want to use a month-to-month rental agreement instead of a lease.

Rental Red Light!

A rental agreement is very similar to a lease; the only thing that's different is the length of time that the agreement is binding. The format for a rental agreement can be exactly the same as a lease as long as the title is referred to as a rental agreement and the term is month-to-month or shorter. See Appendix A for an example of a rental agreement.

The Lease

A lease is a written rental contract that binds the parties involved for a fixed period of time, typically for one year. A lease has definite beginning and ending dates. A lease protects the tenant against rent increases or changes in terms until it expires unless the lease provides for such changes. As a landlord, you cannot force a tenant to move out of the unit before the expiration of the lease unless the tenant fails to pay the rent or violates some other term of the lease and/or state law. For example, you can evict a tenant for selling drugs or damaging the rental unit. (We will discuss more about evictions in Chapter 17.)

Generally, a lease cannot be terminated without a reason. However, it can be terminated if the tenant or landlord gives proper notice for termination, which is typically 60 days, provided that the lease states as such. However, 60-day clauses are not boilerplate in a standard lease and should only be put in when the owner feels that the amount of rents in his or her area might be going up and needs a way out of the lease to raise the rent, or just might need a way out of the leasee period. It also gives the tenant a way out and, in reality, makes the lease a 60-day lease instead of a year lease. It puts the tenant in a bad position because most tenants can't give 60 days' notice to leave the unit, and the owner usually wants someone to occupy the unit by the first of the next month. When a tenant gives 60 days notice and moves out in 30, the tenant is still liable for the next 30 days' rent by law, and the owner will win in court for the full amount.

This contract can be renewed only if, at the end of the lease, the tenant re-signs the lease. Terms in the lease can also state that the terms stay in effect after the expiration date until the tenant signs a new one. If a lease expires and the tenant has not yet signed a new one but has continued to pay rent, most states will regard the tenant as a month-to-month tenant renting under an oral agreement. We will discuss the different terms and clauses you should have in a lease in a moment. Remember that a lease is not as flexible as a rental agreement and therefore protects a tenant for a fixed period of time. The tenant is protected not only with the current owner but with any new owner of the property, including a bank in the event the property is foreclosed upon. This is a good sales pitch to obtain good tenants looking to rent in your area for a long period of time.

> **Rental Red Light!**
>
> One word of caution: A smart tenant will have a lease recorded on the land records in the town in which he or she rents for added protection. By recording a lease on the public land records, it further binds the owner to the conditions of the lease and makes the document a matter of public record.

For a lease to be valid, it must meet certain requirements, much the same as any other contract:

- ◆ **Offer and acceptance.** The parties must reach a mutual agreement regarding all the terms of the contract.

- ◆ **Consideration.** The contract must be supported by some form of legal payment, typically rent.

- ◆ **Capacity to contract.** The parties involved must have the legal capacity to contract.

- ◆ **Legal objectives.** The objectives of the contract must be legal.

A Pause for Lease Clauses

The lease provides a level of protection for the *tenant*, but it also can be designed to protect the landlord. The lease lists personal information about the tenant such as his or her full name, date of birth, and automobile make and model. The lease should also list the address of the property being rented. There should be a place on a lease for personal signatures of the *lessor* and the lessee, and a place to date the signatures. The lease also should state the term of years and should list all the terms of the rental contract—such as the rental amount for the term of years, the amount of security, and when the rent is due—as well as the rules and responsibilities expected to be adhered to by the tenant and the landlord.

Leases might have 100 other pages filled with clauses that are not much more than a concoction of ideas from whoever designed it. It's important to understand that private companies write an assortment of boilerplate leases that are available for purchase. If you obtain a copy of a lease such as the one we offer in this book, you should read it thoroughly, make sure it protects your interests, and make changes accordingly to fit your needs.

Landlord Lingo

Before you can begin to understand the lease, you first need to take a language lesson in legalese. A lease uses certain terminology that you are not accustomed to using. First you need to know what it means to be a **lessor**. The lessor in a lease is you, the owner or person giving someone else a lease. Next you need to know who the lessee is. The lessee in any rental contract is the person or persons being given a lease, the tenant(s). So far so good? Now, what do you call a **tenant** who sublets an apartment for rent? Complicated? Not really. The tenant who is subletting to another becomes a lessor, and that new tenant becomes a lessee. Remember that the lessor is the person who gives a lease to another.

Some clauses found in rental agreements and leases should definitely be considered boilerplate (a legal term that means "standard") simply because they better protect you as a landlord. You will find these clauses in the copy of the sample lease in Appendix A.

Notice that some of the clauses in the lease require a separate signature from the tenant. This is because of the importance of the information to which the tenant is agreeing. The lease in Appendix A has been divided into sections. Section 1 identifies the names and addresses of the landlord and tenant; this is necessary in every lease. Section 2 refers to the terms of years of the lease and the rent to be paid, again a requirement for any lease. Section 3 refers to the security deposits paid. We will now discuss certain other important clauses in the lease:

♦ **Unit to be used as** _____. It is important to indicate in the agreement how the rental is to be used (as a dwelling, an office, and so on).

♦ **An additional fee of $50 per month will be charged for each additional person unrelated to the occupant and not on the lease.** This is a good idea to mention in your lease because you have set a rental rate for your apartment based on the number of occupants. An increase in the number of occupants increases expenses for which you might be responsible such as water and sewer. By adjusting the rent accordingly, you will offset expenses.

◆ **Are you or any occupants now in the military service?** This clause is referred to as the Military Representation. The purpose of this clause is to determine whether people living in the unit are members of the armed forces. Other information required by this clause includes the branch of the armed forces, the date of discharge, and the individual's ID number. This information is important to you because military personnel will be treated differently in an eviction process. A signature is required for this clause. (See Chapter 16 for more details on evictions of tenants serving in the military.)

◆ **Appliances in the unit.** You should list any appliances you have supplied to the unit. This helps resolve any disputes about who owns the refrigerator or who is going to repair it.

◆ **Lessee to pay for _____.** Listing the different expenses associated with living in the unit will help you to clarify who is responsible for paying what.

◆ **Number of smoke detectors in the unit.** This is one of the most important clauses in a lease or rental agreement. List how many smoke detectors are in the unit and state that the tenant has inspected and found the smoke detectors to be in good condition. Make sure that the tenant understands that the smoke detectors are not to be tampered with and that you must be contacted in writing if the detectors need repair. A signature is required for this clause.

◆ **Lessee understands _____.** This is where the terms that apply to rules at the property begin. The tenant should be made aware that taking occupancy makes the tenant the controlling factor of the unit. By taking occupancy, tenants are now responsible for taking reasonable care of their unit and not creating unnecessary code violations. In this section, it should state that the tenant will not hold the landlord responsible for violations that the tenant causes or for losses that the tenant incurs at the property. The lease requires that the tenant obtain tenant insurance and name the landlord additionally insured on the policy. In this section, it also states that the tenant will hold the landlord harmless from legal action resulting from environmental conditions at the property and agrees to move if the property is determined to be a hazard to the safety of occupants. A signature is required for this clause.

◆ **Lessee agrees _____.** This is the list of rules at the property by which the landlord wants the tenant to abide.

◆ **Severability clause.** This is another extremely important clause to have in a lease because it keeps the lease in effect even if some part of the lease is found to be unenforceable.

Edwards' Advice

Beware of utilities that are the tenant's metered responsibility but not exclusively in the tenant's control. Many states do not allow common-area lights such as hallways or basement lights to be on a tenant's utility bill. This situation often is common in older housing stock that was probably owner occupied years ago. When these instances are found to exist, an absentee rental owner may be forced to rewire the common areas and add an owner's meter to the building.

◆ **Subordination to mortgages.** This clause explains that the lease is affected by mortgages and will subordinate to a new mortgage.

◆ **Disaster clause.** This explains to the tenant what will happen to his or her tenancy in the event of a disaster.

◆ **Holdover tenancy clause.** This explains what happens to the lease and the tenancy in the event that the tenant moves to another unit that you own or the lease terminates by running to the end date and the tenant stays.

Rental Red Light!

The liquidated-damages clause is something to consider in a lease even though courts might not always look favorably upon it. A liquidated-damages clause states that if a tenant moves out of the unit before the lease expires, he or she will owe you a predetermined amount of money for the losses you incur. Keeping the amount of money that's owed for breaking the lease to a low amount will better your chances of receiving it. In most states, tenants are responsible for paying the landlord for actual losses they cause. However, you as a landlord are, in most states, legally obligated to try to re-rent the unit as quickly as possible and to minimize your own losses.

◆ **Hand and seal.** This is where the landlord and tenant date and sign the lease and bind the rental contract.

◆ **Co-signer.** If for some reason the tenant does not have good references or can not come up with the proper security-deposit amount, a co-signer may be allowed to financially back the tenant. This section is where the co-signer would sign the agreement and give the landlord recourse against the co-signer if the tenant violates the terms and conditions of the lease.

◆ **Addendum to lease.** This is an area of the lease in which special terms may be added at the tenant's or landlord's request.

The lease clauses mentioned here are useful in just about every area in the country. Some rules, such as regarding snow removal, may not be necessary in some climates and may conflict with local code that makes the owner responsible for the removal. Farm property might have special livestock and crop clauses; other areas might be concerned with mineral rights clauses. Some landlords even have added clauses to prevent against such things as pets and waterbeds. Remember that every property differs and so does every property owner; a lease should be unique to the property and its owner's needs.

Rental Red Light!

Occupancy limits are legal as long as they have to do with the health and safety needs of other occupants, as determined by state building or fire code.

You may want to add policies regarding pets or guests. There may also be reason for a provision, such as an option to buy the unit. However you decide to construct a lease, you should try to keep the lease short and to the point. Try to create something that is user-friendly for the tenant and that offers protection for both you and the tenant.

Rental Red Light!

Beware of illegal clauses in rental agreements and leases that courts will not enforce. Some such clauses do the following:

◆ Indicate that the lease will terminate if the tenant files for bankruptcy.

◆ Give the right to take a tenant's personal property without court action if he or she owes rent.

◆ Make the tenant responsible for major repairs such as a roof or heating system.

◆ State that a tenant is waving his or her right to summary process or any other waiver of rights.

Who Can Sign a Lease?

Anyone can sign a lease, but not everyone will be legally responsible for the signing. For two parties to be in a rental contract, each party must be considered a competent adult at least 18 years of age. As a landlord, you can legally contract with someone under the age of 18 if that person has been declared a legal adult through a court order called emancipation, military service, marriage, or court order.

Only allow the person or persons who will be responsible for the rent to sign the agreement. Be sure to get two forms of identification from each person who signs the agreement. If a co-signer is necessary, be sure that this person signs as the co-signer in a separate space and be sure that all signatures are dated. You might also want to have the signing notarized by a notary public to make it even more legal.

Beware of Oral Agreements

In the movies, John Wayne used to shake hands with someone and say something like, "A man's word is his bond." Well, partner, there are a few things you should know about oral agreements before entering one.

Although oral agreements are legal for month-to-month tenancies and, in most states, for leases up to a year, they can sometimes lead to disputes. Memories have been known to fade as time passes. Remember the details of the Iran-Contra Hearings? Of course not!

Tenants have been known to forget the terms of a lease even when the terms are written down. How can you expect them to remember an oral agreement? And if you wind up in court over monies owed such as rent or security deposits, there will be nothing to refer to except lacking memories. This most likely is not going to help you win your case.

If your mind is set on using only oral agreements, however, there are certain things you should know:

- If you give a tenant an oral lease exceeding one year, it will become an oral month-to-month agreement at the end of the first year.

- When using oral agreements, the amount of notice you give tenants regarding rental increases or terminations typically depends on the period of time between rent payments. For example, if you get paid monthly, you must give 30 days' notice in most states.

Check your state and local statutes regarding oral agreements. Not all states and local governments have laws about oral agreements, but it's better to know before an agreement is made than after the fact.

Written rental agreements and lease contracts are available at local stationery stores for purchase, or you can draw one up for yourself. Your local property owner's organization may also have samples of leases and agreements. Copies of the forms we discuss in this book are available for your convenience in Appendix A.

Roommates: Can't Live with 'Em ...

Roommates, to put it nicely, are a pain in the neck. Typical roommates come and go without your knowledge and without your getting an opportunity to properly screen and interview them before they take occupancy. You can put in your lease or rental agreement that you are to be notified if there is a change or addition of roommates and that you will make the final decision regarding the admission of a new roommate, but chances are it will never happen. If you notice a new face on the property and suspect that a new roommate has been invited by your tenant to live in the unit, you will have no choice but to confront the tenant. You may want to allow it, especially if the person seems quiet and pays the rent in a timely manner, but you still need to find out who this individual is and maybe adjust the rent accordingly. The biggest problem with roommates is that each one believes that they are only responsible for an equal portion of the rent. This, however, is not the case, but it's your responsibility to make it clear to them at the time they enter the lease agreement and every other time the subject comes up. Always, always, always, treat the roommate situation as one family entity just as you would any other family or person who rented from you.

> **Rental Red Light!**
>
> Watch out for the "letter of understanding." A letter of understanding is a letter that a smart tenant might send after entering into an oral rental contract with you. This letter expresses the tenant's understanding of the terms of the contract. This is an attempt to put the agreement in writing by the tenant. In the letter, the tenant usually asks the landlord to sign it and send it back. The letter itself is not the problem, but you should make certain upon receipt of the letter that the terms are expressed correctly by the tenant and promptly reply if the terms are not. These letters have been used successfully against landlords to enforce certain issues, especially in instances in which the landlord didn't pay close attention to the details of the letter or simply didn't reply. If you do receive a letter of understanding, be sure to review it carefully, reply back promptly, and keep a copy for yourself.

The Roommate Clause

Be sure to add a clause to your lease or rental agreement stating the following provisions: In the event that the occupant or occupants occupying the unit decide to vacate the unit and want to be removed from the lease or rental agreement or want to substitute another person who will take their place for the remaining term of the lease and assume the terms and conditions of the lease or rental agreement, then the option of replacement will be the lessors, and the lessor will have the right to interview and accept or deny the applicant as per the policy of the lessor. In the event of a security-deposit transfer, the transfer will take place between changing occupants and will not affect the existing deposit on file with the lessor or owner in the case of a rental agreement.

Let Your Tenant Sublet? Not!

Subletting rental units and lease assignment should be forbidden in the lease or rental agreement. These types of activities undermine your authority as the property owner and exclude you from the process of determining who is renting your units. If these kinds of activities are permitted, it can lead to a loss of control at the property, something you cannot afford to let happen.

Subletting occurs when a tenant to whom you have rented in turn rents the unit to someone else. Normally, if you rent a unit to someone and the person decides to sublet, the rent charged in the sublet is higher than what you're charging. For instance, you rent the unit to a tenant for $500 per month, but now the tenant sublets the same unit for $600 per month to pocket an extra $100. You will have no idea who the new tenant actually is because you never had an opportunity to screen the person. And what happens if either the original tenant or the subletting tenant stops paying the rent or causes a nuisance at the property? The answer is that you will have to evict. In many states, however, you have to evict both the original and the subletting tenants separately to have them removed from the property. Subletting is a bad idea and is not good business on your part.

Facts for Rent

A "tenancy at will" usually refers to agreements in which tenants rent for a very short period of time such as in rooming or lodging houses. Certain states such as Massachusetts and other states that have a high concentration of college students have particular provisions for tenancies at will such as a shorter time required for termination of tenancy.

Lease assignments occur when the tenant finds a new tenant to take his or her place at the unit and simply transfers the tenancy to that person. Again, this activity will undermine your screening procedures and possibly lead to trouble.

Make sure your lease specifically prohibits subletting and lease assignments; otherwise, in most states, a tenant will be allowed to do so without your consent.

In some states, subleasing is prohibited; in others, state law leaves it up to the landlord. If your state is not listed in the following table, then there is no statute or provision for subletting.

Subleasing Laws

State	Laws
Alaska	Sublessee must apply in same manner as new Tenant (T). Landlord (LL) has 14 days to respond to request in writing; no response is taken as consent. LL must give legal reason for denial.
Arizona	Subleasing is allowed. Same rules apply to sublessee as to the tenant.
Arkansas	T must get prior approval of LL.
California	T must get consent of LL.
Colorado	LL can prohibit subleasing, but it must be stated in the lease or rental agreement.
Delaware	LL may prohibit or restrict subleasing if stated in agreement. If LL allows subleasing, then consent cannot be "unreasonably withheld."
Florida	LL may prohibit subletting. If allowed, T must get consent from LL to sublet.
Hawaii	Allowed only with LL's consent.
Idaho	Allowed only with LL's consent.
Missouri	Subleasing is allowed, but original T must get consent of LL. If consent is not requested, sublessee can be charged double the rent.
Nebraska	Subleasing allowed. Up to the LL to prohibit.
Nevada	Allowed per rental or lease agreement.
New York	T in a building with four or more units is allowed to sublet, even if prohibited in the lease or agreement.
Pennsylvania	Allowed sublessees are equally responsible to the LL-T laws as the original T.
South Dakota	Not prohibited. Statutes state that "assignees" of lessees are equally responsible to owner for damages/breach of contract.
Texas	T must have prior consent of LL or subletting is prohibited.
Utah	Not prohibited.
Virginia	LL must respond to written request by current T to approve/disapprove sublessee within 10 days or consent is given.

Breaking the Rental Contract

Whoever said "Breaking up is hard to do" must have been a landlord. As we already mentioned in this chapter, rental agreements and leases are a little different. Either the tenant or the landlord can terminate month-to-month rental agreements at any time as long as proper notice is given, typically 30 days. Breaking a lease can be a little more difficult, especially if you as the landlord are not inclined to break the rental contract. This is the part of the lease issue that gets a little sticky. You see, tenant advocates are quick to point out any possible illegal clauses you may have in your lease, but for some reason they fail to recognize that a lease is an enforceable contract between two competent parties.

Facts for Rent _____

In states such as New York and Texas, the law does not allow for subletting and lease assignments without the landlord's consent. In other states, including Rhode Island and Hawaii, provisions are not made in regards to lease assignments and subletting. A smart landlord will protect him- or herself by including language regarding subletting and assignments in lease or rental agreements.

Rental Red Light! _____

Residential and commercial rental property use different leases. Even though the two leases might appear to be very similar to each other, the enforcement procedures can be quite different. In many states, if a commercial tenant breaks a lease with a landlord before the lease expires, that tenant may be held liable for the cost of the entire term of the lease. In most cases, a commercial lease is negotiated for a longer term of years than a residential lease.

The lease should be designed to protect the tenant and the landlord as a fair and legally binding contract. If a person buys a car from a dealer and then, after several months, decides that he or she no longer likes the automobile, he or she cannot simply bring it back to the dealership and demand his or her money back. The dealership would have no responsibility whatsoever to even listen to the individual. Unfortunately, this is not the case with leases. Courts and arbitrators occasionally interpret the document differently, and the outcome might be more different than you would expect.

It becomes a matter of personal decision whether you want to allow a tenant to break a lease before it expires. Why did you go through the trouble of preparing a lease if you weren't going to enforce it? You wanted to make sure that you would have a tenant for a predetermined period of time. If the tenant hasn't any choice but to break a lease, then rather than argue and create a worse situation with the tenant, it might be in your best interest to release the tenant from his or her obligation and quickly try to re-rent the unit—even though you can still hold the tenant responsible for damages incurred by the early exit.

A smart landlord should be careful to consistently enforce the provisions of the lease in an equal manner with all tenants. If you list provisions in your lease, you had better be prepared to enforce those rules. In some landlord-tenant disputes, courts have awarded in favor of the tenant even if the tenant violated a legal provision because the landlord did not consistently enforce the provision such as a no-pets clause or limits on occupants.

Lead Paint Disclosure Documents

Landlords and property managers are required to inform tenants before they sign or renew a lease or rental agreement as to any information pertinent to the safety of conditions at the rental unit. For example, if lead paint hazards have been identified at a property, the tenant must be notified of such a condition. Lead paint is commonly found in buildings built prior to 1978. A lead disclosure form should be included in your lease or rental agreement package. The lead disclosure form must meet the requirements set by the Environmental Protection Agency. A copy of this form has been included in Appendix A of this book. If you have had your property inspected or tested by certified inspectors, a copy of the report must also be shown to the tenant.

All tenants must also receive a copy of the booklet entitled "Protect Your Family from Lead in Your Home," published by the Environmental Protection Agency.

Penalties for not complying with these disclosure regulations can range from a mild reprimand to criminal fines of up to $11,000 per violation. You also may be ordered to pay up to three times an injured party's actual damages. Don't fool around with this requirement; it only will take you a minute to fill out the disclosure form and present it to the tenant. Make a copy for yourself and keep it on file. For more information regarding lead or other environmental concerns, contact your local and state health agencies; contact information is listed in Appendix C. Copies of the disclosure form and the booklet can be obtained from either the U.S. Environmental Protection Agency or the U.S. Department of Housing and Urban Development; contact information is also listed in Appendix C.

Lead Paint Addendum

If you are renting older housing stock that might contain lead paint, you may want to consider adding a clause similar to the example called "Lead Paint Addendum," which you can find in Appendix A, to help try to curb future potential problems. The clause should basically indicate that the tenant and other occupants are only allowed to use and occupy the area within the painted surfaces of the unit. Also state that they have no authority to allow anyone to test any areas within the painted surfaces and that they shall not in any way pierce, break, or tear any of the painted surfaces. This clause at the very least might be able to help you if a problem arises.

The Least You Need to Know

- Rental agreements differ from leases primarily because of the length of tenancy.
- Oral rental agreements are legal to use but are not as clear or as concise as written agreements.
- Rental agreements offer more flexibility within the terms of the tenancy than a lease.
- A lease will primarily protect a tenant from periodic rent increases, but it better assures a landlord of tenant longevity.
- Any legal adult, typically 18 years of age, can enter into a rental agreement. Anyone can sign a lease, but not everyone is liable for it if he or she is not of legal age.
- Subletting and lease assignments can lead to aggravation and loss of control at the property.

Chapter 9

Fair Housing

In This Chapter

- ◆ Knowing the details of the Federal Fair Housing Act
- ◆ Avoiding discriminatory language in advertising and lease/rental agreements
- ◆ Fair housing laws specific to your local and state government
- ◆ Penalties and fines levied as a result of successful discriminatory lawsuits

You have a two-bedroom apartment available in a four-unit building that you own. The other three units are rented by tenants who are single and over the age of 50. Your tenants are very quiet, and one of them last week praised the building for how peaceful it is to live there. The yard is clean, and there is enough parking for everyone because each tenant only has one car. The only pets you have in the building are a cat and a couple of fish that belong to the 56-year-old woman renting upstairs. One 51-year-old woman on the first floor has been busy planting some flowers in the yard, while a 65-year-old elderly man who lives in another unit on the first floor has been making arrangements to plant a small garden. If you can get another tenant similar to these fine people to fill the vacancy, you'll be made in the shade. But can that be done?

The answer is "yes" if you're lucky and someone who fits the description you're look-ing for applies for that unit. But what if a young woman with two small boys applies for the rental? A mom with kids may not be what you hoped for, but if this prospect meets certain requirements, there isn't a thing you can do about it. You will have no choice but to rent to this person and hope your luck with renting to good tenants continues.

Federal Laws

There are federal, state, and local laws that all forbid various types of discrimination. The most common types of discrimination prohibited by federal law are against race and disability. The main federal laws that landlords must adhere to are the Fair Housing Acts, 42 U.S.C. 3601–3619, 3631.

Most states also have discrimination laws, although some are not quite as comprehen-sive as the federal laws. In some cases, however, the state law will surpass federal guidelines to address something not covered by federal laws such as discrimination based on sexual orientation.

Federal law applies to every state in the country. Therefore, it's a good place to start discussing what you, as a landlord, cannot do. The Federal Fair Housing Act protects the following categories from discrimination:

◆ Race and color

◆ Religion

◆ National origin

◆ Handicap or disability

◆ Age or familial status, including families with children under the age of 18 and pregnant women

◆ Gender, including sexual harassment

The landlord-tenant relationship is also affected by the Fair Housing Act in the following ways. As a landlord you must not …

◆ Advertise or make a statement that violates any of the protected categories previously mentioned. For example, you must not advertise a property as a "looking for Catholics only."

◆ Falsely deny the availability of a rental unit. In our example, you could not tell the mother that the apartment has been taken when it has not.

- Initiate stricter policies when selecting certain tenants. You cannot require more reference checks or paperwork just because this isn't your ideal tenant.

- Provide services, such as repairs, to only selected tenants.

- Refuse to rent to members of certain groups. For instance, the mom in the example belongs to a tenant advocacy group. This just isn't your day!

- Terminate a tenancy for discriminatory reasons. You can't evict a tenant just because she belongs to that strange church down the street.

Facts for Rent _____

Two types of elderly housing are exempted from the Federal Fair Housing Act: communities for tenants who are 62 years or older and those for tenants who are 55 years or older. To qualify for the 55-year-old housing exemption, at least 80 percent of the occupied housing units must be occupied by at least one person who is 55 years or older.

Federal Law Exemptions

There are some exemptions to the federal acts dealing with the types of property as they relate to discrimination. The exemptions are as follows:

- Owner-occupied buildings with four or fewer rental units

- Single-family housing units rented without discriminatory advertising and without the help of a real-estate broker

- Housing operated by certain types of religious organizations and private clubs that limit occupancy to their own members

- Housing reserved exclusively for senior citizens in which certain qualifications must be met

Keep in mind that just because there aren't any federal laws covering these exemptions, it doesn't mean they are not covered by state law. For instance, owner-occupied buildings with four or fewer rental units may be exempt under the federal guidelines but not under the state law of California. Before you attempt to fall into one of these categories, you had better be sure that the exemption applies in your state. Most law-abiding landlords like you follow the basic rules of discrimination laws such as renting to all races, religions, ages, and genders. Knowing all the boundaries of the laws including the levels of nonblatant discrimination, however, will keep you out of court.

The Many Levels of Discrimination

There are many different types of federal and state discrimination laws that landlords must be careful not to violate. Penalties for discrimination can become quite costly and can be damaging to your reputation as a good landlord. In addition to some of the obvious forms of discrimination such as judging someone based on race or color, there are some other more subtle forms of prejudice that can get you into trouble if you're not careful. Whether discrimination is done intentionally or unintentionally, it is still illegal. No matter how well-intentioned a landlord might be when initiating certain policies, it does not justify discrimination.

A smart landlord must be careful when advertising rental units. Ads that are worded incorrectly can lead to trouble if they indicate a desired preference. Special events or policies that a landlord may initiate at a property could violate some of the protected categories listed in the federal and state guidelines. Let's explore the federal guidelines in more detail and list some possible discrimination mistakes that you as a landlord should be cautious not to make.

Race and Religion

A person's personal belief, no matter how strange it may seem, is not reason enough to not rent to that person. If a Catholic landlord were offended by someone's atheistic convictions, it would not be reason enough to refuse renting to that person. An advertisement that reads "quiet Catholic neighborhood" could be perceived as an attempt to discriminate against non-Catholics, and it is in violation of the federal law. A landlord must also be cautious not to accidentally send subtle messages with forms of written or oral communication that would benefit, support, or discriminate against any race or religious group.

Facts for Rent

Advertising and language used in a lease, if not worded correctly, can be a direct violation of fair housing laws. For instance, if you own property in an area with a heavy Spanish influence, and you advertise and offer leases only in Spanish, you could offend English- or other language-speaking people who do not speak Spanish. Unless your state requires lease translations for Spanish-speaking individuals, as California does, English is the only language that you may advertise and write leases in that does not violate fair housing laws.

National Origin

As a landlord, you must not discriminate against a person's national origin. A landlord cannot require that all tenants be U.S. citizens or give discounts to people who belong to special clubs of origin such as the Polish American Club. If you own prop-

erty in an area where immigration issues are a concern, such as in Texas and California where there are problems with illegal aliens and a heavy Hispanic population, and you are accustomed to asking for the proper papers as proof of citizenship, you must make sure you ask every applicant for this proof, not just Hispanic applicants. You cannot single out one group of people based on their origin. However, if you ask every applicant for acceptable proof of identity and work eligibility, you will be sure not to single out specific people.

Landlord's Toolbox
For information about how landlords can legally verify an applicant's citizenship or immigration status, contact the Immigration and Naturalization Service (INS) at 1-800-375-5283 or contact the local INS office listed in any metropolitan phone book under the U.S. Department of Justice.

Familial Status and Age

Landlords cannot refuse to rent to families with children. A landlord also must not set unreasonable limits on the number of occupants who can occupy a unit, which might prevent children from living in the unit. By the same token, a landlord cannot advertise for, initiate policies for, and accept applicants classified as families only. Landlords must not refuse to rent to someone based on the applicant's age unless the applicant is not a legal adult or the housing is legally categorized as senior housing only.

Occupancy limits and setting up rules that determine how many people can live in a rental unit can be identified as a form of discrimination. Landlords must be sure that limits set regarding the number of occupants are reasonable to that unit and are in accordance with state and local health and safety codes. State and local building, housing, and health codes will set minimum requirements of gross living space in a unit for occupants as well as the number of bedrooms and bathrooms.

Regardless of the requirements listed in the codes, it is still not legal to advertise for occupancy preference of any type. A landlord may set an occupancy limit that is lower than federal, state, or local standards if it is for legitimate business reasons, such as if some aspect of the property will not support more occupants (for example, a septic system with limited capacity).

Landlords must be careful to avoid age discrimination violations. A landlord cannot refuse to rent to older persons or impose special terms on the tenancy unless the same standards are applied to all the other tenants. If, however, a reference check reveals that an older applicant is suffering from advanced senility or has no means by which to undertake basic house-cleaning chores, you as a landlord may be allowed to refuse to rent to that person based on age-neutral evidence that the applicant is not stable or reliable. Be aware, however, that certain conditions may warrant special modifications of the unit or your policies if the elderly tenant can qualify for disabled status.

Minors cannot be discriminated against if they have reached legal adult status through emancipation. An emancipated minor is a 16- or 17-year-old who is legally married, has a court order of emancipation, or is in the military. Minors who are not emancipated can be refused a rental based on their age because, legally, they do not have the legal capacity to enter a valid binding rental agreement.

Rental Red Light! _____

The Department of Housing and Urban Development (HUD) issues and enforces the federal guidelines. HUD normally considers an occupancy limit of two people per bedroom as reasonable. The federal test is referred to as the "two-per-bedroom plus" standard. HUD also considers the size of the bedrooms and the rest of the unit in occupancy considerations. State and local governments can set their own occupancy limits as long as they are more generous than the federal guidelines, meaning that they allow more people to live in the unit. In states in which the rule is more generous than the federal rule, landlords are bound to uphold the state law. Here is a list of 32 states that have adopted all or part of the federal "two-per-bedroom plus" standard:

Arizona	Kansas	Pennsylvania
California	Kentucky	Rhode Island
Colorado	Louisiana	South Carolina
Connecticut	Maryland	Tennessee
Delaware	Massachusetts	Texas
Florida	Missouri	Utah
Georgia	New Mexico	Virginia
Hawaii	New York	West Virginia
Illinois	Ohio	Wisconsin
Indiana	Oklahoma	Wyoming
Iowa	Oregon	

Some of these states have cities and counties with ordinances and/or have expanded the federal rule with their own legislation.

Disability

Federal law prohibits discrimination against any person affected with the following types of disability:

- ◆ Anyone who has a physical or mental disability, including but not limited to hearing, mobility, and visual impairments. Also protected in this category are people suffering from mental illness, AIDS and AIDS-related complex, mental retardation, and alcoholism (but only if being treated in a recovery program).

- ◆ Anyone who has had a history or record of such a disability.

- ◆ Anyone who is regarded by others as though he or she has such a disability.

A landlord must be cautious to evaluate and treat a tenant with a disability on the basis of his or her financial stability and history as a tenant, not on the person's mental health. A landlord can refuse to rent or can evict a tenant on the grounds of the disability if the tenant has shown specific instances in his or her behavior in which he or she posed a threat to the health and safety of other residents or the property. For example, if a reference check reveals that a tenant repeatedly assaulted or threatened other residents or destroyed the previous property, that tenant may be refused.

Rental Red Light!

Federal fair housing laws also extend protection to alcoholics and drug users. However, protection is limited to two specifically defined groups:

- ◆ Recovering alcoholics who are actively and regularly participating in a medically based treatment or AA program
- ◆ Former drug addicts including anyone with prior convictions for illegal drug use, but not for drug dealing or manufacturing

There may be other reasons why housing can be refused legally to recovering alcoholics or drug users, but housing cannot be refused solely on the basis that the person is a former addict.

Landlords cannot ask tenants whether they have disabilities of any sort. A landlord's questions and actions must treat every tenant the same. No matter how well-intentioned you are as a landlord, you cannot make decisions regarding where and how a disabled tenant will live in a building. For example, if you have two apartments for rent on the ground and second floors of a building, you must show a prospective tenant in a wheelchair both units if he or she wants to see them, no matter how reasonable it might seem for the applicant to see only the ground-floor unit.

Disabled tenants have the right to live in an accessible place. Federal law protects disabled tenants after they have moved into a rental unit. Landlords must …

◆ Accommodate the needs of disabled tenants at the landlord's own expense. 42 U.S.C. 3604(f)(B)

◆ Allow disabled tenants to make reasonable modifications to their units to accommodate their own comfort and safety needs, at the tenant's expense. 42 U.S.C. 3604(f)(3)(A)

The key to the issue of the landlord making a building and unit accommodate a disabled tenant is if the desired accommodations are reasonable. Some reasonable modifications to a rental property and rental policies include …

◆ Installing a ramp to help a wheelchair-bound tenant negotiate two steps up to an entrance to a building or a room inside a unit.

◆ A special rent payment plan for tenants who have their finances managed by someone else or by a government agency.

◆ Allowing service animals such as guide dogs or hearing dogs in rental properties even where there are "no pet" policies.

◆ Modifying kitchen appliances to accommodate a blind tenant or installing special faucets or door handles for persons with limited hand use.

◆ Installing special smoke detectors for the hearing impaired.

◆ Making arrangements for blind tenants to have all communications from management read to them.

A landlord does not have to change every rule or policy and make unnecessary modifications that are not reasonable requests from disabled tenants. A landlord does not have to make a change that would seriously affect his or her capability to run his or her business. For example, you cannot be made to rip apart your building to install an elevator because a disabled, wheelchair-bound applicant prefers the second-floor unit as opposed to the ground-floor unit you have available. HUD would consider the expense to be unreasonable.

If a tenant attempts to make modifications, the changes to the unit must also be reasonable and be made with prior approval. A landlord is entitled to know what the proposed modifications will be, that they will be done in a workmanlike manner, and that the disabled tenant has obtained any necessary building permits. If such changes to the unit will require the restoration of the unit in the event that the tenant leaves, a landlord can require that the tenant pay into an interest-bearing escrow account for the estimated cost for restoration. The interest, of course, belongs to the tenant. (For more information about regulations regarding permitted modifications and accommodations for disabled persons, contact the Department of Housing and Urban Development. For more information regarding handicapped access requirements, check out HUD's website at www.hud.gov or contact the Department of Housing and Urban Development in the state you own property.)

Edwards' Advice

Landlords are permitted to ask for proof that the accommodations and modifications requested by a disabled tenant are truly needed. Some disabilities, such as mental ones, are not always obvious to detect, and neither is the accommodation. Proof is necessary to know whether the request is legitimate.

Gender

A landlord must not discriminate against people based solely on the fact they are male or female. Once again, a landlord must not make decisions about where a person lives in a rental unit based on the person's gender (for example, trying to protect female tenants from burglary by only allowing them to live in the upper floors of a building). Even though the decision was based on good intentions, it is still considered illegal. In this example, a landlord would be discriminating against women by not allowing them to occupy lower-level units and discriminating against men who want upper-story units.

Edwards' Advice

Keep the relationship between you and your tenants based solely on business. You should never become involved personally with people you do business with. It usually leads to confusion and bad business decisions, not to mention that it could probably get you into trouble. If you really want to ask the tenant out to the movies, wait until he or she no longer is a tenant!

Landlords must be especially careful of sexual harassment charges. It is illegal to refuse to rent to someone because he or she has resisted a landlord's sexual advances. Courts have defined sexual harassment as …

◆ A pattern of persistent, unwanted attention of a sexual nature, including the making of sexual remarks and physical advances or a single instance of highly egregious behavior.

◆ Persistent requests for social contact with a tenant or constant remarks concerning the tenant's appearance or behavior. (This could be a single offensive remark or instance.)

◆ A situation in which the tenant's rights are conditioned on the acceptance of the landlord's or manager's attentions.

A landlord or manager must not refuse to make a repair simply because a tenant does not agree to go on a date.

State and Local Discrimination Laws

Most of the time, state and local antidiscrimination laws mirror the federal laws, making it illegal to discriminate against race, color, national origin, familial status, disability, or gender. However, state and local laws often are more detailed and sometimes forbid other types of discrimination not covered by the federal guidelines. The following sections profile some common antidiscrimination laws that some states and localities have adopted. For more information, refer to Appendix B, which lists the contact information for your state Fair Housing agency.

Source of Income

In many states, it is illegal to refuse to rent to a person based on the source by which his or her income is earned. This means that a tenant who collects some form of public assistance must be rented to if the amount meets the standard necessary for renting the unit.

Marital Status

In many states, it is legal for landlords to refuse to rent to a couple that is not married. Some landlords will refuse to rent to unmarried couples based on the idea that unmarried cohabitation violates religious beliefs. Only about 20 states actually ban discrimination based on marital status. Only a few states—Massachusetts, California, New Jersey, and Alaska—recognize the term "marital status" as pertaining to unmarried couples. Courts in Maryland, Minnesota, New York, and Washington have ruled that "marital status" only protects single people and married couples from being discriminated against but does not protect unmarried couples.

Sexual Orientation

Discrimination based on sexual orientation is illegal in some states including California, Connecticut, the District of Columbia, Massachusetts, Minnesota, New Jersey, Rhode Island, Vermont, and Wisconsin. In addition, many cities prohibit discrimination against sexual orientation including Atlanta, Detroit, New York, Seattle, Chicago, and Miami. For more information about laws that deal with sexual orientation, contact the National Gay & Lesbian Task Force, 1700 Kaloroma Rd. NW, Washington, D.C. 20004 (202-332-6483).

The Penalties

If you are brought up on charges of discrimination, there are several possible penalties if you are found guilty:

♦ You might be required to rent the unit to the aggrieved person.

♦ You might have to pay actual compensatory damages. This amount may reflect the cost of the aggrieved to find another unit, the additional rent the person had to pay elsewhere, and damages that would reflect the humiliation and distress suffered by the aggrieved person.

♦ You might be required to pay punitive damages, meaning extra money paid as punishment for outlandish and intentional discrimination. Rewards can be $25,000 and up for persistent, outlandish discrimination.

♦ You might be required to pay the aggrieved person's attorney fees.

♦ You might be required to pay a penalty to the federal government. The maximum penalty under the Federal Fair Housing Act is $10,000 for a first violation and $50,000 for a third violation within seven years. Many states have comparable penalties.

Terrorism Concerns

Fair Housing laws did not cease to exist on September 11, 2001. The civil rights of individuals remain protected regardless of the heightened threat of terrorism. National origin is a federally protected class and must not be used as a reason to refuse renting to an individual. However, as a matter of civic duty and vigilance, there are things a rental owner must consider when concerned by the unusual habits or actions of a suspect tenant. If you suspect terrorist activity by one of your tenants, notify local law enforcement who will then contact your state's homeland security office. Some states also sponsor seminars on terrorism to help the public learn more about what kind of activity should be suspected.

Facts for Rent _____

The Fair Housing Act says, according to an article published by Housing and Urban Development, www.hud.gov 1-6-2003 titled "Response to concerns about housing security following September 11, 2001":

> The Act does not prohibit discrimination based solely on a person's citizenship status.

Federal Fair Housing law permits landlords to ask housing applicants for documentation of their citizenship or immigration status during the screening process but only if you do so with every tenant. However, each state may have more detailed laws protecting noncitizenship status. Check with your states Equal Rights and Opportunities Department regarding rights of refusal based on citizenship status.

The Least You Need to Know

♦ The protected categories of the Federal Fair Housing Act are not to be discriminated against in any state of the United States.

♦ Some states and localities have more detailed antidiscrimination laws than the federal government.

♦ Landlords must be very careful that they don't discriminate when advertising rental units or drafting lease/rental agreements.

♦ There are few exemptions to the federal guidelines, and landlords must be sure that the specific exemptions apply in their state before claiming one.

♦ Discrimination is a serious crime that can result in fines and imprisonment.

♦ In spite of a heightened threat of terrorism, Fair Housing laws did not cease to exist on September 11, 2001.

Rent Control: Not in Your Control

In This Chapter

◆ What rent control can control

◆ Phasing out of regulations through vacancy decontrol

◆ Investing in a rent-controlled property

◆ Future of rent control

Today, four states—Maryland, New York, New Jersey, and California—and the District of Columbia have rent-controlled cities or areas. Areas with rent regulations are usually citywide but can include exemptions such as luxury units or buildings with a small number of units. Rent control can be imposed on apartment units (mostly), single-family homes, mobile homes, or commercial property. It can stick to an entire building for its life, or it can be removed when certain conditions occur such as a tenant kicking the bucket or voluntarily moving out. Co-ops, condos, and town-houses ("luxury rentals") are typically exempt because the intention of rent regulation is to aid lower-income renters, even though it rarely fulfills this objective.

Worthy of noting is the fact that 46 states have no rent control and 34 of those states have enacted preemptions to prevent future regulations from taking effect. Why do some select areas continue to use rent control? Most explanations are political, not economic. The past decade has brought a noticeable shift away from municipalities imposing new rent regulations. Unhealthy housing markets in rent-regulated areas, often located next to healthier markets that do not impose regulations, have shown that rent control does not solve housing shortages or vacancy rates.

The Roots of Rent Control

What is rent control and where did it come from? Rent control is just what it sounds like: regulations enacted to prevent or stabilize the increased payment of rent. Rent-control rules can also affect how a landlord manages his or her property, handles security deposits, and evicts tenants. Other names used are "rent stabilization" and "statutory tenancy."

In the case of New York City, rent control and rent stabilization are two different terms. For New York, rent stabilization refers to rent-controlled apartments that become vacant and then are subject to the Rent Stabilization Law enacted in 1969. For the purposes of this chapter, we will use the most common term, rent control, to define rent that is regulated by law.

Facts for Rent _____

Subletting is common in New York City and other rent controlled areas. Consider the story of Katherine, the tenant who decided to become a landlord. Katherine rented a "railroad apartment," a unit with each room connected end-to-end (hence the name), with a shower and small tub in the kitchen between the fridge and stove. When Katherine got a new job in Philadelphia, she didn't want to lose her $550-a-month rent-stabilized New York apartment located in a popular downtown neighborhood. She soon had prospective subletters fighting over the place and eventually rented out the unit at $1,200. Katherine's inventive moneymaking opportunity was short-lived. She failed to obtain consent of the landlord to sublet, a required stipulation in New York, and she charged a sublessee more than the stabilized rent, another infraction. With proof of Katherine's violations, the landlord was soon able to terminate her lease and re-rent the unit. In New York City, certain other rules also apply pertaining to rent stabilization, such as that sublessees in furnished apartments cannot be charged more than stabilized rent plus 10 percent.

Uncle Sam Adopts

We all recognize the importance of housing, and when there is a housing shortage, it tremendously impacts the economy and well-being of an area. A massive housing shortage during World War II caused the federal government to impose widespread rent controls on the entire nation. The federal government concluded that having a low supply of housing and a high demand for it would cause landlords to hike up rents to their hearts' desire (and in some instances, it did). The federal government soon handed the rent-control baton to the individual states who then either abolished rent control laws or handed the power to cities and municipalities. Rent regulations saw a surge in popularity in the 1970s and '80s as a result of an inflated U.S. economy. What remains of rent control is primarily a result of regulations that took effect during this time.

If you have ever taken an economics class, you know that the first lesson involves a lecture on supply and demand. When there is a healthy demand for a product—let's use soap as an example—this generates and dictates the manufacturing and distribution to the consumer. Too much soap in the market causes the demand to decrease, and too little soap causes the demand to increase. Housing is like soap. There is always a demand for it, and we all hope everyone uses it. Have you ever heard of a law that regulated the price of soap? Sounds ridiculous, right? Rent control is the regulation of housing, which also is a product. When rental property ownership is viewed as a business, like the manufacturing of any other product, then the laws of economics apply. Or should.

> **CAUTION**
>
> ### Rental Red Light! _____
>
> The most common way that a landlord can remove rent control from a unit (and this varies from state to state) is when a tenant voluntarily leaves or is evicted for "just cause." However, in some municipalities, such as New York City, an apartment may be subjected to another type of regulation after it is no longer controlled, such as rent stabilization. Vacant units under rent control are scarce, however. If tenants do not move out, they often sublet the unit, retaining the market value or more for themselves when it should go to the property owner. (For more on subletting, see Chapter 8.)

Over 50 and Still Going

Although the original intentions of rent control laws—to ensure equal housing rights—were nothing but good, the current situation in the remaining municipalities is nothing but out of control. Rent control was enacted to protect the poor and elderly, and in some cases this works. Usually, however, people living in rent-controlled units are able to pay the market rent or more. Rent control does not discriminate. Regulation of rent is not a public-sector program such as Section 8, so it is the rental unit that is regulated, not what the tenant is able to pay for rent. Therefore, cheap housing, at the cost of the landlord, is provided for anyone who is lucky enough to get it.

Rent control affects not only the landlord's pocket but also the surrounding town or city. New housing construction is considerably less common in rent-control areas. Why would a developer invest in an area subject to capped rents and other restrictions? And, as Massachusetts determined in 1994 when deciding to remove rent control state-wide, property values decline in rent-controlled areas because owners are able to get lower property assessments. This leads to less money going to the local government, which is then absorbed by nonlandlord taxpayers.

Facts for Rent

According to testimony by the National Multi Housing Council to the Washington DC City Council on Rent Control in October 2000, "In the District of Columbia, the DC Authority's study confirms that rent control primarily benefits moderate- and upper-income residents. Some 61,100 of 101,463 units under rent control had household income of $25,000 or more per year. Remarkably, 5,202 units under rent control had household income of $50,000 or more per year."

Is Investing Possible?

If you are considering the purchase of property that you suspect might be under rent control, your next order of business, after finishing this chapter, is to find out for certain. Controlling what you can charge for rent is definitely enough to make you think twice about a property investment, not to mention the other restrictions and special landlord-tenant rules.

Facts for Rent

According to the May 2003 report, "Rent Control and Housing Investment: Evidence from Deregulation in Cambridge, Massachusetts," by Henry Pollakowski, rent regulations in New York City, either rent control or rent stabilization, apply toward over half of the city's 2.1 million privately-owned rental units.

Don't be discouraged instantly if you find out that a property is in a rent-regulated area. There's a chance that the property is not under regulation.

If, for example, you invest in a vacant property previously subjected to rent control in Oakland, California, and you plan to spend the equivalent of 50 percent of similar new construction costs to refurbish the house, then rent controls are permanently removed for that property. In most rent-control cities such as Los Angeles, San Jose, and Washington D.C., units constructed after a particular date are exempt. A lot of rent-control areas exempt buildings with six or fewer units.

What about an investment property with tenants who have lived there for 20 years who are still paying only $300 per month while some new tenants are rent regulated but paying close to market rent? Are you willing to invest in a waiting game? If a rent-controlled property that normally would sell at market rate is listed at a dirt-cheap price, beware. The phrase "You get what you pay for" just might apply in this instance. A frustrated owner with rent-controlled units may be willing to sell the property at any cost to get rid of a headache.

The key to investing in rent-controlled properties is the key to investing in any property: Know all the facts about a property as well as the state and local laws affecting it before putting money on the table.

Facts for Rent

Rent-control boards are not allowed to give legal advice on state or city laws that don't relate to rent control. In most situations, however, they are allowed to provide mediation services to solve landlord-tenant disputes regarding rent-control regulations.

Not-So-Ordinary Ordinances

In most areas, an elected or appointed board of officials enforces rent control. The board is responsible for interpreting the rent-control ordinances set forth by the local government. Some rent-control boards have even more power because they are allowed to approve or disapprove landlords' requests for rent increases, determine penalties, and request that landlords ask for permission when making any changes to a unit.

The following are the most common factors affected by rent-control ordinances:

- Rent increases
- Eviction
- Security deposits
- Re-renting units
- Making improvements to units

Just a Phase

The common term for phasing out or removing rent regulations is "vacancy decontrol." As traditional rent control begins to fade out, vacancy decontrol is often applied as a transition to reverting units back to market rent. In vacancy decontrol, rent rules can only be lifted when one of the following occurs: a tenant voluntarily leaves a unit and a new tenant moves in, a tenant is evicted with "just cause," the lease is renewed, new construction is permitted to a unit (or a new property is constructed in a rent regulated area), or regulations allow an annual increase. In many cases, permitted rent increases with a new tenant will continue to be regulated.

In areas looking to phase out strict rent regulations slowly, vacancy decontrol is used. "Slowly" is the key word here because vacancy decontrol can take years and usually does not entirely permit for removal of regulations at any time in the future.

Extra-Special Evictions

A regular (non-rent-control) eviction will seem boring and dull compared to the process of evicting rent-regulated tenants. Evicting tenants requires time, effort, and perseverance. Evicting rent-control tenants requires all this plus as much patience as you can muster. Rent-control evictions are possible, but the restrictions and requirements plaguing them make them more difficult than a "typical" eviction.

Strict eviction procedures are imposed because the deregulation of rent or rent increases typically occur only when the original tenants move out and new tenants move in. Some landlords are allowed to raise the rent and revise their lease or month-to-month agreement only when a new tenant arrives on the scene. Although eviction laws in most states allow landlords to evict month-to-month tenants without a reason as long as proper notice is given, it's very, very rarely allowed in rent control. Rent-control regulations would lose all power if landlords were allowed to evict tenants just by giving them the required notice.

In most rent-control situations, you can evict tenants under the following circumstances:

Rental Red Light!

In some areas with rent control, a landlord cannot refuse to renew a lease without just cause. This can mean that the same terms and conditions of the old lease will apply to the new one, leaving the landlord stuck with a low-paying renter for possibly a very long time.

◆ **You have a reason.** Reasons for "just cause" evictions include nonpayment of rent, other violation of the lease or month-to-month agreement, damage to the property, causing a nuisance, or moving in others without permission. In some areas, landlords are required to let the

rent-control tenant fix the violation
or to get permission from the rent-
control board before proceeding
with eviction.

◆ **Uncle Joe needs a place to crash.**
You can evict a tenant if you decide
to move a relative or yourself into one of
your occupied units. Some areas require
that the relative (or you) remain in the
unit for a specified amount of time—
sometimes up to three years! This regulation is imposed to deter landlords from
evicting tenants with the promise of moving in a relative and then re-renting the
unit to a nonrelative at a higher rent.

Facts for Rent

In San Francisco, evictions of
residents 60 or older, 10-year
residents who are disabled, or
5-year residents who have "cat-
astrophic illnesses" are prohibited if the reason is to move
yourself or an immediate family
member into the unit. Exempt
from this provision are condos
with only one unit and single-
family homes. Landlords in San
Francisco must pay any tenant
eligible for an owner-occupancy
eviction $1,000 to move out.

◆ **This Old Unit.** If major repairs need to be made to a rent-controlled unit,
landlords can, in most areas, evict the tenant with proper notice and then raise
the rent. You might be required to move the tenant to another unit or let him
or her have first dibs on the new and improved place.

Always, always check your local codes and regulations regarding a rent-control
eviction before proceeding. And if you seek legal advice, make sure that your lawyer
knows more about the ordinances than you do.

Raising the Rent

If rents can be raised, the typical required
notice given to tenants is usually not less than
30 days. Required petitioning to raise rents
and show proof of increased costs is common
in some rent-controlled areas. Others allow for
annual percentage increases or increases when a
lease agreement ends.

New amendments in many rent-controlled
areas to allow for higher annual increases are
coming into effect. Some even allow landlords
to request permission to charge even higher
rents due to increased costs, in addition to the
increase set by the rent control board.

Rental Red Light!

Most regulated rents
can be overturned only with
the permission of the rent-control
board or at a designated
annual increase. Tenants can be
allowed, in some areas, to peti-
tion against any rent increases.
Withholding rent in protest might
also be permitted.

Security Deposits and Charging Fees

Some states do not require owners to place security deposits in bank accounts. As an owner with rent-controlled property, however, you might be required to place security deposits into accounts and pay interest due to local rent regulations. Some rent regulations may also have restrictions on what you can charge for a security deposit.

Rental Red Light!

Some rent-control boards require that landlords pay a mandatory annual fee to cover the costs incurred by the board. Most allow this fee to be passed along to the tenant.

If late rent fees are allowed, you guessed it: Regulations may apply. A cap or a set percentage may prevent landlords from charging what they want.

Be sure to find out all the fees, if any, associated with funding the rent-control board or city/state division in charge of enforcing rent regulations.

Facts for Rent

In New York rent-controlled areas, luxury decontrol has lowered its standards. Originally set at $250,000, property owners of buildings estimated at $175,000 with a minimum rent of $2,000 per month are now exempt from rent control.

Living the High Life

Because rent-control regulations, in most areas, do not apply to higher-priced units, converting a property to fit into the "luxury apartment" or "condo" category might be an appealing option.

Before getting a building permit for conversion, landlords typically must first get approval from the rent-control board or the local government.

Regulations of conversion can include the following:

Rental Red Light!

Some states allow landlords to add a clause in their rental agreements to require tenants to buy renters' insurance. Some rent-control ordinances might not allow this requirement because it is perceived as additional rent.

◆ Notice of tenancy termination can be longer than in normal circumstances. Sometimes lease tenants are allowed to remain in the unit through term. Because the entire conversion process can take months, most leases will expire before any layover occurs.

◆ Existing tenants might be allowed to have first right of refusal to purchase a condo or luxury unit at market rate. Other privileges for current tenants might also be given.

◆ When proposing a conversion at a town planning, zoning, or rent-control board meeting, owners may be required to give existing tenants notice of when the meeting will take place.

◆ Relocation fees or an extended notice of termination may be required, especially for the elderly or people with small kids.

Face to Face with Violations

Violating a rent-control law might mean heavy fines. Tenants may also be able to sue you or use the violation against you to prevent an eviction. Again, your best protection is to know your rent-control laws inside and out.

In rent control, not knowing what you can charge for rent can be hazardous to your checkbook even months or years after a tenant moves in. If you overcharge a tenant for rent and the tenant files a valid complaint, you might have to return the overcharges in full.

Rental Red Light! _____

Even if no rent-control regulations are imposed in your area, there could be a Fair Rent Commission. The Fair Rent Commission is created by the local municipality and, like areas with rent control, has the power to investigate tenant complaints and hold hearings on those complaints. A Fair Rent Commission can order the landlord to reduce the rent or, if the apartment needs repairs, order the tenant to pay the rent to the Fair Rent Commission until the landlord has made all repairs needed. Find out if your area has a Fair Rent Commission by contacting your local town hall.

Dying Breed: The Future of Rent Control

The trend to remove rent control from some cities is growing. Vacancy decontrol is being used in most areas to phase out rent control or to amend current rent regulations. In areas like Santa Monica, however, vacancy decontrol actually decontrols very little. Beginning January 1, 1999, only tenants who moved into single-family homes and condominiums on or after January 1, 1996, are exempt from rent control. Landlords with new tenants who moved in after January 1, 1999, are allowed to negotiate a rent. After the rent is set, however, it is then under rent control.

In 1997, after a two-year phase-out, Massachusetts completely deregulated all rental units. In fighting to keep rent control in Massachusetts, tenant activists and some politicians predicted a widespread havoc of major rent hikes and homeless ex-rent-controlled tenants lining the streets. What happened instead was the increase of rents to market value, allowing for more competition among landlords and higher property assessments. Also, for the first time in over 20 years, construction of new apartment units began in the state.

Since each rent-control area can vary drastically as far as what is controlled and how much, we'd need another book to list them all. Protect your investment by keeping on top of your local politics. Get involved to prevent further regulations by attending rent-control board meetings (if possible) and voicing complaints. The squeaky wheel gets the most grease, and that grease could save your business.

The Least You Need to Know

♦ Born out of a housing shortage during World War II, rent control was imposed nationwide. Since then, rent control has been delegated to local municipalities. Currently only New York, New Jersey, California, Maryland, and Washington, D.C., have municipalities with regulations on the books.

♦ Rent control can affect rent charges, rent increases, eviction procedures, security deposits, re-renting of units, and making improvements to a property.

♦ Regulations and exemptions can vary drastically in each area with rent control. Most areas allow for buildings with a small number of units, luxury apartments, and condos as exemptions.

♦ Choose your investments wisely. If an area is under rent control, certain buildings can still be exempt. Know all the facts and the history of a rent-controlled building before investing.

♦ Deemed economically unsound by most local governments, rent control is a dying breed. Fighting tighter regulations on residential rental property in the private sector could save your business and improve your local economy.

Part 3

The Money Accounts

The only reason you bought the rental property was to make money with it. When this begins to happen, you're going to have to keep precise accounting of the rent money collected. However, there are many other things to consider. For instance, what will you do with the security deposits? How will you handle collecting rents, paying bills, and obtaining insurance for the property?

A smart landlord understands that the rent he or she collects is not necessarily a profit. A smart landlord also realizes that to maximize the return on an investment, money received must be handled with care.

Chapter 11

Dealing with Deposits and Fees

In This Chapter

- ◆ The purpose of security deposits and other fees
- ◆ The do's and don'ts of security deposits and interest, combining with rent, and giving back
- ◆ Protecting against penalties by following your state and local laws
- ◆ Charging nonrefundable fees

A smart landlord will ask for a sum of money before allowing a tenant to use a property possibly worth hundreds of thousands of dollars. Security deposits are taken by landlords to try to create an interest in the property for a tenant. The theory is that if a tenant has a portion of his or her own money tied up in the property, it will be more important to the tenant to be responsible and to keep the surroundings in reasonably good condition. Many state and city laws, however, strictly regulate how security deposits are to be handled and applied. A landlord can charge other types of fees to new and potentially new tenants, though, fees designed to protect the property from damage such as pet deposits, cleaning fees, and credit-check fees.

The Nature of the Security Deposit

A security deposit is money paid to a landlord before use and occupancy of a rental unit; it assures the landlord that the tenant will pay rent on time and will keep the rental unit in good condition. This money should be kept in a special escrow account. In the event that the tenancy is terminated without money owed or damage to the unit, the security deposit is returned to the tenant plus interest. The interest rate to be paid on the security deposit will vary but will be dictated by state law. Interest is owed to the tenant for only the number of months that the rent is paid in full and on time. Some states require that the security deposit account be put jointly in the names of both the landlord and the tenant. In states with this type of requirement, most banks are accustomed to handling rental security deposit accounts and can prepare one for the landlord.

It is important to understand that rent you collect in advance of the first month is not considered part of the security deposit agreement.

Edwards' Advice

When setting up a joint bank account for a rental security deposit in both the tenant's and landlord's names, it is a good idea to have the tenant's Social Security number available for the bank. In many instances, the bank will be able to report the interest earned on the account directly to the tenant so that the landlord does not have to pay the taxes on the accruing interest.

How much you can charge and how the security deposits are to be returned to the tenant are typically regulated by state law. Although state laws vary, there is often a set amount of money a landlord can charge for a security deposit and a set amount of time in which a landlord must return either the entire deposit or an itemized statement explaining deductions from the security.

Although state laws vary, security deposits can typically be held to pay for …

Facts for Rent

Some states also allow you to use a security deposit to pay for any utilities that the tenant was responsible for but did not pay. For more information, check state statutes or contact the Banking Commission in the state where the property is located.

- Damage to a rental unit caused by the tenant, a family member, or a guest. This damage does not include normal wear and tear.

- Unpaid rent.

- Replacing any property that may have been taken by the tenant.

- Any necessary cleaning required to restore the unit to its original condition before the tenant took occupancy (excluding ordinary wear and tear).

How to Use a Security Deposit

You must always remember that a security deposit is not rent and that you cannot use it for rent during the course of the occupancy. A security deposit can only be used if proper notice has been sent to the tenant. State laws vary regarding the notice requirements for security deposits; however, an owner usually must give a tenant written notice regarding the deposit between 14 and 30 days after the tenant vacates the unit. The notice should be in the form of a written letter. If a tenant has not given the owner a new address where he or she can be reached, the landlord must send the notification in the form of a registered letter to the old address requesting a return address.

The letter should spell out to the tenant in exact amounts how much money was in the security and how much interest is due on the security. Then the written letter should itemize any deductions taken out of the security for damages and repairs to the unit or money owed as back rent during the tenancy. At the bottom of the letter, the amount owed either to the tenant or to the landlord should be listed. If money is owed to the tenant, a check for the amount should be placed in an envelope along with the notice and sent to the tenant. If a tenant neglects to pay rent for one of the months he or she occupied the unit, the owner is not permitted to subtract the amount owed from the security deposit until the tenant vacates the unit and proper notice is sent explaining to the tenant what amount of money is owed. Only then can the money be removed from the security deposit and the balance returned to the tenant. Appendix A includes an example of a security deposit itemization letter.

If a tenant asks you to apply a portion of the security deposit toward the last month's rent, you don't have to unless it was labeled as last month's rent. You may not want to apply security money toward the last month's rent primarily because you won't know at this point in what condition the tenant will leave the unit. If the tenant leaves the unit a mess and removes items that he or she doesn't have any right to take, you may need the total security amount to cover the expenses for repair or replacement to the unit. If the tenant is adamant about using this money to cover the rent owed for the last month, the only other options you may have are to …

◆ Agree to allow the tenant to use this money to cover the last month's rent. You should tell the tenant, however, that you would first like to inspect the unit for damage. If you believe that the tenant will leave the unit in good condition, you won't have to worry about the last month's rent payment. Of course, you still have to send the tenant the proper notice for returning the security deposit.

◆ Treat the nonpayment of the last month's rent as you would any other case of nonpayment and begin eviction procedures. This means that you will have to terminate the tenancy with all the proper notices and carry out the eviction until you receive judgment for the money owed. This enables you to use the security for cleaning, repair, and back rent owed. You will have to then start other procedures for suing the tenant for any other outstanding balance owed.

Landlords don't always need to wait for a tenant to move out before using part or all of a tenant's security deposit. You may be able to use a security deposit if a tenant, for example, breaks a window and doesn't pay to have it fixed. In this case, you should make the tenant repay the amount to replenish the security deposit. Take steps to protect yourself by avoiding any misunderstandings with your tenants regarding the use of security deposits; make sure that it is clearly explained in your lease or rental agreement.

CAUTION

Rental Red Light!

Landlords must send security deposit notification itemization letters even if they don't intend to send any money. Just because the tenant has broken the lease or has been evicted from the unit, it does not entitle the landlord to keep the security deposit without explaining why in the proper form of notification. Even if a tenant leaves while owing several months of back rent valuing more than the total deposit, landlords must notify the tenant in writing within the proper time periods as to what charges the deposit has been applied toward.

Assessing the Damage

It will be necessary for you to do an inspection of the unit after the tenant has vacated it to determine what, if anything, has been damaged in the unit. If you used the apartment checklist when the tenant moved in (see Chapter 7), bring it with you during your inspection to help you determine what the condition is compared to when the tenant moved in.

You may want to do the inspection alone and then simply send the tenant the itemization statement with any remaining security deposit balance. Some states, specifically Arizona, Maryland, and Virginia, actually give the tenant the right to be present at the time of inspection. You may want to allow the tenant to accompany you during the inspection so that you can discuss the damages and explain why there will be certain deductions. This way, the tenant won't be so unpleasantly surprised when he or she receives the itemization statement indicating the amount of deposit being withheld. Regardless of whether or not the tenant inspects the unit with you, it's a good idea to take photos and bring a neutral person along with you as a witness who will be available to testify in court if necessary.

Considering Deductions

Any deductions from the security deposit as charges for cleaning and repair must be necessary and reasonable. Ordinary wear and tear to a unit does not constitute a reasonable charge even though the unit may need to be cleaned along with certain repairs. Unreasonable wear and tear to a unit constitutes charges for which the tenant will be responsible. Replacing stained or ripped carpets and fixing and cleaning appliances, walls, ceilings, and fixtures in the unit can prove to be costly and necessary for the re-rent of the unit. You may have to fumigate for fleas left behind from the tenant's cat or dog or repaint walls on which the tenant's child has drawn graffiti. Every tenant move-out is different and so is the responsibility of the tenant to the unit, so it is difficult to define "ordinary wear and tear." Here are some basic guidelines for landlords to follow when considering how to charge for damage:

◆ Consider how long the tenant lived in the unit. If the tenant lived there a long time, more wear and tear should be expected. Therefore, you can't charge the tenant for repainting the unit simply because the walls appear to need it.

◆ Don't charge tenants for damage or filth that was there before they moved in.

◆ If you can repair an item rather than replace it, you should do so if it means saving the tenant some money.

◆ Don't charge for cleaning if the tenant has already paid a nonrefundable cleaning fee.

A smart landlord will not overestimate deductions from security deposits. Tenants very often will feel they have been wronged, even if it isn't true, and will waste no time filing a claim against the landlord in small claims court. Win or lose, you will most likely waste time and money preparing your defense and spending the day in court. It may be worth it to you not to withhold that much money in the first place.

Some states give the tenant the right to inspect the unit to determine the accuracy of the landlord's list of damages to the unit. If the tenant disagrees with the deductions, he or she has a specific amount of time to send the landlord a written explanation regarding the disagreement after which the tenant can sue for the deductions he or she feels are improper.

Edwards' Advice

Landlords can deduct a reasonable hourly rate for repairs done by either the landlord or a work crew. Landlords should also keep records of work done by other services such as exterminators and cleaning companies, as well as contractors such as plumbers and painters. Try to get a detailed report of the work performed as proof in case you wind up in court with a lawsuit from a tenant contesting the deductions.

How Much Deposit Can I Charge?

The amount that can be charged for a security deposit is limited in many states. Typically, states will allow a security deposit to equal one or two months' rent payment. Sometimes, the state limit is based on other factors such as the age of the tenant, whether the unit is furnished, what kind of rental agreement is being used, or whether a pet or waterbed is being permitted.

So how much can you charge for a security deposit? The best advice is to charge as much as the legal limit and the market will allow. The bigger the deposit you get, the less of a financial burden it will be if the tenant leaves owing you rent or if you have to repair damage. The more a tenant has at stake, the better the chances are that the tenant will respect the property. In reality, you can only charge as much as the market can afford to pay, which is usually below any legal limit set by state and local law.

In situations such as areas with high tenant turnover or applicants with poor credit, or if you are concerned about a pet causing damage, it may be worth it for you to charge the highest legal limit to try to offset and recoup any potential losses. In areas that are hard to rent, some landlords may not require a security deposit. This practice should be avoided if possible. Tenants who jump at this type of offer

Rental Red Light!

Unless security deposit policies remain consistent with every tenant, they can lead to big trouble. A claim of discrimination could be held against you in a lawsuit if you were to charge different security deposit rates to different people. Refer to Chapter 9 for more information regarding discrimination and fair housing laws.

might be destructive and have nothing to lose by damaging the unit. No security deposit will mean there is nothing to help pay for any potential damage that may result from careless tenants.

Here is a list of states and the limits each currently has set on security deposit amounts. Be sure to double-check security deposit laws in the applicable state before charging tenants.

The following table lists states that limit the amount of security deposit you can charge, exemptions of certain owners (such as owners with a small amount of units), and other provisions. If your state is not listed, then the statutes do not explicitly state limitations or exemptions. Your local government might, however, have its own limits on security deposits.

Security Deposit Limits and Exemptions

State	Limits and Exemptions
Alaska	Rents above $2,000 are exempt from security deposit laws.
Arizona	Not more than 1½ months' rent.
Arkansas	Not more than 2 months' rent. Owners with five or fewer dwelling units are exempt.
California	Can charge up to 2 months' rent for unfurnished units and 3 months' rent for furnished units. If T has a waterbed or a lease of 6 months or longer, a larger deposit can be requested.
Colorado	Prepayment of rent to hold a unit cannot be considered a security deposit.
Connecticut	Not more than 2 months' rent for tenants under 62 years of age and not more than 1 month's rent for tenants over 62.
Delaware	Not more than 1 month's rent for agreements of 1 year (or more). Can charge more than 1 month's rent for M-M or indefinite term agreements, but after 1 year the excess deposit amount must be returned to the tenant. No limit on deposit charged for furnished units. Can charge a pet deposit but cannot be more than 1 month's rent regardless of the agreement.
Georgia	LLs with fewer than 10 units (unless managed by an outside company) are exempt from security deposit laws.
Hawaii	No more than 1 month's rent.
Illinois	LLs who own four or fewer units are exempt from security deposit laws.

continues

Security Deposit Limits and Exemptions (continued)

State	Limits and Exemptions
Iowa	Not more than 2 months' rent.
Kansas	Not more than 1 month's rent and not more than 1½ months' rent for furnished units. No more than ½ month's rent for pet deposit.
Maine	Not more than 2 months' rent. Owner-occupied buildings with five or fewer units are exempt.
Maryland	Not more than 2 months' rent.
Massachusetts	Not more than 1 month's rent.
Michigan	Not more than 1½ months' rent.
Missouri	Not more than 2 months' rent. T may not use security deposit as last month's rent.
Nebraska	Not more than 1 month's rent. LL can charge an extra deposit, one quarter of rent, for a pet.
Nevada	Not more than 3 months' rent.
New Hampshire	Not more than 1 month's rent or $100, whichever is more.
New Jersey	Not more than 1½ months' rent.
New Mexico	Not more than 1 month's rent for rental agreements under 1 year.
New York	No limit except for rent-stabilized units in New York City where the limit is 1 month's rent. Advance rent is considered a security deposit. Exempt from security deposit laws are LLs who own fewer than six rental units.
Oregon	Prepaid last month's rent is considered a security deposit.
Pennsylvania	Not more than 2 months' rent during the first year of tenancy. At the start of the second year, the LL may only keep the amount equivalent to 1 month's rent.
Rhode Island	Not more than 1 month's rent.
South Carolina	LL must post or send letter of how security deposits are calculated if 1) LL rents more than four units on a property and 2) LL imposes different standards among units.
South Dakota	Not more than 1 month's rent.
Virginia	Not more than 2 months' rent.
Washington D.C.	Deposits cannot be received from Ts renting in buildings built before December 31, 1975. Buildings with five or more units cannot collect a security deposit.

How Do I Increase the Security Deposit?

A landlord may want to increase a security deposit if the tenant has lived in a unit for many years or has obtained a pet. Whether or not this practice is legally permissible depends on the situation.

If you are using a fixed-term lease, you cannot raise the security deposit during the term of the lease unless the lease allows it. Otherwise, you must wait for the lease renewal date to increase the security deposit.

If you are using a written rental agreement in a month-to-month tenancy, the security deposit can be increased the same way that the rent is increased—by giving the tenant proper notice (typically 30 days). Landlords are also allowed to raise the security deposit without raising the rent as long as they do not surpass the legal limitations for deposits. If you own properties under rent control (see Chapter 10), raising the security deposit may have even more restrictions.

Interest on Security Deposits

Many states require that landlords pay interest on deposits, and some states require that security deposits be placed in separate accounts. State laws vary regarding security deposit requirements. Common requirements typically established by state laws are …

- ◆ The rate of interest to be paid.
- ◆ When the interest must be paid.
- ◆ The notification landlords must give tenants regarding security deposits.

Usually, the interest rates mandated by state laws to be paid on security deposits are lower than the rate the bank will actually pay. This is to help cover any cost and trouble incurred by the landlord for setting up the account. Typical state laws require that the interest be paid either annually or with the termination of the tenancy.

Many responsible landlords pay interest at the time of lease renewal or on the anniversary date of the tenant's occupancy. This can be very difficult for property owners, especially if they rent many apartments; each unit will have different renewal dates, and this procedure can become very taxing. For that reason, many property owners will only return any interest due on a security deposit when the tenant finally vacates the unit. However, this practice may be in violation of certain state laws that require interest payments to be paid every year; this is why it is recommended that you base your interest payments to tenants on a calendar year to be paid out around the time of the holidays. The holidays can serve as a reminder for this task, and the payment to the tenant will most certainly be welcomed by its recipient. Interest on the security deposit is only owed to the tenant for the number of months the tenant is current with full payment of rent. If, however, you charge a late fee for late rental payments, then interest will usually be owed to the tenant regardless of whether he or she is late with the rent payment.

The following table lists the states that require interest to accrue on security deposits. Most require that landlords pay the tenant interest, but a select few allow the landlords to keep the interest.

Security Deposit Interest

State	Interest
Alaska	LL is required to pay T interest only if the deposit accrues interest in an interest-bearing account, unless specified otherwise in the agreement.
Connecticut	LL is required to pay interest to T on the deposit. Disabled persons and senior citizens residing in assisted housing for at least 1 year must receive a minimum of 5.25 percent annual interest.
Florida	If the deposit accrues interest in an account, LL must pay T either 5 percent or 75 percent of the annualized average interest rate.
Illinois	If a building contains 25 or more units, LL must pay interest on any deposits held more than 67 months. Any interest to be paid must equal the interest paid by the largest commercial bank in Illinois on a passbook savings account as of December 31 of the previous year.
Iowa	Any interest earned during the first five years of tenancy belongs to LL.
Maryland	Deposits of more than $50 are required to accrue 4 percent interest at 6-month intervals.
Massachusetts	For tenancies of 1 year or more, deposits are required to accrue 5 percent annual interest.
Minnesota	LLs are required to pay interest, which begins accruing the month after the security deposit was paid.
New Hampshire	Interest is required if LL holds a deposit for more than a year. If held for more than 3 years, T can ask for the interest if the request is made 30 days before the 3-year term is up.

State	Interest
New Jersey	Deposits are required to accrue interest at least quarterly.
New Mexico	If LL asks for more than 1 month's rent, then annual interest must be paid.
New York	Buildings with six or more units are required to have interest accrue. T gets the interest less 1 percent that LL is allowed to remove for expenses.
Ohio	If a deposit is $50 or 1 month's rent (whichever is greater) and T will remain in the unit 6 months or more, LL is required to pay interest to T.
Pennsylvania	At the end of the third year of tenancy, LL must pay T the interest accrued from that year and must do so for every year of tenancy to follow.
Virginia	Interest is required and must be at an annual rate equal to the Federal Reserve Board Discount Rate.
Washington	Unless specified in the lease or agreement, LL gets any interest accrued.

Several states require that landlords put security deposits in special security accounts. The purpose for this is to help keep the money from being mixed with the landlord's personal and business accounts. This makes the money more readily available to the tenant upon his or her move-out date if he or she is entitled to it. The separate account also makes it easier for the landlord to trace the security money if there is a dispute between the tenant and the landlord about the handling of these funds. Some states require that the account be placed in a joint bank account in the names of both the tenant and the landlord. This type of account works like a trust, and the tenants are not permitted to remove the money on their own. Most states do not require a separate account for every tenant; instead, landlords are permitted to open one security deposit account but must keep careful records of each tenant's deposit.

Not all states that require interest to accrue require that security accounts be placed in a bank account and vice versa. The following table lists the states that have provisions regarding deposits and placing them in accounts.

Rental Red Light!

Many cities with rent control require landlords to pay interest to tenants on security deposits even if state law does not impose a regulation.

Separate Account Required for Security Deposits

State	Required
Alaska	A separate account is required. Exemptions are made for properties in towns without banks.
Connecticut	LL must put the deposit into an escrow account.
Delaware	LL must inform T in writing within 20 days of receipt of deposit as to where the deposit is being held. LL must return the deposit if he or she fails to notify T of the location within 20 days.
Florida	Deposits are required to be held in either interest-bearing or noninterest-bearing accounts, not mixed with LL's other accounts.
Georgia	LLs who own 10 or more units or who employ a management company must give T written notice of the account where the deposit is being held.
Iowa	All security deposits can be in one account, interest-bearing or not, but they must not be mixed with LL's other accounts.
Kentucky	Must be placed in an account for only security deposits. If not, LL is unable to retain any portion of the deposit at the end of tenancy.
Maine	Must have a separate account but can escrow each T's security deposits together.
Maryland	Must be deposited in an account for only security deposits within 30 days of receipt.
Massachusetts	Must be deposited in an account for only security deposits. LL's and T's name on bank account.
New Hampshire	Must be deposited into an interest-bearing account for only security deposits.
New Jersey	For owners with more than 10 rental units, deposits must be either invested in an insured money market fund or placed in a savings account. For fewer than 10 units, deposits must be placed in a savings account. Notice of location must be sent to T within 30 days of receipt.
New York	Buildings with six or more units are required to place deposits in separate accounts and inform Ts of where the deposit is being held.

State	Required
North Carolina	Must be placed in an account for only security deposits or a special bond from an NC insurance company. Wherever held, written notification of the deposit's location must be given to T within 30 days at the beginning of tenancy.
Oklahoma	Required to be kept in an interest-bearing account.
Pennsylvania	A deposit of more than $100, or at the beginning of the third year of tenancy, must be placed in an interest-bearing account, and T must be notified of location in writing.
Washington	A separate account is required, and LL must inform T in writing as to where the deposit is being kept.

Last Month's Rent

Many times, an owner will charge the first month's rent, the last month's rent, and one month's security deposit. There are a couple of different views about the policy of collecting money labeled "last month's rent." Collecting last month's rent is often considered a bad idea because landlords tend to use this money much the same way they would a security deposit. Problems typically will arise when …

♦ Landlords try to use this money to cover repairs or cleaning.

♦ Landlords periodically increase the rent and try to get the tenant to increase the last month's rent.

However, some tenants will prefer to pay the last month's rent up front before they take occupancy because they may not want to worry about paying the last month's rent when it is due. Also, the landlord is assured that at least one month's rent is paid in the event the tenant makes an early exit from the agreement and owes the landlord rent.

Many states allow landlords to treat the last month's rent as part of the security deposit and to use all or part of the money for repairs and damages. A few states, such as Massachusetts and New York, restrict how the money labeled as last month's rent can be used. In these states, the last month's rent can only be used as rent

Rental Red Light!

Interest earned on the security deposit and the last month's rent should be paid to the tenant. However, interest on the *last month's rent* is not to be paid for the *last month* that the rent is being used.

money paid for the last month that the tenant occupies the unit. In states where the last month's rent is considered part of the security agreement, tenants may think that the last month has been paid when in fact it has been used to cover repairs.

Many landlords charge the first and last month's rent plus a one-month security deposit. In this instance, the security deposit and the last month's rent will be perceived as two months of security deposit, and the owner cannot try to charge an additional month's security.

Whatever you decide to charge a new tenant, make sure that both you and the tenant are clear on first and last month's rent and security deposits. Always keep a record of what the tenant has paid so that no questions will be asked later on!

What if the Tenant Leaves?

Under normal circumstances, when the tenant has stayed until the end of his or her lease agreement, a landlord has to return the security deposit minus any applicable deductions. If the tenant breaks the lease—leaves before it expires and does not give proper notice—the rental owner will have to decide what to do with the security deposit. The owner or property manager should immediately send a letter to the tenant regarding the tenant's early departure and lease violation. The letter should state what the landlord intends to do with the security in regard to any damages to the unit or money owed.

The owner must actively try to re-rent the apartment to minimize both tenant and landlord losses. In the event of a month-to-month tenancy, the rental owner will only be able to charge rent for the days of the month that the tenant did not pay. This amount is called the "per-diem rate," and it is figured by taking the amount of rent and dividing it by the number of days in the month to determine the daily rate. The daily rate is then multiplied by the number of days the tenant still owes for rent.

What if I Sell the Property?

In some states, the owner selling a rental property is to do one of two things with tenant security deposits: Either return the deposit to the tenant or transfer the deposit to the new owner. If you are purchasing property with existing tenants, be sure you know the exact dollar amounts of security deposits and make sure the deposits are transferred over to you. Read your state statute regarding the handling of security deposit transfers. Also familiarize yourself with the notification requirements to tenants regarding the new owner's name, address, and phone number. If the past owner simply keeps the security deposits, most states will not allow the new owner to demand that the tenant repay the deposit money. Most states also require that the current owner at the time of tenancy termination be legally responsible for the return of security deposits to tenants.

The following table lists the time limits that states require for returning the security deposit and/or a list of deductions at the end of a tenancy. Only Alabama, Washington, D.C., and West Virginia do not have a statute on returning security deposits. (Unless noted, the grace period begins when tenancy terminates and includes the time in which the deposit must be returned with the list of deductions if any.)

Provisions for Returning Deposits

State	Provisions
Alaska	14 days; 30 days if T abandons property.
Arizona	14 days (excluding Saturdays, Sundays, and legal holidays).
Arkansas	30 days.
California	Three weeks from move-out date. Failure to send deposit and/or list within three weeks results in a $600 penalty.
Colorado	30 days; 60 days if written into the agreement. More than 60 days is not permitted.
Connecticut	30 days.
Delaware	20 days.
Florida	15 days.
Georgia	30 days.
Hawaii	14 days; T has 1 year from termination to recover all or part of deposit through legal action.
Idaho	21 days; this can be extended to 30 days if LL and T both agree but no longer.
Illinois	30 days; if itemized list is not sent within 30 days, LL must send full deposit within 45 days of the tenant vacating the unit.
Indiana	45 days.
Iowa	30 days.
Kansas	14 to 30 days.
Kentucky	If, after 60 days of sending notice to T of the deposit owed, T does not respond, then LL can keep the deposit. If T leaves owing rent, LL can take deposit after 30 days.

continues

Provisions for Returning Deposits (continued)

State	Provisions
Louisiana	One month; if T abandons property without giving notice or leaves before the lease ends, then T is not entitled to deposit.
Maine	30 days; 21 days for tenancy-at-will.
Maryland	45 days.
Massachusetts	30 days.
Michigan	14 days from notification by T of forwarding address (which must be sent to LL four days after removal from unit).
Minnesota	21 days; if LL fails to deliver on time, LL must pay up to two times the deposit plus interest.
Mississippi	45 days.
Missouri	30 days.
Montana	30 days.
Nebraska	14 days.
Nevada	30 days.
New Hampshire	30 days.
New Jersey	30 days.
New Mexico	30 days.
New York	Within a "reasonable" amount of time after termination.
North Carolina	30 days.
North Dakota	30 days.
Ohio	30 days.
Oklahoma	30 days.
Oregon	31 days.
Pennsylvania	30 days.
Rhode Island	20 days from termination or when tenant provides forwarding address.
South Carolina	30 days; if T fails to provide forwarding address and is unreachable, T is not entitled to deposit. If LL fails to provide deposit and/or itemized list, T can claim up to three times the amount owed.
South Dakota	2 weeks.

State	Provisions
Tennessee	If T leaves owing rent, LL may, after 30 days, take deposit. If T leaves not owing rent but does not collect deposit, LL may, after 60 days of sending notice, take deposit. If deducting deposit from damages, LL must have T sign itemized list (no time limit specified).
Texas	30 days; T must provide forwarding address.
Utah	30 days from termination or 15 days from receiving forwarding address, whichever is later.
Vermont	14 days.
Virginia	30 days.
Washington	14 days.
Wisconsin	21 days.
Wyoming	30 days from termination or 15 days from when T gives forwarding address.

 Rental Red Light!

Security deposit laws differ in many states, and a smart landlord must take the time to understand the state laws that apply to him or her. If you do not carefully follow the state laws and you get sued by a tenant and lose, the loss may prove to be quite costly. In many states, if it is determined that you willfully violated a security deposit statute, you may not be able to retain any of the security deposit money, and you may be liable for two to three times the amount, referred to as double or triple damages, plus court costs and attorney fees to the tenant. In some instances in which a judge has determined that the defendant has acted outrageously, punitive damages may also be awarded to the tenant.

Other Types of Deposits and Nonrefundable Fees

Security deposits are not the only kind of monetary deposit that a landlord is permitted to require from an applicant or tenant.

Deposits for having pets are becoming more popular due in part to the fact that more and more people these days have pets, very often dogs, which are a well-recognized source of damage to rental units. Instead of refusing to rent to pet owners, landlords who are having difficulty renting units may allow pets but ask for a special security deposit to cover the anticipated damage done by the pet.

Many times, when an applicant is offered a rental unit, he or she will leave a sum of money with the landlord to hold the unit for a predetermined period of time. This way, the applicant is assured that the unit cannot be rented to someone else, and the applicant has first right of refusal to take the unit. If, however, the applicant does not rent the unit within the allotted period of time, he or she often risks losing the deposit. Landlords should be sure to clarify, in writing, which deposits are refundable and nonrefundable.

Credit-check fees are often charged to applicants for the processing of the credit check. The company that performs the credit checks will charge the landlord a fee, and most landlords pass this cost along to the applicant. Some landlords absorb the cost of this processing fee, and others have been known to apply the money paid for the fee to the first month's rent in the event that the application is approved. We recommend that the applicant pay the fee because a bad applicant will not want to waste his or her money on a credit report that he or she knows will not come back in his or her favor. This policy works as an excellent screening procedure that will eliminate most bad tenants from wasting your valuable time. Credit check fees are usually nonrefundable.

Some fees are considered nonrefundable, such as fees for credit checks, cleaning, or pet deposits. If a fee is to be nonrefundable, it should be specifically spelled out in the lease or rental agreement. Some states, such as California, specifically prohibit landlords from charging any fee that is nonrefundable. Landlords should check state statutes regarding deposits and fees or should contact the consumer protection agency in their state for rules and regulations regarding nonrefundable fees and deposits.

The following table lists the states that have statutes and provisions on nonrefundable fees.

Statutes Regarding Nonrefundable Fees

State	Statutes
Alaska	Application fee is allowed but cannot be substituted for a security deposit. LL cannot charge a nonrefundable cleaning fee.
Arizona	Fees are allowed but only if they're written into the agreement or lease as nonrefundable.
Delaware	LL may not charge any nonrefundable fee as a condition to living in a unit. Nonrefundable fees that are optional to a T for services are allowed.
Florida	Nonrefundable fees or deposits must be written into the agreement or lease.

State	Statutes
Georgia	LL can charge an application fee and a cleaning fee. Pet deposit and advance rent deposit are allowed but are considered to be security deposits and refundable.
Massachusetts	LL can charge new lock and key costs.
Minnesota	Nonrefundable fees are allowed. LL can also charge a prelease deposit, refundable if no agreement is signed but applicable to security deposit if an agreement is signed.
New Mexico	LL may not request a fee for a "reasonable number of guests for a reasonable length of time."
Pennsylvania	Nonrefundable fees are allowed.
Utah	Any nonrefundable deposit or fee must be explained in writing.
Vermont	Nonrefundable fees are allowed.
Virginia	A nonrefundable application fee is allowed. If the fee exceeds $10 and T fails to rent unit or is rejected, money in excess of expenses plus a list of costs must be returned to T within 20 days.
Washington	Nonrefundable fees are allowed only with written agreements, and the agreement must state that the fee will not be refunded.
Wisconsin	LL can charge up to $20 for a credit-check fee. If T provides LL with a credit check not older than 30 days, then LL cannot charge for a credit check.
Wyoming	Any nonrefundable fee must be in writing and given to the T.

The Least You Need to Know

- Security deposits are required to create an interest in the property for the tenant, which will hopefully dissuade the tenant from intentionally doing damage to a rental unit.

- Rent you collect in advance of the first month is not considered part of the security deposit.

- The security deposit should be carefully explained to the tenant in your lease or rental agreement.

- Security deposits should be kept separate from your personal and business accounts because security deposits are technically not your money.

- Penalties for violating security deposit laws can be quite expensive, sometimes costing the equivalent of two or three times the original amount of the deposit.

Chapter 12

Increasing Your Income

In This Chapter

- ◆ Stashing cash for bills and expenses
- ◆ Organizing your accounts and taxes to maximize profit
- ◆ Renting out nonliving space for extra income
- ◆ Decreasing expenses to increase profit

A tenant just handed you $500 cash for the rent she owes this month. You write the tenant a receipt, thank her for the payment, and stuff the wad of money into your front pants pocket. Next, you hop in your truck, drive to the local mall, and buy yourself a brand new color TV set with the cash the tenant paid you. Is this wrong? After all, you bought the property, fixed it up, and rented the units to tenants. You have worked hard and want to get paid. Why not? Everyone else gets paid when they work, so why can't you?

Well, you can, but just like everything else in the world, there is a right way and a wrong way to do things. Remember that owning and operating rental property is a business, and when you are a landlord, you are also the boss. A good boss always gets paid last, after the overhead and expenses for running the business have been satisfied. Good accounting methods and record keeping are essential for tracking and operating your investment. In this chapter, we reveal some disciplined accounting methods and examine some other areas of the rental business that affect the income generated from a property and enable you to get paid. In the meantime, you might want to consider returning that TV set.

Escrow Your Expenses

Setting up a rental escrow account is the most important thing a smart landlord will do to make sure money is available to pay bills against the property as they come due. As you are probably already aware, bills will come due on a monthly, quarterly, and yearly basis. For instance, a utility company might not send a water bill to a customer on a monthly basis; instead, the company might send it quarterly. This means that, in the month of April, you could receive a bill that reflects water usage for the months of January, February, and March. In this instance, you would need to make sure money was put aside and made available to pay the bill.

> **Edwards' Advice**
>
> The money you decide to escrow for bills is still your money, even though it should not be considered as such. Treat the escrowed amount as a monthly bill and pay this bill religiously every month.

> **Edwards' Advice**
>
> Rather than escrowing for monthly bills, you may just want to pay them out of the properties' checking account as the bills come due.

The idea of rent escrowing is really quite simple. You must estimate the bills associated with operating your property, deduct the proper estimated amounts from the rent received every month, and either pay the monthly bill or place the money in a separate account where it will sit safely until its time to pay future bills. Whatever is left over from the rent received after the monthly bills and escrow have been satisfied is your profit, but if you take your share of the profit first, you risk not having money available for paying the bills. This can lead to some big headaches down the road.

To correctly escrow, you first need to determine what the expenses are and approximately how much each bill will cost. You can refer to the expense estimates on the operating statement you hopefully used when you purchased the building to help in these determinations, or you can estimate by following some of the tips we mentioned in Chapter 5 about how to gather this type of information.

If a bill is scheduled to come on a quarterly basis, you need to divide the bill by three months to reach a monthly number that will indicate how much money should be escrowed each month to satisfy that bill. This procedure should be followed with every bill that affects your property. You then deduct the proper amount of money from the rent received every month and deposit it into a separate account each and every month. You should earmark each amount in a separate ledger so you can keep a record of how much is available for each bill.

" " Edwards' Advice

You should reconcile the escrow account once a year. Add up the amounts left over per escrowed category to determine how much is really needed monthly for that category. If it is determined that too much money has been escrowed for water bills during the year, adjust the amount and either take the balance for yourself or place it into a different category where you feel it could be better used.

We like to call the escrow account the BST account. BST stands for blood, sweat, and tears because it is not easy to save for long-term expenses, and when doing so, you reduce the amount of money you would like to take from the property. However, having the money available to pay bills sure beats having to reach into your own pocket to pay bills when the time comes.

Remember that you started this account procedure by guessing the amounts you expected to pay every month. These numbers could be slightly off, could vary with time, or could change dramatically depending on the bill. The water bill we mentioned before might be $50 a month during the winter but $75 or more a month during the summer. Other types of bills will fluctuate during different times of the year. When you pay a bill against the property, you will have to make adjustments as necessary to either compensate for or reduce the monthly amounts being escrowed for certain expenses. In the event that there isn't enough rent money collected to meet your monthly escrow amounts, you will need to personally subsidize the account with your own funds. If you realize that there is an abundance of money available in the account after the bills have been paid, it will be your decision to either keep it in the account or move it to your profit.

If the cost of the bill fluctuates monthly, such as a heating fuel bill in an area where climate changes are frequent, the formula for escrow can get a little tricky. Basically, the only way to handle it is to estimate the charge for the year and divide it by 12 to get a monthly amount. If a property was purchased in December, the first heating bill is due in January, and the amount is estimated to cost $500, you will need to subsidize this amount from your personal funds to start the account off right.

Even if you have estimated that your monthly escrow amount is $280 for heating fuel for the year, you will need to subsidize the account until there is more money in the account than what is needed to pay the monthly bills. So, for example, if the February bill for heating fuel is $540 and you have escrowed only $280, you will be $260 short and will need to subsidize the amount. For a heating bill, the difference in the escrowed balance probably won't be noticed until the summer months. Remember that the escrowing system is not a perfect science, but it's a necessary one for your peace of mind while you own the property.

Landlord's Toolbox

One category we suggest adding to the escrow account is for miscellaneous repairs. Repair is a costly expense that needs to be reckoned with. For smaller properties, this category can prove particularly useful. In the event that a water heater or another big-ticket item needs to be replaced, money may be readily available to purchase it if you have escrowed for a period of time. Typically, a minimum of $100 per month for four or fewer units is a reasonable amount to escrow every month. If you can put a little more away for repair purposes, you will be ahead of the game, especially if a heating boiler bursts.

Escrow Categories

The most important aspect of the escrow account is being able to separate and categorize the money in the account.

Let's say for a moment that there are four categories for which you are escrowing, and the total amount equals $1,000 per month. The four categories you are concerned about are taxes, water, sewer, and insurance. Each category has an amount of money attached for which you are escrowing every month. If the monthly water bill escrowed amount is $100 per month and you escrow this amount for three months and then receive a bill for $330, where will you get the extra $30? Even if the escrow account has a total of $3,000 available to you for paying bills, the $30 cannot come from this account. All the money you have placed in this account is spoken for. In other words, it is put there to pay other bills.

You will need to once again subsidize the account and pay the extra $30 from personal funds. If you go ahead and take the $30 from the escrow account, you will only be stealing it from another category. This is referred to as "robbing Peter to pay Paul," and it will not work. You must be careful to deposit money by category and to separate it accordingly, perhaps by recording it in a ledger book or a computer accounting program. If you don't keep track of your money, you will risk mingling the amounts and messing up the account.

All Accounted For

Many computer programs are available on the market today for accounting purposes. We recommend that you use a PC program that's comfortable for you, but for those of you who are not computer savvy, the old-fashioned method of a ledger book and a pencil with an eraser will work just fine. It is very important that you always keep a record of expenses, because you will want to be able to track the costs associated with the property such as repairs, utilities, and supplies. Many, many rental-property owners haven't the slightest idea whether their property is making any money. This is because many of these owners don't keep very good accounting records.

If you own many properties and use only one account to handle the money that each generates, it will be very difficult to separate the income and expenses for an accurate portrayal of how each property is performing. The best way to handle this dilemma is to have a separate bank account for each property. Unfortunately, the actual task of separate bookkeeping for each separate property can be quite tedious and time consuming as well as seemingly impossible at times.

Facts for Rent

Here's some food for thought: If the money you make off the sale of a property can be put into a bank with a rate of interest that will equal the amount of money you could make from renting it, then it might be a good time to sell. Good luck with the kind of rates being paid these days!

Luckily, this is the twenty-first century, and the PC is available for use in the rental industry. There are many different rental-property-management computer programs as well as accounting programs on the market. A computer accounting program such as Microsoft Money or Quicken will enable you to use one account and separate each deposit and expense by category and property. This type of program also enables you to switch back and forth between other important accounts such as your escrow or personal accounts. Reports are available regarding inflows and outflows either for the business as a whole or for each individual property. Most computer-accounting programs offer the option of detailed reports for accounts that can track the performance of properties over certain lengths of time; this type of information is important because it will help you determine how your investment is doing and whether it's time to sell. One of the hardest decisions for an investor to make is to know when to buy and when to sell. A good accounting system might assist in making a decision.

Taxing Taxes

The only thing you can count on in life is death and taxes. Rental-property owner-ship will introduce you to some taxes with which you may not be that familiar. You might not know it, but you have a silent partner in your investment who shares none of the liability, hard work, or headaches associated with rental property ownership, but he most certainly gets a share of the profit. His name is Uncle Sam.

If you purchase a property for $100,000, sell it for $200,000, and have a profit of $100,000, you will pay taxes on the profit. This is called a capital-gains tax.

Each year that you own the property, you will need to attach a Schedule E form to your 1040 tax return to the Internal Revenue Service. This form will show how much income you received for the time you owned the property and how much the expenses were. There is also a depreciating factor that you will apply to the prop-erty that will reduce the profit you made during the year that you owned it. Many investors will purchase a property and take advantage of depreciation factors to reduce the amount of money they must pay for taxes during a year, but remember that when the property is sold, the depreciation used is added back into the property, which reduces the base and increases the profit on the sale.

Also keep in mind that only the building value is subject to depreciation, not the land value. The IRS allows you to determine what the value of the land and the building is, but if you become involved in an audit by the IRS, the value you assign may become subject to verification. If this happens, you had better be able to substan-tiate the numbers you chose to use. The assessor's office in the town where the prop-erty is located will have assessments for your property that will separate the land and the building. You might choose to use the numbers provided by these valuations.

Let's take a closer look at the rental property-tax dilemma. Remember that only the building value is subject to depreciation. Let's say the purchase price is $100,000; this is also known as the "base price upon purchase." Next, you separate the building value from the land value and make the decision of whether to use a residential rate of 27.5 years or a commercial depreciation rate of 39 years; check with an accountant regarding current depreciation rates. For the purpose of our example, we will use a residential depreciation term of 27.5 years and a land value of $10,000. This means that the building value equals $90,000 and is subject to depreciation. This shows us a depreciation of $3,273 the first year. The base price is now $96,727. If you then sell the property for $200,000, you will have a profit of $103,273. This is true because you must add back the first years of depreciation that you deducted on that first year's 1040, only to now pay capital-gains taxes on the depreciated amount. Uncle Sam is always one step ahead of you!

Now, if the building makes a yearly income of $20,000 and has an expense of $10,000, the profit from the property will be $10,000 for the year before income taxes. If you then take a depreciation of $10,000, it will indicate to the Feds that you have not made any money with the property so there is no profit to pay taxes on.

The Schedule E Profit and Loss Example	
Income	$20,000
Expense	$10,000
Profit	$10,000 subject to tax
Depreciation	$10,000
=	
Adjusted profit of $0 subject to tax	

If your depreciation is even greater, not only will you not pay any taxes on the property income, but you also reduce any taxes you would have to pay on any other income earned. This is a good trick as long as you never sell the property, but it's not so good the day you do.

Now let's take a moment and look at the same example only from a different angle. This time, instead of taking the expense as a loss, you instead choose to apply it to the base price of the property. The purchase price was $100,000, and the applied expense is $10,000. The new base is now $110,000. You then sell the property for $200,000, so your profit is $90,000, which is then subject to taxes. Once again, you should always check with a qualified accountant to be sure that the expense you are choosing to add to your base is allowed under the IRS code.

Capital Improvement vs. the Capital Gain

Some expenses for capital improvements can be added to your basis (purchase price), and can reduce the capital gain on the sale. Some expenses, such as a new roof, fall into a category called a "capital repair" and will be subject to their own depreciation rate. You should consult with an accountant about how to depreciate your property and the expenses associated with it.

Property Tax Assessments

Since we're already on the subject of taxes, let's discuss property taxes. Every town that charges a yearly tax will need to base that tax on a value, and this value is known as an assessment. The assessment of value separates the value of the land and the value of the building at a property. Then both values are added together for the total value of a property, which is subject to a property tax. Let's take a moment to look at the system of property-tax valuations and what it means to rental-property owners.

First, you must think of your town as a business that needs money to operate. Money is necessary to operate schools and other public buildings, to pay employees, and to maintain streets and utilities provided to the public within the town. Every year, a budget is prepared for the upcoming year that forecasts how much money the town will need to function. The town obtains money in the form of the property tax, which it requires property owners to pay.

Second, you need to understand how property is taxed. The first thing that happens is that a fair-market value is assigned to your property. Next, the town will determine what portion of that value it will tax, usually 70 percent of the total value. If you take the value assigned to your property, divide it by 7, and then multiply it by 10, you can figure out how much the town believes your property is worth. Then the town will decide what percentage of the 70 percent assessment it will charge. This is referred to as the mill rate.

Rental Red Light!

The mill rate is equal to $\frac{1}{10}$ of a cent. It is used in expressing a tax rate. Ten mills would be the same as $10 per thousand dollars of value.

For example:

Fair-market value	=	$100,000
70 percent of value	=	$70,000 subject to tax
20 mills	=	$1,400 yearly tax

The 20 mills is equal to $20 per thousand of value. Your property value subject to tax is $70,000, so you must multiply $20 by 70 because the town is using a rate of 70 percent of value. In this example, your yearly tax on the property would be $1,400.

By increasing or decreasing the mill rate, a town can increase or decrease the amount you will spend on property taxes.

Most towns will have what is called a revaluation in which the town attempts to determine what the values of properties are that will be subject to taxes. The "reval," as it is sometimes called, is usually done every 10 years. This is done because property has a way of increasing in value over time. A property that was worth $50,000 in 1990 might be worth $100,000 by the year 2000; this is called appreciation of value. While your property value is increasing, so is the cost of running the town. The way the town keeps up with associated expenses is by assigning new values to the property in the town. A town may also increase the mill rate until the reval is done. Then, if the total value of all the properties in the town increases, the mill rate may be lowered.

The town's assessor may do a reval, or a town might hire out the reval work to a special appraisal company that does revaluations. Whether done by the assessor or an appraisal company, it will require someone to visit each and every taxable property in the town to list property conditions and additions for the interior and exterior. If the individual cannot gain entry to the property, he or she will attempt to place a value on the property without actually seeing it. It's important that property owners review such valuations and make sure the facts about the property are correct to guard against the *"golden toilet seat approach"* appraisal and overvalued property taxes.

Landlord Lingo

When either an assessor or an appraisal company conducting the revaluation cannot gain entry but attempts to place a value on the property, this appraisal is often referred to as **the golden toilet seat approach.** If every property on your street has a Jacuzzi tub, the appraiser will assume that you have one, too, and might value it accordingly.

It is important to connect with the people who do the revaluations and allow them to look at your property to help avoid such discrepancies and to obtain a correct valuation for your property.

The amount of work associated with a revaluation is quite considerable. Often there isn't time for the individuals conducting the reval to visit each and every property or to see every facet of a property. Often, the individuals must rely on help from special appraisal books designed to assign values for specific square footages and building supplies used in construction to help them assign a value to your property.

The problem therein is that your property may not conform to the categories used to best describe your property. If you can change the information used to determine your property's valuation, you might be able to lower the overall assessment, which will lower the amount you will have to pay in property taxes every year. After the assessment has been completed, you will be given the opportunity to challenge the results, and you should do so if you disagree with the findings. Many times, you can meet with the reval company to review the findings and make corrections.

If for some reason you miss the opportunity to correct the assessment and receive a tax bill that seems way out of whack, you should visit the assessor in the town and discuss the circumstances. The assessor might either adjust the tax or tell you what the procedure is for bringing your case before the tax board of review. Remember that if you intend to dispute your property's tax assessment, you will need to find comparable properties in the area that have lower assessments.

The tax-review committee will hear your case and make the determination as to whether to lower your assessment. This review committee will try to be fair but will also be committed to preserving the tax revenue collected for the town. If you still feel the assessment is wrong after the tax board of review's decision, you will need to further contest the tax by taking the town to court. Speak with a competent accountant and attorney to help decide which the best avenue to pursue the problem is.

Show Me More Money!

Greedy? Of course not. A smart investor will always attempt to optimize the performance of the property to achieve maximum profits. There are several activities that should be considered daily in the constant struggle to increase returns.

First, a smart investor will keep a watchful eye on market rental rates for slight increases. If the rents in the area are increasing, you should not hesitate to try to get an increase as soon as your rental agreement permits and provided that your property is not under rent-control regulations. Some landlords are reluctant to raise the rent because they fear driving out good tenants. This concern has merit, particularly in areas where a large supply of affordable housing is available. Inflation affects every aspect of the economy, including the cost of business operations, property repairs, and upkeep and rental rates. Landlords must try to stay current with the optimum market rental rate.

Investors must also consider other factors besides the rent they charge. For instance, what is the highest and best use for the property? In other words, if your property is being used as apartments when there is a shortage and high demand for office space in the neighborhood, and the office space would warrant a higher price per square foot than the residential use, perhaps a use change is in order.

A smart landlord will also make capital improvements to the property to attempt to attract higher income from higher-paying tenants.

What Else Can You Rent?

Be careful not to give away space for which you might be able to charge. Don't take potential storage space, garage ports, or parking spots for granted by giving them without charge to tenants. These areas can be rented separately to a tenant who is occupying a unit that you own.

You should first try to determine how much you are getting as rent for the use of this type of space, if it is available on the property, by letting the tenants have it as part of the rental agreement. Then try to assess how much could be charged to a tenant or other person if the space was rented separately. You are under no obligation to supply storage or parking spaces as part of a rental agreement to a tenant.

That garage you're not using or the small shed or old barn on the property could be rented as storage space. The empty attic or basement also could be rented to tenants as an area where they can put things. Tenants are always looking for a place to store old clothes, bicycles, and children's toys. These areas that otherwise might not be of any benefit to you or the property can start earning their keep if you charge for the use. If you charge even $50 a month for that garage space, you could earn an extra $600 a year.

In areas where there are parking shortages, rental amounts for automobile space on a property could mean quite a considerable increase to your potential income. If you do decide to rent out nonliving space to residents, always remember to include the rental in a lease or agreement or to write an amendment to a current lease.

Use Every Bit of the Property

There might be many other income possibilities available at your property. Consider for a moment adding vending machines, pay phones, and coin-operated laundry facilities, which could offer a rental property other forms of income. Look for other types of unused space such as for billboards or cellular telephone transmitters. However, be aware that these types of income possibilities often don't live up to the expected potential. The costs associated with renting, buying, supplying, and repairing vending machines can be quite high. And if you have to service areas such as billboards or telephone transmitters, it can become quite an inconvenience. Consult with others who have experience with these types of ventures before committing yourself to one or more of them.

Rental Red Light!

Vending machines and coin-operated laundry appliances ought to pay for themselves in three years to be considered a good investment.

Show Me Even More Money!

One excellent way to increase profits is to reduce expenses. By saving money that is earned, you will increase profits. However, there is a limit to how much you can reduce expenses. You can't save more money on expenses than the absolute minimum amount it takes to operate the property, although it would be hard to do anyway. Nevertheless, there are some expenses and policies that can be tinkered with that will, in the long run, save some money and increase potential profits. The following tips are some examples of how to reduce expenses and save money:

♦ Don't hesitate to start an eviction of a tenant for nonpayment of rent. Tenants who do not pay their rent within the time limits allotted by either a lease or a state law are dead financial losses to the property and an expense to you. Save yourself as much of this expense as you can by taking the appropriate steps to remedy the situation as soon as legally permissible.

♦ Save money by fixing something once. When doing repairs, make sure that you fix things right the first time and avoid the added cost of repeated repairs. Repairs and service contractors can be quite costly, especially if each repair has to be done twice.

Edwards' Advice

Remember that, if you have a public sewer system, you're paying for the water not only on the way into your building but also on the way out. Locating and repairing water leaks can save you a small fortune.

♦ Either do repairs yourself or hire a handyman who can fix odds and ends around the property. If you have to call an electrician every time a light bulb burns out, it will cost you a fortune.

♦ Screening your tenants carefully will save you money. By avoiding destructive tenants and possible nonpayment situations, you will enhance your chances for better profit return by reducing operating costs.

♦ Water bills can really add up to a hefty expense for landlords who pay the bill. Check your building for leaks. Water conservation kits that can help conserve water in your units and save you some money are available from either your area water company or local plumbing-supply stores. Water conservation kits, complete with faucet aerators, showerhead, toilet dam, and color tablets that help identify leaks, can help tremendously reduce high water bills. Many water companies have service technicians available who will gladly visit a property to investigate reasons for high water usage.

A landlord who is never satisfied with a property's cash flow will always be on the lookout for ways to reduce expenses and increase profits.

The Least You Need to Know

◆ Escrow accounts are an excellent accounting method to make sure you don't spend money that would otherwise be used to pay bills.

◆ Accounting records should be kept in either a ledger book or a reliable computer program.

◆ Understanding income tax and property tax is essential for the property owner looking to maximize profits.

◆ There may be other sources available at a rental property—besides the actual rental units—from which to generate income.

◆ Landlords who can reduce careless expenses can eventually fatten the bottom line of profit.

Chapter 3

Receiving Rent

In This Chapter

- ◆ Setting rent payment and rental due dates
- ◆ Getting rent payments on time
- ◆ When to increase rent and how much
- ◆ Managing subsidized rents

The best time of the month is when we collect our rent. Unfortunately, it can also be one of the most aggravating times of the month because it is usually when tenant complaints are most frequent. Setting up good policies with regard to rent collection can alleviate some basic concerns and put the fun back into rent collection.

When Is the Rent Due?

It is completely up to the landlord to decide when rent is due. If you don't specify a due date in your lease, some state laws will dictate what day in the month the rent is due (see the following table).

Traditionally, for a month-to-month or lease agreement, the rent is due on the first day of every month. This is a convenient time in which to require the rent be paid because many people get paychecks at the end of the month. Also, the policy of the first day of the month can serve as a helpful reminder to tenants that the rental bill is due. For week-to-week agreements, the rent traditionally is due on a Friday because this is the day on which many people get paid, and a landlord should be concerned with getting the rent owed before the tenant has a chance to spend it.

The following table lists states that indicate when rent is due, if not specified in your lease or rental agreement, as well as states with late-fee restrictions.

Rent Due and Late Rent Charges

State	Rent Due On	Late Charge Restrictions
Alaska	---	According to written agreement, the landlord can charge a flat rate or a percentage per day, which can be either 10.5 percent or 5 percent plus the Federal Reserve discount rate, if rate is specified. Either must be specified.
Arizona	---	Can charge a late fee but only if written into the lease or agreement.
Connecticut	---	Can't charge a late fee before the tenant's 9-day grace period.
Delaware	---	Can charge a late fee after rent is 5 days late, but the fee cannot exceed 5 percent of the monthly rent.
Florida	Beginning of the month unless otherwise stated.	---
Georgia	---	Can only charge a late fee if it's stated in the agreement.
Hawaii	---	---
Idaho	---	---
Illinois	---	---
Indiana	---	---
Iowa	At the beginning of the month unless otherwise agreed.	---

State	Rent Due On	Late Charge Restrictions
Kansas	At the beginning of the month unless otherwise agreed.	---
Kentucky	At the beginning of the rental term unless otherwise agreed.	---
Maryland	---	Cannot be more than 5 percent.
Michigan	---	Must be reasonable.
Nebraska	Due at the beginning of each rental term for an unwritten lease.	---
Nevada	Due at the beginning of each rental term unless stated in the agreement.	Late charges not allowed.
New Jersey	---	Not allowed to charge a late fee during the 5-day grace period.
New Mexico	---	Landlord can charge a late fee, but it cannot exceed 10 percent of the rent for a rental period.
North Carolina	---	Can charge a late fee after 5 days that is the greater of $15 or 5 percent of the rental payment, but no more.
North Dakota	---	Can charge a late fee only if it's written into the lease or agreement.
Oklahoma	The beginning of the month unless specified in the agreement.	---
Oregon	---	Cannot charge a late fee until midnight of the fourth day after rent is due.

continues

Rent Due and Late Rent Charges (continued)

State	Rent Due On	Late Charge Restrictions
South Carolina	If not specified in the agreement, rent is due at the beginning of the month.	---
South Dakota	If not specified in the agreement, rent is due at the end of the month.	---
Vermont	---	Can charge a late fee to cover expenses. Cannot use a late fee as a penalty.
Virginia	If not specified in the agreement, rent is due at the beginning of the month.	---

If a tenant moves into a unit during the middle of the month (on the fifteenth, for example), the rent will have to be prorated for that shorter month because the tenant should not have to pay for the entire month. You can prorate rent by taking the monthly amount and dividing it by the number of days in the month; this will equal the daily amount.

Next, multiply the daily amount by the number of days the tenant will occupy the unit for the month. This will equal the rental amount the tenant owes for that month. Make sure the tenant understands that the rental due date will convert to a specific day, typically the first day of the month, starting with the next month of the tenancy, and it will continue as such until the rental agreement expires. If, however, you would prefer to simply have the tenant pay for an entire month by making this tenant's rent due on the fifteenth of every month, it is perfectly legal. It is very important that you make the terms regarding the due date very clear. If you find yourself evicting the tenant for nonpayment of rent, one possible defense is that the rent is not due until some other day, which could extend his or her stay while you lose revenue for those days.

Facts for Rent

If the due date for rent falls on a holiday or a weekend, the due date should be extended to the very next business day. This should be mentioned in your lease or rental agreement, and it is legally required in most states.

Public assistance programs in some states have special provisions as to when the rent is due. If the public assistance check is collected by the recipient on the first of the month, the recipient may have no choice but to pay rent on the third day of the month.

Whatever is decided about the rent due date, the date should be mentioned in the rental agreement or lease. If it is not, some state laws will dictate when the rent is due for you. In many states, the rent for month-to-month agreements is due at the beginning of the month, but in a few states, the rent would not be due until the end of the month. Most landlords would not allow a tenant who moved in at the beginning of the month to pay the rent at the end of the month. Make sure you don't accidentally permit this to happen.

Grace Periods for Rental Payments

In some states, the tenant has 10 or fewer days from the first day rent is due to pay the rent without the property owner being able to start an eviction for nonpayment. If you require the tenant to pay the rent on the twentieth of the month, the tenant would have until the thirtieth to pay the rent in these states.

Some tenants will insist that they have until the tenth day (or some other number of days) to legally pay their rent before a late charge can be administered. This is not true. You have a legal right to demand that the rent be paid on the date it is due. Most landlords don't get too upset about late rent until it becomes several days late, but you should send a notice or contact the tenant immediately about the rent and continue to drive home the point that rent must be paid on the due date.

We suggest that you wait no longer than three days to collect the rent that is due; if you do, you are making a mistake and are possibly extending the amount of time a nonpaying tenant can stay. You must remain firm with your tenants in regard to rent. Exceptions to the rule should be avoided. Usually once an exception is made, it is very hard to correct the late-paying behavior of the tenant. The tenant will likely believe that because they got away with it once they can do it again. Also, once tenants are late with the rent, it may be very hard for them to get back on track even if they want to. Only permit exceptions in extreme cases; otherwise, tenants will think you are a pushover and will take

Rental Red Light!

Be sure to give a tenant a rental receipt indicating the amount paid, owed, and the balance. Also include the date the payment is made as well as the name of the tenant and the address of the unit. Remember to sign the receipt. It's best if you use receipt booklets that provide carbon copies.

advantage of your lenient policies. After all, how many operations can their grand-mother really have this year before she finally croaks? God bless her!

Collecting the Rent

You should make sure your lease or rental agreement clearly states to whom and where the rent should be paid.

Should you go and physically collect the rent or require that the money be sent to you? Fortunately, there are a few options for collecting rent, and if you have the means, you should try using them all.

The Check Is in the Mail

Mailing the rental check is a common and convenient way for many tenants to pay their rent. Obviously, this is a necessary form of a payment if you live a great distance from the property. Receiving rent in the mail is the most convenient way for you to receive rent payments. In a perfect world, the tenant would religiously send the rental payment in full to the landlord's address. This way, the landlord would only have to open the mailbox and PRESTO! There the rental money would be. However, this is not always the case in reality, and sometimes the landlord will have to visit the tenant to collect the money.

Some landlords send a monthly statement to each tenant one week or so before the rent is due. Similar to a credit card statement, you can create a form that has a tear-off sheet (or a separate form so that tenants can have one copy to keep, similar to a rent receipt) stating the tenant's name and address, the amount of rent due, and when. If you charge late-rent fees, you can also include what the late fee is and when it will be charged if rent is not received. Sometimes a formal written reminder days before the rent due date would seem imposing. Creating a monthly statement form each month for every tenant might seem like too much work for you. If you are computer literate and have a good word-processing program, creating forms such as this every month will save time. See Chapter 21 for more ideas on running a smooth office.

Edwards' Advice

To make it easier for your tenants to pay rent by mail, give them pre-addressed, stamped envelopes in which to send it to you. This technique might help speed up the rent-collecting process.

Go Get the Rent!

Another time-tested way of collecting rent is to either send someone or physically go and visit each tenant to pick up the rent. This technique proves useful in situations in which you might need to confront the tenant face to face about money owed. It also enables you to have a little personal contact with the tenant, and it gives you the chance to oversee the property firsthand.

There are a couple of downsides to this method. First, tenants are not always home even if you have notified them that you will be coming, and your visit could prove to be a waste of time. Second, physically collecting rent can prove to be very unsafe, especially if you or your collector is carrying a great deal of money. Third, if you must physically collect all your rents, it will complicate your bookkeeping methods because your books will have to remain open until all the rents for the month have been collected.

Allowing a tenant to wait until you visit to pay the rent will become a ritual that will be almost impossible to stop. Although many tenants will not mind sending the rent to you, many others won't be bothered with it if they know you will eventually stop by for the money. This can become quite a nuisance for you, especially when a tenant takes this opportunity to complain about every little aspect of a unit.

Edwards' Advice

Be smart and safe in your rent-collecting policy. Never collect rent by yourself or send someone to collect a rental payment alone. A person who is alone becomes easy prey for thieves who might be familiar with your rent-collection methods.

Drop Off the Money

Some landlords require the rent to be paid by the tenant at a particular place of business. In bigger rental complexes, there is often a rental office in which a mail slot is available for tenants to drop off rent. Sometimes a landlord may run either a real-estate office or a management company office where rent may be collected. By requiring the tenant to bring you the rent, you force the payment to be made on your turf. In other words, it is better to do business in a place of business instead of in a hallway or on a doorstep. This also guarantees at least a little personal contact between you and the tenant, and if by chance the rental agreement has lapsed, it will be easier to have the tenant re-sign a new agreement while he or she is in your office.

If you do not specify in either your lease or your rental agreement where the rent is to be paid, some state laws will decide for you. In several states, rent is due at the rental unit unless specified differently in the rental agreement.

Rent Receipts

More and more states are enacting legislation requiring landlords to give rent receipts to tenants for cash payments. Rent receipts are a good idea as long as certain care is given regarding the payment information on the slip. Rental receipt books, which provide carbon copies for your records, can be purchased at stationery stores. We prefer this to writing a receipt on scrap paper because of the carbon record. Whichever way you prefer, be sure that your receipt includes the following:

◆ Date

◆ Name of person making payment

◆ Address and rental unit of the tenant

◆ Exact amount paid

◆ Your signature

◆ Memo Note: Use and occupancy only (to distinguish from other possible non-rent payments)

Clams, Bananas, or Cash?

You should make sure that your lease or rental agreement clearly states in what form of payment the rent should be. Should you accept only cash? How about checks and money orders? If you're like most landlords, you'll accept all forms of payment and just be happy to get it. However, there are a few circumstances in which you should beware the different types of rental payments.

Cash is nice unless you have to carry it while physically collecting rent from tenants. Always make sure to give a tenant who hands you cash as a rental payment a proper receipt, preferably one that is carbon copied, indicating the exact amount paid and the date it was received. People will know you're carrying cash, and you could become an easy target for robbery. Also, cash can be lost, and if this happens, you will have no one to blame but yourself. Certainly, it is not up to the tenant to replace money you have lost. And here's one other important tidbit of information: If you collect cash knowing that the tenant earned it by illegal methods such as drug dealing, the government may be able to seize it from you.

You should not under any circumstances collect post-dated checks as a form of rent payment. There are never any assurances that there is any money in a checking account to pay the check. A post-dated check may legally be considered a promissory note

Rental Red Light!

If you decide to change the method of collection or the form of rental payment, you must properly notify the tenants about such a change. If you do not send proper notice, you may be held to the terms of your agreement for the remainder of the agreement.

to pay the rent at a certain date, and it can affect an eviction. Let's say you require rent to be paid on the first and a tenant post-dates his or her check for the twenty-fifth of the same month. If you accept the post-dated check, it will delay any attempt to evict the tenant because you have accepted a promissory note to receive rent on the twenty-fifth. Require your tenants to pay the rent in full and on time. If rent is not paid on time, you should not hesitate to send the tenant a late notice or to charge a fee if you have a late-fee policy.

Charge! And How Much ...

You should charge as much as you legally can and as much as the market will bear for rent. It's very important to charge a market rent that is both fair and competitive. You must attempt to obtain the highest rent you can for the unit you are renting. In most states, there is no legal limit for what you can charge for rent. Most landlords attempt to charge a little less than the market rate to try to appeal to good tenants. Whatever rate you decide to charge must be enough to enable you to successfully operate the property and make a profit. In areas where rent is controlled by city ordinance, there will be legal limitations. For more on rent control, refer to Chapter 10.

A smart landlord will always make an effort to stay current with the going market rates for rent. Newspaper ads and networking with other landlords or real-estate agencies are excellent sources for gaining rental rate information. Newly available rentals will have to be advertised and rented at current rates, and existing tenants will have to have their rents adjusted to current standards.

> **Edwards' Advice**
>
> When the need arises and your rental agreement permits it, you should try to raise the rent in small increments. If you don't and you eventually find that it is difficult to continue to operate your property at the current rental rates, it will be very difficult to raise the rents several hundred dollars all at once and still maintain a good relationship with the tenant.

Raising the Rent

The cost of living increases every year. Your costs are going up, and you will need to pass this increase on to your tenants. Whether you can raise the rent depends on the type of rental agreement you use, unless your property resides in an area governed by rent-control laws.

Remember that the definition of a lease is a fixed-term tenancy. This means you cannot change the terms of the lease until the term of the tenancy expires unless the lease permits it or the tenant agrees to the change. So if the lease is for one year and does not specify a rental increase at a specific time during the tenancy, the rent cannot be raised until that year elapses. However, at the time the lease expires, you can change the terms of the lease or increase the rent. If you do plan to increase the rent, it would be best to give the tenant notice regarding the increase, typically 30 days.

In a month-to-month or some other periodic rental agreement, the rent can be raised at any time as long as the tenant has been given proper notice, typically 30 days for a month-to-month and 7 days for a weekly rental.

Some states require that proper notice be given to tenants 45 to 60 days before raising rents, regardless of the type of agreement (month-to-month, week-to-week, or lease). You should read your state statutes regarding rent increase notices and tenant rights.

In areas without rent control, there is no limitation on the amount rent can be raised. Rent for month-to-month or other periodic tenancies can be raised as much and as often as good business will permit. However, you must be careful not to overdo it and create bad relations with tenants due to unfair rental increases. The result will probably be vacant units, and vacant units don't make money!

Facts for Rent

Some states do allow tenants to refuse to accept a perceived unfair rental increase. In these states, it may be acceptable for the tenant to pay a lesser amount than what the landlord asked for. The intent of payment of the lesser amount will nullify any attempt to evict for nonpayment, but other means of eviction may be pursued.

Rental Red Light!

Beware of charges of discrimination and retaliation based on the fact that you have increased one tenant's rent but not others in the building. Make sure if you institute a policy on a property that the same applies to every tenant; otherwise, you could find yourself in a heap of trouble.

What Is a Rental Subsidy?

A rental subsidy is a payment of rent made from a government or other nonprofit agency for the use and occupancy of a rental dwelling for poor and underprivileged citizens who cannot afford living space on their own. There are several different types of rental subsidies; the most popular is the federal Section 8 program that assists the general public in paying rent if the recipient qualifies within very specific guidelines for consideration for the program. Basically, a rental subsidy is a welfare program designed to temporarily help people who are financially troubled until the individual recipients can somehow afford to make the payments on their own. These programs are available in just about every town in the country, but they are most commonly found in larger urban areas where there is a high concentration of poor people.

Particularly in lower-income areas, rental subsidies can be good for landlords because they ensure that payments will be made. The federal and state programs, although different by state and town, will pay close to market rates for rental units. Typically, a portion of the rent money will be sent directly to the landlord, but most welfare subsidy programs do require that the tenants pay a portion themselves. Although every case is different, often the portion that is required by the tenant is much less than what is sent from the welfare agency.

For the most part, the process involved in dealing with tenants who are using rental subsidies is similar to dealing with other tenants. However, some welfare subsidy programs, such as the Section 8 program, require that the landlord and tenant use a special lease provided by the welfare subsidy agency. The Landlord must also sign a Housing Assistance Payment (HAP) contract to receive the funds. A smart landlord should read the lease and HAP contract very carefully before signing it. Landlords should clarify anything that needs better understanding. Usually, the welfare subsidy agency's contract is designed to protect the agency and the tenant. We also suggest that you attach a copy of your own lease to their paperwork to better protect yourself.

Edwards' Advice

Be wary of rental subsidies that promise to pay for only a few months. When time runs out on a tenant who cannot afford to pay on his or her own, usually the tenant no longer pays and has to be evicted.

Rental Red Light!

When giving rent receipts to subsidized tenants for rental payments, only indicate on the receipt what the tenant has actually paid. If the rent is $500 per month with a rental subsidy amount of $400 and the tenant paying the balance of $100, only give a receipt indicating the $100 payment.

Sometimes the welfare subsidy program will require that a certified inspector, usually someone the agency has on staff, complete a physical inspection of the leased premises before the tenant is allowed to take occupancy and any payments are started. This inspector is interested in looking the unit over for quality and cleanliness to better ensure that the agency is not wasting money on substandard rental units. Very often, these inspections are required to be performed on a yearly basis after the tenant has taken occupancy, usually at the time of lease renewal.

Some extra headaches and extra paperwork can arise for landlords when using rental subsidy programs:

♦ With most federal and state welfare programs, a tenant who is arrested for either drug use or drug dealing will be kicked off the program. This does not mean that the tenant must leave the rental unit or that he or she is automatically evicted. The problem tenant becomes the landlord's sole problem, and the welfare agency stops making any rental payments.

◆ If the tenant allows other people to move into the unit who are not of the tenant's agreed-upon immediate family, the tenant risks getting kicked off the program.

◆ Destruction of the rental unit by the occupying tenant is of no consideration to the welfare agency. The yearly inspection will require the landlord to make any and all repairs to the unit to continue in the program and receive payments.

◆ If a landlord starts an eviction on a tenant who is involved with one of these programs, the landlord must supply the welfare agency with copies of all the court paperwork throughout the process of the eviction.

Some property owners dislike rental subsidy programs because they take away some control from the owner that is needed to efficiently operate the property.

Increasing Rental Subsidies

Landlords who are involved with rental subsidy programs may be able to achieve rental increases. You should find out what the highest rate paid for rental subsidies is in the area and try to achieve scale for your size unit. It's important that you make an effort every year to increase the rent for the entire property, including the rental subsidy.

If you try to increase only the rental subsidy, the agency will not pay it based on the fact that the increase is not balanced throughout the building. Some programs will not allow for a sizable increase unless some capital improvement, such as installation of new windows or bath fixtures, warrants the increase. If you go a long period of time without increasing the rent and then decide to do so to achieve fair market value, you may not get it. It's better to try to increase the amount a little every year with every tenant. The Section-8 tenant will not be allowed to be the leader in rent increase at the building; the office that administers payments will always ask about how much you are charging rent for other comparable units at the property.

The Least You Need to Know

◆ Make sure to specify in your lease or rental agreement when the rent is due, where the rental payment should be made, and which forms of payment are allowed.

◆ Always increase rent whenever the market and your agreement will allow.

◆ Set up efficient, safe, and convenient procedures for determining forms of payment and collecting rent.

◆ Look into state and federal rental subsidy programs for steady renting tenants. Also be sure to know what's required before getting involved.

Chapter

14

Insuring Your Investment

In This Chapter

- ◆ Exploring the different kinds of insurance for your investment
- ◆ Understanding fire and liability insurance
- ◆ Learning the insurance process for better protection
- ◆ Understanding claims and adjustments

Insurance is a landlord's double-edged sword. In other words, every landlord must have it, and yet every landlord hopes never to need it.

The risk associated with rental-property ownership is much higher for an
owner than the risk associated with owner-occupied single-family homes.
In addition to the common disasters such as a building burning down or
a roof blowing off, there are many other risks that could affect a rental
property.

Smart landlords must be careful when considering insurance policies
for their rental properties. Large investments such as rental property
require good, protective insurance policies that will protect your investment from the ever-present dangers that seem to loom over rental-
property ownership.

Do I Need Insurance?

You sure do! No lender in his or her right mind is going to lend you money to purchase a property without an insurance policy ready to be placed on the property. Some lenders even require the insurance company to notify them if the policy is cancelled. Many lenders attach the payment of the policy to your monthly mortgage payment and pay the premium for you so they can be sure that the policy is always paid on time.

Some Common Types of Insurance

Most people who own homes are familiar with homeowner insurance, but there are other types of insurance of which homeowners and landlords must be aware:

◆ **Homeowners insurance** covers your personal home, possessions, and people on your property. This type of insurance is required by lenders to be placed on a personal home. Rental property is usually not covered by a homeowner's policy unless the property is owner-occupied.

◆ **Mortgage insurance** protects the lender in case the buyer defaults on the loan. Depending on the financial situation of the buyer, lenders often require this type of insurance. Mortgage insurance is only required when the buyer has less than 20 percent equity in the building.

Rental Red Light! _____

Other types of insurance are also available. For instance, some insurance companies offer insurance referred to as ordinance and law insurance. This insurance protects a property owner in the event that a fire leaves a large asbestos or lead-paint environmental cleanup. However, a claim would have to be sought against the owner for this type of insurance to activate.

◆ **Title insurance** protects the buyer against problems with his or her claim of ownership. The lender also requires this type of insurance.

◆ **Liability insurance** protects the policyholder from claims of liability at the property. This type of insurance is an exclusive requirement for rental property that is not owner-occupied. In other words, landlords must have this kind of insurance to protect themselves from the occasional slip and fall or similar types of accidents that could develop at a rental property.

♦ **Fire insurance** protects the owner's investment from being lost in the event of a fire. This type of insurance is another exclusive requirement for rental-property ownership.

Other types of insurance will be mentioned later in this chapter that may be of interest to landlords to protect against possible environmental concerns.

Liability and Fire Insurance

Liability and fire insurance policies are essential for property owners who own rental property. With the amount of risk and liability associated with the rental industry, these types of insurance are a must for any smart landlord. The last thing you need is to be sued for a personal injury or to have the building burn down and not be covered by a good insurance policy.

Liability insurance protects you against claims from tenants and visitors who get hurt on your property and claim their injury is due to your personal negligence. The old "slip and fall" is a common occurrence from which you will need some form of protection. You can't be everywhere at once, nor can you protect everybody who comes in contact with your property from getting hurt. All you can do is your best to make sure the property is safe and then take the necessary steps to protect your personal assets from lawsuits.

You should try to obtain insurance coverage that is equal to your net worth. In other words, if the total value of your assets is $2 million, then you need $2 million in insurance coverage.

Fire insurance protects the investment from being totally lost in the event of a fire. You must be careful when purchasing fire insurance. Two different types of fire-insurance policies are available: replacement cost and cash value. These are described in more detail a little later in this chapter.

Facts for Rent

Some states are actively pursuing legislation that will require a tenant to obtain insurance if he or she owns dangerous dogs or other types of potentially dangerous pets. Landlords in some states have been held liable for the damages done by a tenant's vicious dog because the landlord allowed the dog to exist at the property.

Rental Red Light!

You will be forced to make many decisions in the wake of a fire. Make sure to take your time and evaluate each decision carefully. Let your insurance company offer a settlement. If you don't agree with the settlement, contact a private adjuster and let him or her do what he or she does best.

Make sure to select an agent who can explain the policy to you in language that is easy for you to understand.

If you have a fire, you might be surprised to hear from an adjuster from your insurance company—sometimes just hours after the fire—but this is a common occurrence. This is because your insurance company will want to speak with you before other adjusters get a chance to. Private adjusters will be climbing over each other to get a chance to speak with you about your policy. A private adjuster is an individual who assesses the damage after a fire and handles the claim with the insurance company for a property owner for a fee. A private adjuster is also known as a "10 percenter" who, for a fee of 10 percent of the loss, will negotiate the loss with your insurance company on your behalf. Often the people who do this type of work understand your policy better than you do and can be of great benefit to you.

The Ins and Outs of Insurance

So you need an insurance policy. The policy will name you as the policyholder and the lender as additionally insured. This means that in the event of a loss, when the insurance company pays the loss, the check will require both your signature and the signature of someone of authority from the lending company to cash the check. So if the property burns down and the insurance company decides to pay a sum of $100,000 to cover the loss, and you have a first mortgage of $75,000, the lender is guaranteed to receive the money it loaned you before you can have any of it.

Insurance can be a very complicated aspect of the rental business to understand. Typically, when you set up a policy, you meet with an insurance agent who will explain the policies available and will quote you a price for the insurance. Many times, the agent doesn't fully understand the policy either and probably cares very little for your investment concerns. Most people buy the insurance policy but never really understand what in fact they have purchased.

When you have a loss, however, you will meet with an insurance adjuster who knows exactly what type of insurance you bought and how the coverage is applied. This is usually a really bad time to learn such a valuable lesson.

Let's try to shed some light on common insurance myths to hopefully help you better understand insurance.

Let's say you have a property worth $100,000, and you simply want to insure the property for $100,000 so that, in the event the property burns down, you can get paid $100,000 without any hassles.

This might seem logical, but it is not how the insurance process works. When you purchase the insurance policy, the insurance company places a value on the property by taking the square footage of the building and multiplying it by a rate the company feels best reflects the cost of reconstructing the building. This value will reflect current construction costs for a similar-size building.

Suppose the insurance company determines it would cost $180,000 to rebuild the building. Great! You think that, if the building burns, you get paid $180,000.

Not quite!

There are a couple of different types of insurance policies that property owners can buy. One is a replacement-cost policy, and the other is a cash-value policy.

A replacement-cost policy does just that; in the event that the building is a total loss, it provides the money it would take to replace the building at current standards.

Rental Red Light!

Make sure to properly insure your property. Property should be insured for at least 80 percent of its actual value. In the event that the building is lost, if the insurance company decides you were not adequately insured, you might be penalized with a percentage deducted from your payment.

A cash-value policy is a little different than replacement cost. In a cash-value policy, if you insure a building for $100,000 and it burns down, the insurance company sends out an appraiser to determine a value for the building. If the appraisal states that the building is only worth $25,000, guess what you get? That's right. You'll only get the $25,000. But what if the appraisal comes in at $125,000? Then you will only get the $100,000. The insurance company will not pay you more than what you have insured.

Choosing either a replacement-cost or cash-value policy depends on you. If you intend to replace the building after a fire, you will want a replacement-cost policy. If you are only interested in the value of the property and don't intend to rebuild, then a cash value might be your best bet.

What Should You Claim?

You have insurance, you pay for it every month, and you should be able to use it whenever you need to, right? This might be true in theory but certainly not in reality. The truth is that if you have repeated claims against your policy, the insurance company eventually will drop you, and you will have to get insurance elsewhere. When you apply for new insurance, the new agent will probably ask you about any recent losses; your answer could affect whether the new company offers insurance to you and how much it will cost. It's not smart for landlords to have several claims against the insurance policy. A good, cost-effective policy is worth its weight in gold, and a smart landlord is careful not to lose it.

Deductibles

When you purchase an insurance policy, you will set the deductible for which you will be responsible at $100, $200, or higher. The higher the deductible you're willing to pay, the lower the cost of the insurance policy.

Try to set a deductible that will work for you financially in case you need to make a claim against the policy.

Adjusting the Adjustment

If you have a loss, the adjuster will take into account the age of the material at time of loss. For example, you have a roof on your building that is 30 years old, is not leaking, and appears to be in good condition. One day, the wind comes along and blows it off the building, and you call the insurance company to report the claim. The insurance company will then send out an adjuster who will meet with you and examine the loss. If the adjuster determines that the life of the roof shingles was 15 years, and it's been up there for 30 years, guess what? That's right, you don't have a loss! If the roof has a life expectancy of 15 years but has only been up there for 10 years, however, you will get one third of the value less your deductible. So if the loss equals $2,000 and your deductible is $1,000, you'll get $1,000.

Rental Red Light!

You can suggest to your insurance agent which company you would like to be insured with, but in most cases, the agent will choose a company with which he or she already does business. If this is definitely not a company you are comfortable with, you can request that the agent use a specific company, but he or she might have to enlist the services of yet another agent with the company you have chosen. Try not to complicate matters; try to use an agent who is already affiliated with the insurance company you want. Your insurance agent will appreciate this.

Renters Insurance

Many insurance companies offer policies to tenants called tenant insurance or renters insurance. The purpose of this type of insurance policy is to insure the tenant against loss at the rental unit due to fire damage, water damage, or other potential mishaps that could occur at the property. This kind of policy is rather inexpensive, and every tenant should have one.

Chapter 8 discussed leases and one specific lease clause that requires the tenant to obtain insurance and to name the landlord as additionally insured on the policy. This is done to protect your property in the event of a loss in the tenant's unit. However, if the insurance company pays the loss at your property and then determines that you were negligent and at fault for the loss, the company may be able to successfully sue you for the money it paid to the tenant.

Edwards' Advice

Inform your tenants about renters insurance. Some landlords will even try to implement a program in which the tenant insurance is paid by a portion of the rent. This is done primarily to attract and keep good tenants. Renter insurance will typically cover the following:

◆ Losses to the tenant's personal property including repair and replacement of property that is damaged or stolen such as furniture and clothing.

◆ Losses that occur both at home and away from home such as in a hotel room or a parked car.

◆ Claims of liability against the tenant (for instance, if a person were to trip over a garbage bag placed in front of the tenant's door).

◆ Additional living expenses incurred because the tenant has to leave the apartment due to fire or flood damage.

Fear for the Worst and Hope for the Best

When you shop for insurance, you should take into consideration factors such as the area in which your property is located. If your property is located in an area that is commonly affected by hurricanes or tornadoes, you may need to have certain types of extra coverage specific to the area. If the property is close to water or is located in a flood plain, you will need flood insurance. Insurance policies are available that can cover you for just about anything if you're willing to pay the premium.

If your property is in a depressed area that suffers high losses on a repeated basis, the premiums may be higher than elsewhere. Often, an insurance company will require that the insured properties in these areas be inspected on a regular basis to make sure you keep your property free from defects that could eventually translate to potential losses.

Remember that an insurance company is a business designed to make money. Insurance companies don't want to pay out more money than they receive; otherwise, they wouldn't be in business very long if they did. These companies play the odds that the property owners will pay them more money than they will ever have to pay for the protection the policies provide.

The Least You Need to Know

- A landlord must have fire and liability insurance policies placed on his or her rental properties to protect the investment and his or her personal assets.

- Several types of insurance are available for property owners to purchase, and they offer a wide variety of coverage.

- Your lender considers itself to be a partner in your investment, and it requires a certain amount of insurance before it will lend you money to purchase a property.

- Cost-replacement and cash-value insurance policies are two types of fire insurance policies.

- Too many claims against an insurance policy may result in the insurance company dropping your coverage.

Part 4

The Tenant-Landlord Relationship

When you own and rent property, you deal with many different people. You have to learn how to interact with tenants and authorities in a polite yet firm manner.

Occasionally, disputes will arise between tenants and you. How well you communicate with others will make the difference in whether disputes can be handled in a way that won't severely alter your investment returns.

Chapter

15

Coping with Tenants, Service, and Repairs

In This Chapter

- ◆ Learning to cope with your new stresses as a landlord
- ◆ Using preventive maintenance to keep the value of your property in tact and to keep good tenants
- ◆ Making repairs and developing good relationships with tenants
- ◆ Winterizing units and avoiding environmental hazards

You happen by your building on the day that your new tenant has moved in. The first thing you notice is a strange car parked on the lawn leading up to the steps. As you walk into the building to investigate, some young people rudely run down the stairs past you yelling obscenities. You notice scratches and black marks on the freshly painted walls leading up the hallway. As you reach the entrance to the apartment you just rented, the door swings open, and loud music and your new tenants (who for some reason look different than they did when you processed their application) greet you.

You are immediately bombarded with comments such as "The sink is dripping, and the toilet won't flush!" and "The drain under the sink is dripping, and there's no place to park!"

What's a smart landlord to do?

Keep Your Sanity and Enjoy the Comedy!

More than one landlord has found him- or herself in situations similar to the one mentioned here, and some have even taken extended leaves of absence at their local loony bin. There is no question that stress can affect a person's health. A lot of normal people in the world rely on medication to help them handle the different stresses in life. It's our opinion, however, that unless you're the president of the United States or that guy who feeds the lions at the zoo, you won't find a more stressful job than landlording.

> **Rental Red Light!**
>
> Some towns with a short supply of rental stock provide classes for people looking for a rental. The class instructs them on what they should wear, what to say, and how they should act. The smart landlord needs to see through this disguise when choosing a new tenant.

Being able to handle stress and anxiety is a requirement if you're going to be a smart landlord. If you need to take medication, then do so, but a much better cure for anxiety associated with rental ownership is the ability to laugh. What else can you do when the tenant tells you that he or she gave the rent money to his or her sister so she could pay her rent? Or when the one bad tenant is complaining about all the other good tenants? You will find that many of the complaints and excuses you hear can be quite humorous. This doesn't mean you should laugh at your tenants every time you see them; just try to recognize the lighter sides of situations that arise and you will feel better.

For example, instead of being overcome with exasperation and anger when faced with a situation such as the one at the beginning of this chapter, take a deep breath, try to relax, and smile at your new tenants. Assure them that you will be happy to look into their concerns and—as if you didn't already know—ask them whose car is on the lawn.

Your Tenants Are Your Best Clients

There are a few different ways to make money with your investment property. You can take advantage of the *appreciation* of the property and sell it for more money than you paid for it. You can *build equity* (the difference between what you owe and the fair-market value of the property) in the property by making payments on the loan you used to purchase the property, thus shrinking your debt, while increasing your potential amount of profit when the property is sold. You can take advantage of a *tax shelter*, called *depreciation*, which occurs when you deduct a portion of the purchase price along with capital improvements and report them as losses to attempt to offset income. And the last way to make money with your property is to let others use and occupy it while you *collect rent*.

Although all these money-making strategies are important to the success of your rental property, if you want to build cash flow to maintain the property and put money in your pocket, you're going to need tenants. Tenants are the people who pay you the money you need to operate the property while you wait for your property to appreciate, build equity, and give you more income to hide in a tax shelter.

Put Yourself in Your Tenants' Shoes

If you think you have crazy tenants, it's a good bet they think they've got a crazy landlord. The truth is that, even if they're crazy or you're crazy, you still need them if you're going to be a landlord. Tenants are your clients, and your apartments are your products.

Remember that you are in a unique business that requires your client to pay you a large sum of money periodically to use your product. At the same time, you must also service your client by continuing to maintain that product.

Most tenants are people who either cannot afford to own their own home or don't want the responsibility of owning a home. Therefore, a tenant might resent the fact that you own something he or she cannot. In areas with housing shortages and big demand, tenants will be very pleased to have found a nice, affordable apartment and might even make some repairs themselves. Imagine that! Well, it does happen. Landlords are always on the hunt for responsible tenants to fill vacancies; unfortunately, the area in which you own property will determine the kind of tenants you get. Through careful screening techniques, you will have to try to select the best you can find from the supply of tenants available.

Welcome New Tenants

A landlord's life is full of challenges, and one of the biggest is being able to handle other people, especially if they're your tenants. Good communication skills are essential, and a little bit of kindness can go a long way. When you rent an apartment to a new tenant, you should try to make that tenant feel as welcome as possible to his or her new home.

Moving can be a big transition for people, and your new tenant will probably be a little anxious and uneasy, so anything you can do to ease this transition will be appreciated. You don't have to throw the person a party or even introduce him or her to everyone in the building. Small things usually mean the most. Take the liberty of putting the tenant's name on the mailbox. If the tenant will pay his or her own utilities, provide the tenant with the electrical and gas meter numbers and the phone numbers for the utility companies. A complimentary shower curtain and roll of toilet paper is a nice gesture as well, and maybe even a fruit basket. The idea here is to let your tenants know that you appreciate their business, and maybe they will appreciate you back.

> ### Rental Red Light! _____
>
> You're probably the tenants' biggest bill every month, and because of that, they will require that the product continue to be worth what they are paying for it. Unfortunately, what usually happens is that the tenant moves into a place and soon after starts to take the unit for granted without remembering why he or she wanted to live there in the first place. Suddenly, the unit is too small and inadequate. There aren't enough outlets, there are too many or too few windows, or the neighborhood isn't safe enough. The bottom line is an unhappy tenant. You can't worry about that, though; all you need to do is try to understand the tenant mentality and do the best job you can.

Hang On to Good Tenants

It is extremely important that you learn how to recognize and keep good tenants because, if you lose one, it can cost you hundreds of dollars. So what makes one tenant better than another? If you think the good tenant is the one who pays the rent on time every month, there are some other things you should consider.

What if that same tenant continues to bring unregistered cars onto the property, or leaves garbage lying around the grounds? What if the tenant attracts police attention and creates a nuisance to the neighborhood? A good tenant is more than a consistent rent check; a good tenant is someone who is responsible and considerate of others.

Let's face it, no one's perfect. But if you're lucky, you might find a tenant who has some of these better qualities and pays the rent religiously every month. If you do, you will have to try to make that good tenant want to stay for as long as possible so that you can continue to charge and collect a market rent. Here are some ideas for keeping good tenants:

♦ Every once in a while, let the tenant know that you're concerned about the safety and well-being of your property. This will indicate to the tenant that you care about more than just the rent he or she owes every month. You are communicating that you actually care about the tenant's home!

♦ Security is important to a tenant. Change the locks on the tenant's door and let the tenant see you do it. It will put the tenant's mind at ease about who has keys to his or her unit. Make sure to provide the same level of security to the unit by willingly changing the locks for the tenant if he or she reasonably requests it. A roommate or a family member might move out and not return the key to the occupant, giving them reason for concern. Changing the lock will put the issue to rest and will make the remaining tenant feel better.

Rental Red Light!

Make sure you understand why the tenant is requesting a change of locks and who exactly the tenant is concerned with keeping out of the unit. You cannot legally lock out someone who has signed your agreement to rent a unit. Roommates and spouses have been known to quarrel. If this situation occurs, don't get caught in the middle. Explain to the tenant about your duties to the other tenant, suggest that the parties involved handle the situation themselves, and remind them to give you a key when they do. However, if the person being locked out is not listed as an occupant in the rental agreement or if the tenant making the request can show you a restraining order against that person, then you do not have to provide access. When in doubt, you should consult with an attorney to prevent getting in trouble for illegal lockout.

♦ Inform your tenant about some little odds and ends at the property like where the electrical panels and water shutoff valves are or how to work the dishwasher or garbage disposal. Provide the tenant with phone numbers for police, fire, and ambulance services as well as utility companies and repair personnel.

Edwards' Advice

Interest on security deposits is usually required to be paid to the tenant once a year. One way to do this and enhance public relations with the tenants at the same time is to send it during the holiday season along with a card thanking them for their continued patronage. Even though the interest payment may be a requirement, it is still a nice gesture to send it at a time of year when people will be looking for a little more money.

♦ Try to memorize your tenants' names as well as a few personal things about them (such as their jobs, birthdays, or hobbies) for conversational purposes. By adding a more personal touch to a conversation, communication efforts will be better.

♦ Familiarize yourself with rental housing assistance programs available from public agencies and charitable organizations in the community. Make your tenants aware of these programs and be willing to assist your tenants who qualify for such programs to obtain them.

♦ Make arrangements with the tenant to repaint or improve the quality of the unit after the tenant has lived there for a year or two. Often, a tenant will want to move simply because the place begins to break down and doesn't look quite as good as it did when he or she moved in. Some new carpet and floor tiles, maybe a toilet seat, or a sink faucet could make all the difference in the decision to stay or leave.

♦ Take time to listen to your tenants' concerns about the property. Make arrangements to service your tenants' needs and make sure you do so.

Service Your Tenants

Servicing your tenant is very important if you want to maintain a good relationship. Even if the relationship is not so good, servicing the tenant will play an important role. Most tenants don't perceive their rental payment as payment for the use and occupancy of the unit; instead, they feel they are paying for a service available to them 24 hours a day. God forbid you have a life of your own. To make this easier, you need to set up some policies for handling repair and service requests.

Edwards' Advice

Make sure the contractors you use are licensed in the state in which they are performing the work and are insured to cover accidents and damages. Most states have specific regulations regarding requirements for independent contractors. Contact your state's agency of consumer protection for more information.

Pick some days in the week and set hours on those days during which you will provide tenant servicing. Create a to-do list labeled by apartment address to record repairs and be sure to date the repairs as they are called in and completed. Keep a record of the repairs you do in the appropriate tenant's file. Hey, it's a fact of life that things break, and there's no use getting upset about it. Repair is a part of the business, so you might as well get used to it.

Taking Care of Business

Remember that landlording is a business; your time is valuable, and all your landlording expenses are tax deductible. You can't do everything yourself, and there will be times when you will need the assistance of a professional because you lack the expertise, can't legally do the job, or don't have time to do the job. Don't be penny wise and pound foolish. Pay to have the job completed and write the expense off come tax time or add the cost to the base of your property, giving you more equity at time of sale.

Hiring Contractors

It would be nice if the cost of hiring out for repair work were never a concern. Truth is, repair and apartment preparation can be quite costly, especially if you hire contractors to do all the work.

Good help is hard to find and so are good, inexpensive contractors. Although contractors will try to charge prices that are competitive with other contractors in the same area, the cost can often still be very high and can seriously alter your rate of profit from the property. This is why it is a good idea to find out what you can and cannot legally work on in a rental property and then get to work on the repairs you can do yourself and try to save some money. The more you can do yourself, the more you will have earned by saving some of the cost of repair. Of course, how you want to approach certain issues such as repair is entirely up to you. If you own or plan to own just one or two small properties, it may be worth it for you to do as much of the repair as you can on your own. If you own several properties, small or large, it probably will be necessary for you to hire work out, spending some money but saving yourself time.

Preventive Maintenance

Preventive maintenance is an extremely important concept for you to grasp as a landlord. The idea here is to save you money in the long run by fixing something correctly before it either breaks or gets worse. Look at your property carefully and correct any problems you find. A leaky roof, faucet, or toilet, if it isn't fixed in a prompt manner, will soon affect the floors or ceilings below, possibly costing quite a bit more than it would have if you had fixed it upon first notice.

Preventive maintenance also means preparing the apartment in such a way as to preserve a long life for the apartment. Because a tenant will occupy and use the unit, wear and tear will eventually take a toll on it. For this reason, certain steps can help prevent future damage to the unit or at least can make it easier to prepare the apartment the next time. And believe me, there will be a next time.

An ounce of caution is worth a pound of cure. Preventive maintenance can protect you from all sorts of liability. Chipping paint should be removed and repainted; this will help protect you from possible lead paint claims that could cost thousands of dollars. Keep an eye on the mortar and cement around the bricks and stone in your chimneys and foundations and be sure to repoint areas if necessary; otherwise, it may break and crumble, causing danger and expensive repair. Look for that dripping oil line or shutoff valve near the boiler; by merely tightening a fitting, you may not only stop a potential hazard but also save yourself a lot of money and headaches.

Edwards' Advice

Here are some items that might help during your quest for preventive maintenance:

- Use commercial-grade carpet and floor tile.
- Use base cove around the perimeter of each room to help make the unit watertight.
- Install doorstops to prevent holes in walls from door handles.
- Self-closing entry doors and cabinet door hinges will ensure that the doors close properly.
- Hardwire battery backup smoke detectors can replace a light fixture on a ceiling.
- Caulking can be used in cracks on ceilings and walls to prevent moisture and bugs from entering a unit and can help the appearance of the unit.
- Insulation used in cubbyholes and around pipes will make the unit more energy efficient and protect the plumbing from freezing.

By using some of these products and techniques, you can save yourself money and help make your property easier to operate by preserving the life of your property's fixtures.

Day-to-Day Upkeep!

It's your responsibility to make sure the property is kept in good condition. If you're lucky, you will have responsible tenants who will keep their own areas clean and safe. We will discuss responsibilities that can be expected of tenants later in this book. The ultimate responsibility is yours, however, and you need to take this duty seriously. The simple fact is that people live in and visit your building on a daily basis, and therefore you need to make sure the premises are reasonably safe at all times.

Visit the property frequently and look your property over to make sure things appear to be in order. The physical appearance of the building is very important to the success you will have renting the property; look for loose garbage to pick up and broken windows to repair. Eyeball corners and crevices of the property for potential problems. Check such things as gutters to make sure they are working correctly and are not clogged, causing water to back up and run down over the facia and soffit boards of the building, which will cause rot at the edge of the roof. Look at the staircases and railings to be sure everything is secure. Check the heating apparatus to make sure it is working properly. Gas appliances should be checked for odors and gases, both of which can be dangerous.

Rental Red Light!

Carbon monoxide is a poisonous gas known as the silent killer. Carbon monoxide can be emitted from heat sources such as oil-, wood-, and gas-burning appliances. Most commonly, it is found emitted from gas appliances such as stoves, water heaters, and boilers. Natural gas is supposed to burn clean when used in these appliances, but occasionally, a burner tube inside the appliance will become corroded, and the result will be that it does not burn clean and creates carbon monoxide. One telltale sign of this is when the flame from the burner is yellow. A clean burner will emit a blue flame. Carbon monoxide testers are available for purchase at local hardware stores and can be strategically placed in the building to alert occupants of a problem. Periodic service by qualified technicians will also help to abate future problems.

Pressure-relief valves on boilers and water heaters should be checked to make sure the valves are not stuck. If the tenant doesn't mind, doing a periodic inspection of the rental units is a good idea. Look for broken outlets and coverplates, bare wires, missing or broken light fixtures, holes in the walls, and chipping paint.

You may not need to visit the property every day, but you certainly shouldn't neglect it. It's up to you how well you manage the property and how successful you will be. At the very least, you or your handyman should visit the property once a week. Pick up any loose garbage, inspect the property, and make sure the tenants see you or your helper.

Edwards' Advice

Check smoke detectors to make sure they work; look for missing batteries; listen for beeping smoke detectors, which usually indicate the need for new batteries, and replace them right away. You should always bring some batteries with you on a unit inspection for replacement purposes. If you have a tenant with a hearing disability, you should use a detector that has a light along with a sound.

Winterizing: Taking the Chill out of Empty Units

Winterizing units is a form of preventive maintenance. In areas where weather temperatures can drop below 32°F, certain cautions should be taken to protect your rental unit from water freeze-up. Here's a little science lesson: At 32°F, water will freeze, and vacant units that are not heated and protected from the cold temperatures can develop frozen and broken pipes. When water freezes, it expands and pushes on the inside of the pipe until the pipe breaks. Unfortunately, you won't notice the broken pipe during the cold temperatures due to the absence of dripping water. The water is frozen in the pipe and has created a dam that will not let water that isn't frozen (perhaps elsewhere in the pipe) flow. But you will notice the problem once the temperature climbs and the pipe thaws; it will probably sound and look a lot like Niagara Falls.

If you have an empty unit in a cold climate, take precautions—insulate your pipes, shut off the water valves, drain the water out of them, and pour a little antifreeze in the drain openings and the toilets. Be sure to drain the water heaters and boilers not in use and leave sink and tub faucets open. Many water valves have a little knob on the side of the valve, called a stop and waste valve, which can open and be used for draining a pipe up to that valve. In some instances, it may be necessary to blow water from the pipe using a compressor. Broken pipes, water heaters, and boilers can be very expensive to repair and hard to replace in cold weather.

Before turning the water to the unit back on, you will need to close the stop and waste valves you may have opened on water valves, and close the faucets and drains on the boilers and hot water heaters. Turn the water back on and see if there are leaks anywhere. After you fill the boiler, you will need to bleed the heating lines to remove any air pockets that can cause blockage of water and restrict heat. If you have questions about winterizing your building and getting that old heating system working again, call a qualified plumber or a seasoned landlord who might be able to guide you through the process.

Edwards' Advice

Be sure to hang a note on the boiler and water heater stating that they have been drained, that there isn't any water inside them, and that they should not be turned on until water is added. This is important because it will protect them from being lit and turned on by someone who doesn't know about adding water. Lack of water can crack and break a boiler or water heater when heat is added. Electric water heaters have elements inside that must be submerged in water when energized; if the elements are not, they will destruct when the power is turned on.

Edwards' Advice

Insulation is a double-edged sword. Although there is no question that a well-insulated building is a warm building, if the building is too well insulated, it can be dangerous. A building needs to be properly vented because oxygen is essential for safety reasons. A building needs to breathe. If a property is over-insulated, a vacuum can be created in the chimney where, instead of the fumes from the boiler or furnace escaping or drafting out, air will actually be sucked in through the chimney and will not allow potentially deadly fumes such as carbon monoxide to escape. So that annoying draft the tenant is complaining about might actually be a blessing.

Dealing with Environmental Hazards

Now for a little bit of fun called finding environmental hazards. It seems like new environmental hazards are popping up every day. Unfortunately, landlords carry the brunt of expense when these hazards are found on their properties. To better protect yourself and your investment, you should familiarize yourself with some of the more common ones such as asbestos, lead, and radon:

♦ **Asbestos** is a product used years ago as insulation on pipes, floor tile, roofing materials, and exterior siding. Two advantages of this substance are that it is fire retardant and a good insulator. Unfortunately, the product emits a dust that has been associated with a form of cancer from a condition known as asbestoses. Most regulations require removal of the substance when it is found to be in living quarters and if it is cracked or broken. In many states, removal can only be done by qualified environmental contractors.

 **Edwards' Advice**

If you are concerned about the possibility of environmental hazards at your property, contact your local or state health agencies for tips and information regarding these and other hazards.

♦ **Lead** is a substance formerly found in products commonly used in different aspects of construction. Lead was known to have special qualities that allowed it to be used in paint, piping, and solder. Until recently, lead also was an additive used in gasoline for automobiles. If lead particles are consumed, they enter the blood stream, and they have been detected as a possible cause of learning disabilities in children under the age of six years. Although lead additives for automobiles can still be purchased, lead paint no longer is available. In some states, lead solder is also still available but can only be used in special situations.

◆ **Mold** has been around since the beginning of time and it is everywhere. In recent years it has become one of the more popular types of hazards related to housing. Mold lawsuits have become quite frequent, and insurance coverage for these instances are either too expensive or impossible to achieve. Therefore, rental owners should acquaint themselves with the hazard and learn how to address it before it becomes problem. Mold is the result of a moisture problem in the building; careful moisture-prevention techniques and quick cleanup of water-damaged materials can help to eliminate potential mold problems from occurring. The existence of mold spores has been linked to ailments such as asthma, sinus congestion, skin rashes, and others. Allergic people can be quite sensitive to mold spores. There are many types of mold and not all of them are dangerous, however the mold *Stachybotrys chartarum* has been distinguished as a kind linked to the creation of *micro toxins* that can lead to serious illness.

Edwards' Advice

Although laws regarding lead paint are different from state to state, one of the best ways to handle this hazard is to abate or encapsulate the paint before receiving an order requiring abatement, preferably during the make-ready stage of the unit before it is rented. Encapsulation paints are now readily available for purchase specifically to be used for covering affected areas of lead paint. This type of preventive maintenance can save you thousands of dollars and can help protect future occupants.

◆ **Radon** is a radioactive, colorless, odorless, and tasteless gas that is emitted from the earth due to decay of uranium. It can penetrate the foundation or pipes of your building. Radon has been associated with illnesses such as lung cancer. Radon poses a serious risk for occupants of poorly ventilated buildings and can enter a building's water supply for consumption or be inhaled as dust particles. Radon detectors can be used to test a building; results must be sent to a laboratory for analysis.

The Least You Need to Know

◆ Try to find the lighter side of situations that occur in the business and enjoy them.

◆ Recognize the importance of tenants to your industry; learn to respect them and understand them.

◆ Initiate policies that enhance your relationship with your tenants and attempt to keep good tenants from moving.

◆ Understand that servicing your tenants creates a better landlord-tenant relationship and helps provide uninterrupted rent payments by eliminating lack-of-repair complaints.

◆ Familiarize yourself with the laws in your state regarding environmental hazards. Find out what you can do to protect your property and its occupants from the effects of hazards such as asbestos, lead, and radon.

Chapter 16

Handling Tenant Disputes

In This Chapter

◆ Avoiding disputes with tenants

◆ Preventing landlord retaliation claims

◆ What to do when tenants dispute each other

◆ When disputes go to court

The best way to handle disputes with your tenant is to avoid having them. However, this is often easier said than done. A tenant complains to you about a leaky sink. A tenant complains to you about another tenant in the building. A neighbor complains to you about your tenants. The authorities call you and complain about the complaints they have received. And you're complaining about all the complaints and problems you're having with all these disputes.

Complaints and disputes are part of the rental industry. Disputes can be quite stressful and create much unneeded anxiety for landlords. Smart landlords learn techniques to not only avoid potential disputes but also manage the stress and anxiety associated with disputes. This helps them make smart decisions and hopefully keep their sanity.

Avoid the Dispute

The best way to avoid having a dispute is to set the ground rules up front and to spell out each of your policies very carefully in your lease or rental agreement before the tenant even signs it. Let the new tenant take as much time as he or she needs to read and understand the lease or rental agreement. Give tenants the opportunity to ask questions, and make an effort to answer the questions asked with clear and honest responses. Most potential tenants never fully read the lease or rental agreement. Sometimes leases can be rather on the long side, complete with complicated languages and conditions.

A smart landlord will take the time to read over the lease or rental agreement line by line with the new tenant. This gives the tenant a chance to thoroughly understand the terms and conditions of the agreement, and it gives you the chance to stress the more important elements of the agreement with the new tenant. Let the new tenant have a copy of the lease or rental agreement, but be sure to keep the original for your own records.

Communication Breakdown

Poor communication is the usual cause of many disputes. When a tenant asks you a question regarding a policy or a repair, make sure to answer the question in a clear manner to avoid potential problems. Here are some examples of how conversations can be interpreted:

> **Rental Red Light!**
>
> If the new tenant does not speak English, you need to make an effort to interpret the lease or rental agreement to him of her. This may mean finding someone who speaks both English and the tenant's language to do the interpreting. Make sure to have the interpreter sign the end of the lease as proof that he or she was the interpreter.

Question: What will you do about the stains in the carpet?

Answer: You reply that you will have someone try to clean it, and if that doesn't work, you will consider replacing it.

Tenant Interpretation: You will replace the carpet if the stain doesn't completely disappear.

Question: Are you going to paint the outside of the house?

Answer: You reply that you're considering vinyl siding for the exterior.

Tenant Interpretation: You are siding the house.

Question: Is it okay if I pay the rent late?

Answer: Silence.

Tenant Interpretation: Yes.

As you can see, the answers you give to questions had better be clear; otherwise, they could lead to problems down the road. Disputes are coming. The world is not a perfect place, and disputes between landlords and tenants have been happening since the first caveman tenant withheld rent because his landlord didn't fix the cave door. The fact is that if you own rental property, you can count on at least one thing—disputes!

> **Edwards' Advice**
>
> Whatever the situation, try to keep the lease or rental agreement in simple language that is easy to read and understand. In other words, if you don't have a Philadelphia lawyer draw up the agreement, you might not need a Philadelphia lawyer to represent you in court.

When Bad Disputes Happen to Good People

Even if you do make an effort to completely review and clarify points in the lease or rental agreement with the new tenant, sometimes a dispute may still arise. Tenants very often misplace the copy of the written agreement you give them and do not have it available for consultation in the event that they question one of your policies. Sometimes the tenants simply do not remember the terms to which they agreed; sometimes they choose not to remember. Whatever the situation, listen to your tenants' concerns and try to address each problem in a prompt and friendly manner.

Maybe the tenant asked you to repair the drippy faucet, and you said you would but then forgot to take care of it or *jury rigged* it and it broke again. Maybe there is a crack in a window or a closet door that needs a handle, but you haven't had time to make the repairs, and the tenant has become annoyed by this. If repairs become outstanding and the tenant continues to complain about your apparent lack of interest, you might become agitated. Don't. Try to remember that the tenant is also your customer, and the customer is always right.

> **Landlord Lingo**
>
> **Jury rig** is a way of fixing something broken without fixing it entirely correctly. This can be a good way to fix something temporarily, but it usually requires you to fix it correctly at a later date. It's always better to fix something right the first time.

Do your best to prevent this type of unpleasantness by taking care of repairs in a timely fashion. Make sure the repairs are done correctly. Lend an ear to your tenants about problems they may have and be willing to work out solutions with them. Be

Facts for Rent _____

If you don't understand a problem as it is conveyed or if the problem seems confusing, you're probably not being told the truth.

careful in your communication not to make representations that might be misunderstood by the tenant. Remain friendly.

Whatever the dispute, it is extremely important for you as a landlord to keep a level head and not get emotional about the problem. Once again, we must remind you that you are running a business, and you must make decisions based on the success of your business.

Rental Red Light! _____

Some states have "presumed retaliation" laws that protect the tenant for a period of time, sometimes six months, after a complaint is made. Under this time limit, if a tenant makes a complaint in May and you start an eviction in July, the law presumes landlord retaliation, and you will face penalties. Retaliation is not presumed in every state—be sure to check your statutes before making any move.

When a dispute arises and the tenant's perceived point of view doesn't seem to make sense or the situation is becoming increasingly complicated, perhaps the problem is not what it appears to be. You need to take a step back from the situation and review it again. Try to see every angle of the problem. Often the problem, no matter what you're being told by the tenant, stems from some other reason. The reason is usually something rather simple, such as the tenant's inability to pay rent that month or the tenant's interest in breaking the agreement early.

Retaliation

Most states have laws that protect tenants from acts of landlord retaliation. The act of retaliation is considered to have been committed when a landlord has done something to a tenant, such as file for an eviction, after a tenant has done one of the following:

◆ Filed a complaint with you or a government agency

◆ Joined or formed a tenants' organization

◆ Exercised a legal right

Tenants can be viewed as retaliating against a landlord and often do, but there are far more laws protecting tenants than protecting landlords from the same kinds of acts.

If a tenant calls the housing code official and makes a complaint against a landlord, the landlord cannot then attempt to evict the tenant because the tenant made a complaint. If an eviction were to be started, the tenant could argue that the eviction was an act of retaliation. In many instances, the court would find in the tenant's favor and not allow the eviction to continue.

Protect yourself and get to know your state's landlord retaliation laws. The states listed in the following table recognize "presumed retaliation." This means that you could be accused of retaliation if you try to evict a tenant or act in some way against the tenant after a period of time during which the tenant has exercised a right, joined a tenants' group, or filed a complaint against you. Almost all states have laws against retaliation. Check with your state about what you can and can't do.

Presumed Retaliation			
Arizona	6 months	Minnesota	90 days
California	180 days	Montana	6 months
Connecticut	6 months	New Hampshire	6 months
Delaware	90 days	New Jersey	90 days
Iowa	1 year	New Mexico	3 months
Kentucky	1 year	New York	6 months
Maine	6 months	Rhode Island	6 months
Massachusetts	6 months	Washington	90 days
Michigan	90 days	Washington, D.C.	6 months

Let's Get Ready to Rumble!

Disputes between you and your tenants will happen from time to time. Ultimately, there isn't much you can do to keep a tenant from making complaints about you as a landlord. Most common are complaints to housing and building code officials regarding the condition of a landlord's property.

Many towns enact housing-code ordinances that dictate the condition in which housing must be maintained in the area. When violations are found to exist, there is normally a period of time extended to the property owner to remediate. Usually punishable by a fine and/or imprisonment if found to be in noncompliance, the housing-code ordinance also prescribes a procedure in which housing-code inspections and appeal processes are to be carried out by officials. Although the theory of such an ordinance may appear to be good, in reality it is often misused against good, responsible landlords. Housing-code ordinances usually dictate what certain

Facts for Rent _____

Many towns and states are looking into other ways to more fairly regulate housing conditions instead of using housing codes. Many areas are considering ways in which to hold residents accountable for housing damage.

Rental Red Light! _____

In some states, tenants can sue a landlord for double damages equal to the amount of their rent if a code violation is not corrected within the appropriate time given to do the repair.

conditions of housing will be. Commonly unacceptable conditions that violate housing codes are cracks in plaster, chipping paint, broken gutters, peeling wallpaper, a torn or missing screen, or anything else the authorities want to mention.

It is commonly agreed by seasoned landlords that a builder could build a new building, have a building inspector inspect it, issue a certificate of occupancy, and then 10 minutes later have the same property inspected by a housing-code inspector who will find housing-code violations. Even the most prestigious house in America, the White House, is believed to have housing-code violations, but the Feds shouldn't worry. The code is usually not enforced against single-family homes. Whew!

This type of ordinance usually does not safeguard against irresponsible tenants who haven't any intention of paying their rent. These tenants call a local official and report housing-code violations such as a hole in a wall, a broken window, or trash strewn about at the property. They know that they do not have the money for rent, and they need to buy time to raise money for another place to live before they are evicted. There is usually nothing the landlord can do to safeguard the rental unit from destructive tenants. Once a unit is rented, the tenant is the controlling factor in the unit and can often willfully do damage without the landlord even knowing about it.

Record Everything

Once again, you as the property owner should make an effort to keep records of any and all complaints and to be sure your lease or rental agreement requires that all complaints be in writing. If you have a complaint placed against you, you will have to find out what the substance of the complaint is and how much time you have to satisfy the complaint. Don't get angry and attempt to fight back. Take the necessary steps to promptly satisfy the problem and carefully document everything in the process. If the complaint is a housing-code violation, this means arrange to quickly make the necessary repairs and take some photos of the completed work. Above all else, always attempt to keep the relationship between you and the tenant civil.

Avoiding the Courtroom Battle

The best way to avoid a courtroom battle is to take special care when screening and selecting your tenants in an effort to weed out bad or *professional tenants* who might be inclined to cause you grief at the property. Follow the techniques mentioned in Chapter 7 for screening tenants.

If you can attend to repair concerns in a timely manner, you will reduce the likelihood of complaints to authorities. You must understand that the tenant is paying you a large amount of money, and he or she expects to have the product you rented serviced. If you fail to do so, poor relationships will result that eventually could lead to court.

Landlord Lingo

The term **professional tenants** refers to renters who move from one rental property to the next and specialize in causing trouble for landlords.

Welcome to Court!

If you do find yourself in court with your tenant, you will need to be prepared. This is where all those records you have been keeping will come in handy. The unfortunate truth is that many states have passed laws that are not in favor of the landlord. A tremendous amount of sympathy is generated for tenants, especially low-income tenants, and today's landlords have to be extra meticulous with the steps taken to defend themselves against complaints that wind up in court. It is advisable to be represented by an attorney who specializes in handling landlord-tenant disputes.

Landlord's Toolbox

A picture is worth a thousand words. The camera is steadily becoming an important tool of the trade for landlords. Landlords should always carry one in their automobiles, complete with film and a fresh battery. Photographing damage and repairs can help provide visual aids and proof in court that will assist you in explaining a situation clearly. A judge is not a plumber or a carpenter and will need to see the damage for him- or herself to make a fair determination regarding the situation. Photos will help. If you consider taking video footage, you might want to think twice. Photos are much easier to present in court, especially if a judge doesn't want to waste time with a VCR to view your directorial debut.

When you are in court, you must be courteous at all times and understand that you most likely will be required to appear during working hours. You must understand that the court personnel who handle your case also handle hundreds of cases like yours every year, and they will probably seem unsympathetic to you. When you're in court, you will be given a chance to explain your side of the story, but be careful not to let your emotions get out of control. Don't bother to labor on about how bad the tenant is; it's not in your best interest. You must act like the professional that you are. This is a game, and the best player will win. If you have carefully documented yourself and have done your homework, you'll stand a better chance of winning the case.

Tenant vs. Tenant

Tenants sometimes have disputes with other tenants in the building. Very often, the complaint will come to a landlord first, and if the landlord doesn't act, the scene can get rather ugly. For some reason, tenants (and the rest of society, for that matter) seem to think landlords should be able to do something about disputes between the people who occupy the building.

Facts for Rent

Some states have passed legislation that allows for the state authorities to confiscate properties that are deemed a nuisance in a neighborhood. Landlords are forced in these states to work with authorities to keep track of the daily activities at their properties to protect property from being confiscated.

The truth is that most state laws restrict the amount of control and power a landlord actually has at a property. Even if you wanted to do something about the source of the complaint, there wouldn't be much you could do. If a tenant in the building is annoying other tenants by playing the radio too loud every night, you could certainly speak with the tenant or perhaps send a letter regarding his or her behavior, but that's about the extent of what you can do. You certainly cannot walk into the unit and turn the volume down or take the radio, because you risk being arrested.

Eviction of the tenant is always a possibility, but if the tenant pays the rent on time, you would have to evict for reason of nuisance. (See Chapter 17 for more on evictions.) Although you may not want other tenants to be annoyed by the irresponsible behavior of one tenant, you also don't want to lose an otherwise good tenant or create a bad situation with an eviction. The best advice is to explain to the complaining tenant that you plan to contact the tenant in question, but if the matter does not clear up, the complaining tenant should contact the police and report the behavior of the problem tenant to authorities.

Working with Authorities

If you have a dispute with a tenant, you most likely will be dealing with local authorities charged with enforcing the housing code, building code, health code, and penal code. It's important not to get upset when you receive a call or letter regarding a dispute at a property. These authorities are just people who have jobs and, like you, they want to do their jobs as best they can. When these people receive a call from a tenant with a complaint, it is their job to inspect the unit and report their findings. The authorities usually do not want to get involved in an argument between you and your tenant. The landlord should be contacted either before or after an inspection regarding the complaint. After the inspection, the landlord should then be contacted regarding the proper procedures for resolving any listed concerns at the unit or for appealing any violations of which the owner is cited.

Rental Red Light!

Appealing the order from a housing official does not exempt a landlord from performing a repair. Regardless of an appeal, the landlord is still responsible for making the repair. A landlord may, however, be able to appeal an order with a "stay." If this is granted, it allows the landlord to not perform the repair until the appeal has been decided. Because a landlord will probably have to make the repair anyway, it is in the landlord's best interest to make the appropriate repair in a timely fashion.

In many instances, a problem arises because a tenant uses the authorities as a tool in his or her defense against a landlord. Many times, an irresponsible tenant will not report any problems to the landlord and instead will report problems directly to an inspector who can then be summoned to report his or her findings as testimony to be used against you in court.

The Game

Sometimes the dispute between a landlord and a tenant can resemble a game of chess. The move you make can win or lose the game. At times, you may have to ask yourself these questions: Do I want to win? Or do I want to lose?

Let's say the tenant is destroying the unit on purpose to create an ugly situation that will enable him or her to remain in your unit. Tenant advocates have educated the tenant to call on the local housing, building, health, and fire authorities to make complaints. All this puts the landlord in a bad spot, and the tenant knows it. If the landlord starts an eviction, it may be deemed an act of retaliation, and worse, there is nothing you can do to stop the tenant from destroying the unit and calling housing authorities. Although this may infuriate you, you must not take out your anger on the inspector who does the inspection, even though you may not appreciate the inspector's attitude regarding your property. It's true that the tenant has sucker-punched you by using the inspector. In some states, noncompliance with the inspector's findings may cost the landlord damages equal to double the amount of the rent owed. The inspector will request that the landlord be in compliance within a prescribed period of time.

Win the Game

If you are faced with this kind of dilemma, you must remain friendly with the inspector, come within compliance as quickly as possible, keep the inspector informed regarding the repairs, and keep excellent records of the entire affair. After the repairs are completed, get the inspector to reinspect the unit as quickly as possible. This at least allows the inspector to testify in court that you complied with the order in a timely fashion, and it proves to the court that you are a responsible landlord trying to work with the tenant. Throughout the entire dispute, it's important to remain cordial with the tenant and not attempt to upset the tenant, because it may only make matters worse for you.

Facts for Rent

Some localities require an occupancy permit, a certificate given to a rental owner from a housing official that allows a unit to be rented. Normally, the appropriate authorities first inspect the unit before the certificate of occupancy is awarded. In some areas, the occupancy permit must be renewed every time the unit is rerented; other areas require occupancy permits after certain prescribed periods of time such as every five years. Landlords who rent property in these areas must be sure to obtain the necessary permit; otherwise, they risk having the defense raised against them in an eviction case that the unit was rented illegally due to the lack of a permit.

If you want to win, you need to present yourself in a professional manner at all times and not let your emotions get the best of you. If you can stay calm and make well-calculated moves, you stand a better chance of winning. The landlord wins the game when the tenant either leaves or is successfully evicted from the unit with a minimal loss of revenue as a result.

The Least You Need to Know

- The best way to handle a dispute is to avoid the dispute.

- Good communication is an essential key to avoiding landlord-tenant disputes.

- Landlords must be careful not to react to a situation in a way that could be deemed an act of retaliation against a tenant.

- It's better to try to settle a dispute before the situation ends up in court.

- Always be willing to lend an ear to a tenant's concerns about the property.

- Remain calm and friendly during the dispute and keep careful records regarding the dispute.

Chapter 17

Dealing with Evictions

In This Chapter

- ◆ Knowing when to evict a tenant
- ◆ Understanding the eviction process before the court date and beyond
- ◆ Representing yourself in court
- ◆ The several types of evictions

In a perfect world, no one would ever have to experience the hardship of paying rent to secure a place to live nor would they have to comply with rules regarding how they should live in or care for another person's property.

In reality, however, when someone steps outside the parameters a landlord has set, a consequence occurs. The consequence that occurs in rental properties is called eviction.

The removal of a family or an individual from the place where he or she lives does not sit well with society. To protect a family's home, states have designed laws that protect the tenant and that set demands on the owner of the building.

Edwards' Advice

Before beginning an eviction, a smart landlord will weigh the odds of winning and will try to negotiate a meeting of the minds with the tenant. Sometimes this will result in a better outcome.

The laws, usually specified as residential or landlord-tenant, are different in every state, but they offer similar protections for the tenant and have similar rules that force the owner to prove any allegations made against the tenant in a court of law.

Understand that an action brought to court for eviction will give a tenant a chance to defend the complaint made against him or her, and the decision of the court might be in favor of the tenant.

An eviction case is like a game with many rules of play, and the player who knows the rules and can use them to win the case will have a better chance of winning the game. The player who fails to know the rules stands a greater chance of losing. Study the rules in the state where your property is located; don't make a mistake, or the price you pay will be costly. Mistakes may cause you to restart your case all over again.

You might find the courts very sympathetic to the tenant and very critical of your points for bringing the action for eviction. The action can reach beyond the issue being brought before the court and explore other areas such as a claim of retaliation against the tenant because he or she contacted the authorities and made a complaint against you as the owner. As in any game, there is a winner and a loser. The winner is not always the best player but sometimes the player with the most luck.

Time for Evictions

A tenant has not paid the rent this month. The rent was due on the first, and you sent a notice to the tenant on the third. Now it's the tenth of the month; according to your state statutes, you can file for an eviction. You haven't heard a word from the tenant, and realizing that it's time to make a decision regarding this individual's future at your property, you sadly begin to prepare the paperwork necessary for terminating tenancy.

This is just one situation that may result in an eviction procedure. But what if the tenant violates other terms of the agreement? Or what if you simply no longer want to rent to an individual because you might want to use the unit for personal reasons? There are other reasons for evicting tenants; therefore, there are different types of evictions of which smart landlords should be aware.

I Hate Evictions

The unfortunate occasion of having to evict a tenant sometimes occurs. Many people perceive the landlord as the bad guy based on the fact that landlords receive money for rent while maintaining the power to evict the very same people who pay the rent. The perception of power that some tenants perceive landlords to have might make those tenants uneasy. The landlord is perceived as the guy or gal who can throw the tenant out of his or her home. It's true that the landlord collects rent money and has the right to terminate the agreement with the tenant if certain conditions are not met, but many more laws have been developed to protect tenant rights in these types of instances than to protect the landlord's rights.

The landlord is by no means a bad guy; some people just don't comprehend the whole process of the rental business. Rightfully so—the rental business is a very complex one, filled with emotions and complicated concepts. The truth of the matter about evictions is that landlords don't want to evict people. Evictions cost rental owners valuable time and money. As landlords, we would much rather continue to rent to a tenant who pays the rent on time and is not a nuisance, even if we don't like the individual. Remember that landlords need tenants to survive in this business; without tenants, the investment property doesn't do quite so well.

> **Rental Red Light!**
>
> Some landlords prefer to avoid evictions and lawsuits by simply offering the problem tenant money to vacate the unit. If this can be done successfully without high cost, it may prove to be a good compromise to protect the landlord from the tenant winning an eviction case as well as possibly receiving a judgment for court and attorney fees. If you do this, be sure to carefully document the transaction and make the payment only when the tenant vacates the unit and hands you the keys.

Getting the Apartment Back

The sole purpose of the eviction process, from a smart landlord's point of view, is to get the rental unit back into his or her possession. You can't very well make any money with a rental unit if someone who refuses to pay rent is occupying it. A landlord might want to take back possession of the unit for different reasons. Perhaps there is a family member such as an in-law who needs a place to live. Maybe the landlord feels that the rent being charged is not sufficient and wants to raise the rate. Of course, as described in Chapter 8, a lease protects a tenant until the end of the leased term from rental increases unless the lease allows for such increases. Most of the time, the landlord will want to take the unit back because the occupant is doing something that violates the rental agreement. The landlord will, of course, hope to re-rent the unit to an individual who is more responsible. But in every case in which you are forced to evict a tenant for some reason, the bottom line is that you want to re-rent or use the unit as quickly as possible.

CAUTION

Rental Red Light!

Beware of charges of landlord retaliation. Only a dumb landlord will evict for the sake of vengeance because he or she is simply mad at a tenant for some reason. Sure, it can be argued that the landlord is mad about the rent not being paid or a lease violation, but the eviction action should be a business decision according to set policies and should be based on dollars and cents, not emotion. Some states even have "presumption" laws. This means that if, for instance, a tenant joins a tenant organization and you serve him or her with an eviction notice soon after, you can be charged with retaliation. See Chapter 16 for more on retaliation.

The Terminator

There are two parts to the eviction process: the termination and the eviction itself.

The termination is the first part of any eviction process. This is usually done in the form of a notice sent to the tenant or occupant in possession of the unit. The notice announces that the tenancy is terminated and instructs the tenant that if he or she does not either vacate the unit or remedy the situation that provoked the notice, the landlord will file an eviction lawsuit.

The eviction itself is the actual removal of the occupant from the rental unit. This is usually accomplished after successfully navigating through the eviction process, obtaining a judgment and execution, and repossessing the unit legally by the legal authority such as a court-recognized sheriff.

Types of Evictions

There are different reasons for starting eviction procedures. Most states have devised a few specific types of evictions that are recognized by the state laws. These types of evictions also have specific procedures and requirements that differ from one another.

Nonpayment of Rent

Nonpayment is one of the most common types of eviction procedure. In an eviction for nonpayment, a landlord attempts to evict a tenant for not paying the rent. A lease or rental agreement will state the due date for rent payment; some state laws extend the due date for a tenant to pay the rent by a certain amount of days. If the rent is paid in full within the legal grace period of these states, an eviction for nonpayment cannot be started. In other words, a landlord cannot start an eviction until the legal grace period has lapsed.

Rental Red Light!

Remember that, in states where there is a legally prescribed grace period for rent payment, the grace period will not begin until after the set due date. This means that if the tenant is paying you on the fifteenth day of the month and the legal grace period for the state where the property is located is 10 days, the rent will not be due until the twenty-fifth of that month. The eviction then could not begin until the twenty-sixth of that month.

Lapse-of-Time

Lapse-of-time evictions come in a close second as the most common type of eviction. In a lapse-of-time eviction, a landlord evicts the tenant on the basis that the lease or rental agreement has expired. Although a lapse-of-time eviction can be done when a lease is in its final month, landlords who give month-to-month tenancies most commonly use this type of eviction procedure.

A lapse-of-time eviction can be done without giving any other reason than the owner wants his or her unit back. Many landlords prefer to use this type of eviction and to have month-to-month or even week-to-week tenancies because no reason needs to be given for the eviction. (See Appendix B for state statutes regarding the amount of time needed to terminate or change a month-to-month or week-to-week tenancy.)

Nuisance

Causing a nuisance is another reason that landlords can evict tenants. A landlord might want to evict a tenant if the tenant has become a nuisance to the property. A nuisance can be defined as an individual who continuously violates terms of the lease or rental agreement (if the agreement includes a nuisance clause) and/or state and local laws.

CAUTION

Rental Red Light! _____

A lapse-of-time eviction procedure will limit any possible defense that a tenant may try to raise when attempting to dispute the eviction unless the landlord is also seeking rent arrears. In a nonpayment eviction, the tenant may try to show that the rental unit was sub par as a defense for not paying rent. But in a lapse-of-time eviction, the contract is terminated because of its expiration only. In this instance, it doesn't matter what condition the tenant claims the unit is in because the condition has no relevance to the expiration of the agreement. For this reason, many landlords who use month-to-month agreements prefer to evict for lapse of time even if the tenant has not paid the rent.

A nuisance could be someone who throws loud parties every night or who continuously disturbs the neighbors, resulting in police visits to the property. In fact, the police visit often is what will determine whether the tenant behavior is a nuisance. Tenants have a right to use and occupy a rental unit in any way they want as long as it does not infringe on the quiet enjoyment of other tenants in the building or violate federal, state, and local laws.

Facts for Rent _____

Many states have enacted laws that hold property owners responsible for continued and documented irresponsible behavior by tenants. The laws are normally called nuisance laws, sometimes referred to as the "three-strikes rule." The legislation was designed to crack down on illegal activity such as drug dealing at certain properties. It is important for landlords who own property in these areas to be aware of this legislation and to be willing to work with authorities to help stop illegal activity at their properties by taking the appropriate measures to evict these criminals.

Breach of Lease

A tenant causing a nuisance might be breaking your lease, but what about the other parts of your lease? Most states allow for landlords to evict due to "breach of lease," which means anything that you and the tenant have agreed on, such as a no-pet rule or moving people into a unit without your permission. If the tenant doesn't leave when you ask him or her to, you may have to evict according to some state laws. Make sure that you know the grace period that tenants have to fix the breach before filing an eviction notice (if there is a grace period and if the breach is fixable).

The "Other" Category

The building may become damaged by fire, and tenants will have to leave. If the building is damaged and the tenant does not want to leave, he or she may have to be evicted.

What if the roof blows off the building? What if a flood makes the building uninhabitable? What if the health department condemns the building? These are all possible situations that could occur, and they should be considered when you draw up your lease or rental agreement.

John and Jane Doe

You didn't rent to a John and Jane Doe? Maybe you did, but didn't know it! These are the names of people who occupy your building even though you didn't rent to them. Maybe the tenant you did rent to allowed them to move in, or maybe they moved in after the last tenant moved out. Regardless of how they obtained occupancy of the unit, if you didn't rent to them and don't know who they are, you don't want them living there unless the proper methods are used for renting to them.

Many times, these individuals know that there isn't any way they could possibly be approved for renting the unit, or could pay the rental amount being asked, and so they sneak in and set up residence. These individuals must be removed. In some states, however, laws require that the landlord evict the occupant regardless of whether he or she has a legal right to the unit guaranteed by a rental agreement.

Johns and Janes make themselves known only when you start seeing several strange cars at the property or many unfamiliar faces entering and leaving the building on a regular basis. To evict somebody from a rental unit, you will always need to know the individual's name. However, since you didn't rent to the individual and probably don't have any information about the person (including his or her name), the eviction glitches on a technicality.

If you can, you should try to obtain the names of the people who live in your building regardless of whether you rented to them or not. In the event that you cannot get their names, you

Edwards' Advice

Don't waste time dealing with individuals who move in and occupy your unit without your consent. Either get rid of them or put them through your screening process. The policies and procedures you have developed for renting units should always be adhered to. You're only asking for trouble if you start to get lax and allow tenants to violate policies, especially important ones.

can refer to these individuals as John and Jane Doe and evict them accordingly. The Doe family can be increased if more than two individuals are occupying the unit without your consent. There are some complications with the strategy of evicting John and Jane Does, and we will mention them in the next section.

Giving the Tenant Another Chance

Fool me once, shame on you; fool me twice, shame on me.

Giving a tenant a second chance not only is nice to do, it sometimes is mandatory by state statute. The statute will allow a tenant to remain in the unit if the rent is paid after an eviction proceeding has begun.

If a tenant is evicted for failure to pay the rent and you decide to re-rent to him or her in the future, remember that a person who gets fooled twice has no one but him- or herself to blame.

State Laws

Landlord-tenant laws differ in every state. Because of the complexity of the laws, it would require a book within this book to list all the laws and all the do's and don'ts associated with eviction. However, we have researched the main landlord-tenant statutes and have collected them in Appendix B. These statutes may not include every case law that can dictate certain revised provisions, so be sure to start with our research and take it further.

A smart landlord will get a copy of the landlord-tenant act governing the state in which he or she owns property and will read it thoroughly. If you are faced with the need to do an eviction, you should contact a competent attorney familiar with the laws governing eviction in your state and perhaps obtain his or her representation.

It only takes a few hours of work to interview and screen a prospective tenant, and the cost associated with it is minimal, but the time required to evict a tenant can drag on for months, and the cost can be in the thousands of dollars.

The Process in a Nutshell

The eviction process begins when the tenant breaks a provision of the lease or agreement between the owner and the tenant, the two parties aren't able to agree how to handle the dispute, and the tenant refuses to vacate the unit that he or she occupies. The eviction forms differ by state; copies of the appropriate forms you will need are available at your local court.

Notice to Quit

The owner will serve upon the tenant a notice to vacate the unit. This notice has different names, but we will use the most common term, "*notice to quit.*"

The notice to quit (again, depending on the state in which you own property) will have to be served on the tenant in a manner allowed by the state in which your property is located. The notice will have the name or names of the tenant, the address of the unit, and the reason the notice is being sent. You should also include the names of John and Jane Doe if you think other people might be occupying the unit along with your tenant.

Facts for Rent

Some states allow the **notice to quit** to be handed in person to a tenant in the household who is over a certain age, such as 12.

Some states allow the notice to be served by an impartial person, a law-enforcement official, or a sheriff. Some states allow the notice to be mailed by a specific method; again, this depends on the rules of your state.

The notice can give the tenant an amount of time in which to cure the problem (such as in a nonpayment of rent notice, by paying the rent), or it can tell the tenant that he or she must vacate the unit by a certain date as prescribed by law.

Rental Red Light!

Some states require that evicted tenants' belongings be stored in professional bonded and secured storage facilities where contents can be made available to the tenant. Typically the cost is the responsibility of the landlord. Typically when this law exists, fewer movers are available because fewer will be bonded or have the capacity to store items. Also, the cost of the movers may increase due to the demand for their services, frequently charging as much as six months' storage fees in advance.

Summons and Complaint

The next step begins after the date listed in the notice to quit. This step is referred to as the summons and complaint (however, in other states it can be called something else) of the suit being brought against the tenant in a court of law.

This summons will be served on the tenant, will give the tenant the name and address of the plaintiff (you), and will list him or her as the defendant. The summons and complaint will also explain the reason for the action and will allow a period of time, usually known as an "answer date," to respond to the complaint.

How the summons is delivered to the defendant will depend on the rules of the state in which you own property.

Rental Red Light!

Some states require you to prove to the court (by way of a military affidavit) that the tenant and/or the John and Jane Does are not serving military service for the United States. Check with the court, if this is requested, to determine how to substantiate a military affidavit to them.

Edwards' Advice

"Never let them see you sweat!" It's important to once again remain calm, cool, and collected regardless of any allegations made by a tenant or a tenant's witness. If you document yourself and present your case carefully, clearly, and concisely, you stand a good chance of winning.

The next step is to file the summons with court. This needs to be done before the answer date so that the court will be ready to proceed with the case when replies are made.

What happens next differs by state. In some states, a court date will be set. In others, the date is dictated by law. In still others, it is not dictated by law and will be set by a clerk of the court. Some courts hear housing matters on a certain day of the week or every other week, so you will need to know the workings of the court with which you are dealing. If you are dealing with an area of the country that is extremely rural, you might have a circuit judge who only holds court on certain days.

In some states, different papers need to be delivered to the court by both the defendant and the plaintiff. These might be called an answer to the complaint and a pleading to the case, but again, check with the state in which your property is located to be sure of the steps.

Whatever your state's procedures, the outcome is the same. A court date will be set, and both the plaintiff and the defendant need to be in court on that day at a time set by the court to hear the case.

Your Day in Court

The day you go to court, you should bring with you all the proof you need to prove your case to the court.

Bring the pictures you took of the damage or your original records of the payments made by the tenant as well as the lease and/or rental agreement that the tenant signed. You may also need a certified copy of your deed and a certified copy of your certificate of occupancy (if one exists).

If you have a witness, bring him or her with you. If the witness is employed and cannot attend the hearing, you need to subpoena the person to the court. The papers needed to subpoena a witness are available at the court.

Next, the case will be called by a court clerk to determine whether it is ready to go to trial. Upon hearing your name being called, you should answer that you are there and are ready to go ahead.

Depending on the state or the court you are using, what happens next could differ. In some courts, you will be assigned to a mediator or a housing specialist who will speak with you and the tenant to try to arrange a settlement to which both you and the tenant will agree. If an agreement is reached, it is called a stipulated judgment.

Stipulated Agreement

The stipulated agreement, or stip as it is called, will have the terms and conditions to which the tenant will conform as well as specified time periods for the terms and conditions. After the stip is agreed to, you and the tenant will reenter the court. A judge will ask you and the tenant whether you understand the conditions of the stip and whether the agreement is "your free act and deed," meaning that you are doing this of your own free will. If you both say yes, the judge will make the stipulations a court order in the case. (States may differ in what the judgment is called or whether it is a judgment at all.) If you cannot agree to a stip, your case will be assigned to a judge to hear and make a decision as to what will happen in your case.

In some courts, you will not see a housing specialist. Instead, you will appear in front of a judge who will listen to both sides of the argument and make a decision in your case. The judge might make a decision on the spot or might reserve the decision for a later date and mail you (plaintiff) and the tenant (defendant) the decision when it is made.

Failure to Appear

If the tenant fails to appear in court on the day of the hearing, you can request that the court grant you a default judgment for failure to appear. A tenant can request a continuance to another date if he or she can't make it to court that day.

Depending on the reason given and the attitude of the court, the court may assign a new court date, and you will have to come again. The same holds true for you, but don't try it. Your reason for not showing up might not be accepted by the court, and you will lose the case for failure to appear. If this happens, you will need to start all over with the eviction.

Failure to Comply

If the tenant fails to meet a provision of the stipulation agreement, you can file a judgment for failure to comply with the court. The court can sign the judgment or can assign a court date to hear the motion.

If you find yourself back in court, the process starts over with your sitting down with the housing specialist or a judge or a commissioner of the court, and a new agreement between you and the tenant could be made.

It is up to the court as to what it wants to do, and sometimes this can go on and on with the tenant failing to perform to the stip. And the court could continue to give the tenant another chance.

The Judgment and Execution

If the judgment is granted to the plaintiff (don't forget, that's you), this means you are getting near the end but are not there yet. You need an execution to remove the tenant from the dwelling, and some states have a waiting period between the date of judgment and the date you can apply for an execution. The waiting period is usually five days, but your state could be different.

Once you have the execution, you will give it to a law-enforcement official recognized by the court to carry out an eviction of the tenant from the property. This official will notify the tenant and the town that, on a certain date, the tenant will be removed from the premises along with his or her belongings. Some officials require a moving company to remove the belongings from the dwelling to the street; others don't.

 Rental Red Light! _____

Moving companies are often required to remove tenants' personal items from a unit to the street. Even though you may have won the eviction, it does not entitle you to the tenant's personal belongings. The movers are responsible for the actual removal, and you will be forced to pay for this service. This cost can then be calculated into the total damages you will seek when you sue the tenant in small claims court for the money owed.

On the day the official goes to the dwelling to remove the tenant, if he or she finds someone else occupying the unit other than the person you evicted, you might have a problem. This is why you need to evict John and Jane Doe along with your tenant.

The official should make an inventory of what is being removed. After everything is removed, the official will turn the dwelling over to you, and you will be able to change the locks and re-rent the unit.

The sheriff, marshal, or court official will make arrangements for the removal of your evicted tenant's belongings and store them for a period of time for the tenant, sometimes at a cost to the tenant and sometimes without a cost. In some states it is the landlord's responsibility to store the tenant's belongings for a "reasonable period of time."

Tenants can slow down the process by filing all sorts of motions, and a motion to reopen the case can be filed with the court after the judgment. Again, you need to know the laws of your state to determine what you and your tenant can do during the case.

As you can see, the process is complicated, costly, and nerve-racking and is not for the weak of heart.

The Do-It-Yourself Eviction

Going through the eviction process by representing yourself (in other words, without an attorney) is known as a "pro-se" action.

The state your property is located in might not allow you to do a pro-se action if your property is in the name of an LLC or a corporation. Many landlords elect to do evictions without the help of attorneys to save on the initial cost of the eviction. This works well for many who are familiar with the system and the courts in their respective areas and as long as the process moves along without any complications.

For those of you who are not familiar with the process, however, it may be wise to seek legal counsel to handle this type of court action. The explanation of the process in this book has been simplified for understanding, but by no means should the process be taken for granted as being that easy. Complications can easily arise if you're disputing with a professional tenant who is savvy about the system and eviction process in the area or if the tenant has obtained legal counsel to represent him or her. Even the most educated landlords will seek legal representation for evictions when the situation warrants it.

The trick, of course, is to recognize whether the situation does warrant it. You have to remember that eviction preparation costs both money and time, which translates again into money. The smart landlord will take whatever steps are necessary to eliminate this waste of money. For this reason, many landlords prefer to obtain the services of a competent attorney to handle the eviction so that they can dedicate themselves to more important business.

The Least You Need to Know

♦ The sole purpose of any eviction is to get the rental unit back into the possession of the landlord.

♦ An eviction is a two-part process: the termination of the tenancy and the removal of the tenant.

♦ There are different types of eviction processes for different types of leases and law violations.

♦ Some states require landlords to give a tenant a second chance to remedy a lease or rental-agreement violation before attempting to evict.

♦ State laws vary regarding the process to be followed during an eviction. For this reason, a smart landlord will familiarize him- or herself with the landlord-tenant laws governing the state in which he or she owns property.

Understanding Landlord-Tenant Rights and Responsibilities

In This Chapter

- ◆ Provisions of responsibilities for landlords and tenants required by most states
- ◆ Rights for landlords and tenants before, during, and after occupancy
- ◆ Do's and don'ts for landlords and tenants
- ◆ Privacy and avoiding the invasion of privacy

Having been involved in several landlord organizations over the years, we are continuously reminded how few rights seem to be available to landlords and how many responsibilities are required of landlords. Rental owners who belong to these types of groups always seem to ask the same questions when they first join: "What can I do about an unruly tenant?" "Where are my rights?" "What about the tenant's responsibilities?"

At this point in a discussion with seasoned landlords, the new landlord's frustration is evident and he or she needs answers. In this chapter, we attempt to answer some of these questions to alleviate some of these frustrations, although we can't guarantee to eliminate them all.

The Ultimate Responsibility Is Yours

When you purchase property, you also acquire the right to repair and maintain your property. The days of *caveat emptor* are gone. In just about every state, landlords are required by law to provide rental property that meets certain basic structural, safety, and health standards. Some state laws and requirements are stricter than others. It is important for a smart landlord to obtain specific information regarding these standards for the state in which he or she owns rental property. If the landlord does not fulfill the required duties, tenants may be able to legally respond in a number of ways, depending on the state. For instance, a tenant may be able to ...

♦ Withhold rent.

♦ Sue the landlord.

♦ Pay for repairs him- or herself and deduct the cost from the rent.

♦ Move out without giving proper notice.

Landlord Lingo

Caveat emptor refers back to common law and landlord-tenant relationships. The term is New Latin and means, "Let the buyer beware." When applied to landlord-tenant law, it means that, unless agreed upon explicitly, the tenant took the premises as is. Under this principal, the landlord implied nothing about the premises, nor did he or she have a duty to repair any defects to the property during the course of the lease unless such duties were provided for.

It is in the landlord's best interest to learn and understand what property standards are required in the state in which he or she does business and then attempt to surpass those requirements. Good repair and maintenance policies will result in more satisfied tenants and a healthier investment. This point of view will help protect the landlord from complaints from disgruntled tenants and from housing or health-code orders that could result in expensive legal troubles.

Implications of a Fit Habitat

The landlord has always warranted, by implication, that he or she has the legal right to give possession of the rented property to the tenant. This warranty would be violated if it was later determined either that he or she did not have the legal capacity to rent the premises or that the unit had been leased to someone else for the same period.

The "implied warranty of habitability" is a legal doctrine that makes it the responsibility of landlords to maintain and repair their rental premises. This concept has been adopted by nearly every state in the country in either a judicial decision or a statute. Basically, this doctrine states that the landlord implies a warranty to a tenant that the unit is livable and that it will be maintained to that original condition for the life of the tenancy. Prior to 1970, a tenant usually was expected to accept a property "as is," and U.S. courts seldom held that a warranty of habitability could exist where none had been granted contractually.

Facts for Rent _____

> The implied warranty of habitability originated in a court case decided in 1970 in Washington, D.C. (*Jarvins v. First National Realty Corp.*, 428 F.2d 1071 [DC Cir. 1970]). In this case, a landlord sued to evict tenants for nonpayment, but the tenants countered by exposing about 1,500 housing-code violations that the landlord refused to fix. The court ruled in favor of the tenants by allowing the amount of their unpaid rent to be applied to the repairs and by not allowing the landlord to evict the tenants. In this case, the judge ruled on the basis of two sources that made the landlord responsible for the repairs and for maintaining the property to conditions that were habitable. The sources were local building codes and common law.

The implied warranty of habitability refers to …

- ◆ Local building codes that specify the minimum requirements for heat, water, plumbing, and other essential services.
- ◆ Widely held common-law notions of what constitutes decent housing.

It is important to note that many of the states that have adopted the implied warranty of habitability have done so by using one or the other of these approaches.

Housing Laws or Court Decisions

The source of law used in determining whether a landlord has violated the implied warranty of habitability can affect what the landlord's responsibilities are and what remedies are available to tenants. States will differ on the sources they decide to use with regard to the implied warranty of habitability.

Housing laws such as state or local building codes and housing and health codes normally list specific standards by which property should be constructed and maintained by rental property owners. These conditions and requirements vary by state and municipality, but usually they apply to the rental units and common areas of the property.

Some states have ruled that the implied warranty of habitability requires the property owner to maintain the property only according to what is required in the state and local housing codes. In these states, landlords have the benefit of knowing exactly what is required of them. Normally, substantial compliance with the code requirements is viewed as sufficient. Tenants may be able to still withhold rent or seek other remedies if violations affect their health and welfare.

Courts in some states sometimes view the implied warranty of habitability as not being affected by housing codes. The question of the court in these instances isn't whether the property meets specific criteria required by state or local codes, but whether the unit is fit for human occupancy. A housing-code violation doesn't necessarily mean that a unit is unfit for human habitation, but 100 percent compliance doesn't mean it is fit for habitation either. In situations in which the court is allowed to make the determination, requirements may be imposed on a property owner that are more substantial than the local or state codes.

The Covenant of Quiet Enjoyment

In states that have not adopted the implied warranty of habitability by either judicial decision or statute, landlords may not be responsible for offering housing that is *fit* and *habitable* at the time it is rented. Housing codes, however, still make the rental owners responsible for the maintenance of the building and rental unit after it is rented. In areas where there is a lack of housing code, the "covenant of quiet enjoyment" may prevail.

All 50 states have accepted the common-law concept of the "covenant of quiet enjoyment." Courts normally define this concept as an implied promise that a landlord will not act, or fail to act, in a way that interferes with or destroys the capability of the tenant to use and enjoy the rented premises. In other words, if the landlord allows for the following conditions to exist at the property, he or she may be subject to a lawsuit in court under this covenant:

♦ Failing to supply working electrical receptacles so that tenants can use appliances

♦ Allowing for infestations of bugs and rodents in the building or unit

♦ Not providing properly working plumbing and heating fixtures

♦ Not repairing broken or rotted staircases, floors, walls, ceilings, or roofs

Local and State Codes

As previously mentioned, it is extremely important for landlords to stay informed. A smart landlord will contact the state and local housing authorities for complete copies of housing and building-code requirements for the respective areas. Keep in mind that state and local housing codes sometimes differ. In these instances, it is up to the state to decide which code will prevail. In some states, the state code overrides local code requirements; in others, localities are given the freedom to surpass state requirements in imposing the code. Typically, unless specified by state law, the stricter code will prevail.

Rental Red Light!

"Nuisances" and "attractive nuisances" are defined by statutes as whatever can be construed as dangerous to the health and safety of the public. For example, a nuisance could be the existence of poorly ventilated or illuminated areas or drug dealing in the building. Abandoned cars and appliances or unsafe structures on the property that inquisitive children would be drawn to could be considered attractive nuisances. If landlords are found to have tolerated the existence of such nuisances and someone is injured, the property owner could be held liable.

Property Exemptions from Codes

Some state and local codes provide for certain exemptions to code requirements for specific property types. Normally, single-family, owner-occupied properties are exempt from local and state housing codes.

Other exemptions may be applied to older buildings built before a certain date. Because some code requirements may require major structural changes, lawmakers have provided "grandfather clauses" in the codes for all buildings built before a certain date. Sometimes the date of the building is the same as the date of the change in the code, but not always. If the building is undergoing remodeling, it may have to be brought within specific codes. Other code requirements such as door locks and smoke detectors must be adhered to regardless of the age of the building.

The Tenant's Responsibilities

If you have owned rental property for a while, you're probably wondering, "What are the tenant responsibilities?" The truth is that most legislation holds the property owner responsible, not the tenant. As previously mentioned, the property owner is always the bottom line regarding problems that arise at the property.

However, some cities and states do attempt to hold tenants responsible for maintenance to the units they occupy. In these areas, it is the tenant's responsibility to keep the unit in a habitable condition. After all, the tenant is the controlling factor living in the unit. The following unit conditions may be considered the tenant's responsibility in your state:

♦ **The unit should be kept clean and safe.** A tenant should be expected to have at least some cleaning capabilities. Tenants should keep kitchens and bathrooms cleaned and should remove all the garbage they generate to the appropriate receptacles or to the curb for city pickup. It is a tenant's responsibility to maintain living conditions in and around his or her unit that will help promote cleanliness and will prevent infestations and filth.

♦ **Use fixtures and appliances properly in the unit.** Tenants must not abuse the fixtures and appliances supplied to the unit. Tenants must exercise reasonable care by not overloading electrical outlets or flushing large objects down a toilet.

♦ **Tenants must fix or pay for damage for which they are responsible.** If the tenant creates a situation that affects the habitability of the rental unit, he or she can be held responsible. If a tenant puts a hole in a wall, severely stains the carpets, or breaks fixtures and appliances, he or she must make arrangements to either fix or pay to repair the damages.

That's about the extent of the tenant's legal responsibilities. Of course, more detailed tenant responsibilities can and should be listed in your lease or rental agreement (see Appendix A for examples).

It is important to understand that, just because you make an effort to hold a tenant responsible for certain things, it doesn't mean that this shift in responsibility will hold up in court. For instance, in our sample lease, we list the responsibility for snow removal around the tenant's unit as being the tenant's responsibility. If you were to be sued on the basis of someone slipping and falling, the decision could go either way, but don't count on it.

My Rights? What Rights?

Although it may seem like the scales have been tipped in favor of the tenant when it comes to rights at the property, the truth is that landlords do have some. First of all, you have the right to rent the property. Here are some other rights that landlords may exercise if need be:

◆ You have the right to maintain the property. This means that you have the right to make most types of repairs yourself. This right, however, may be restricted to only the owner and not repair personnel. For example, lead legislation in many states allows property owners to actually remove lead paint themselves; however, hired personnel must be licensed.

◆ You have the right to a hearing in a court of law to dispute claims made against you. If a claim of housing-code violations is brought against you, you have the right to defend yourself in a hearing regarding such claims.

◆ You have the right to properly screen for good tenants. This includes requiring permission for the release of credit, criminal, and eviction history from potential tenants as a policy for screening. But landlords must be careful not to discriminate with screening policies.

◆ You have the right to verify a rental application and to refuse to rent to anyone whom you discover has lied on the application.

◆ You have the right to charge a tenant a security deposit and to use this deposit if the tenant does damage to the rental unit.

◆ You have the right to not permit animals or pets in your rental unit unless the animal serves a purpose for handicapped or disabled tenants, such as a seeing-eye dog used by the vision-impaired.

◆ You have the right to have tenants pay for their own utilities as long as the utilities are separately metered and this is properly agreed upon in the lease or rental agreement.

♦ You have the right to sell your rental property.

♦ You have the right to make a profit from your property as well as to not make a profit from your property.

There may be other rights available to rental owners, but we feel that these are the important ones. Once again, the rental business is a complex one with many different possible situations that could arise. It is beyond the scope of this book to explore every possibility that could arise. Common sense should be used in exercising certain rights, and if there is a question, you should consult an attorney. Keep in mind that your rights can be modified by a court decision—you could be prevented from exercising certain rights.

Rental Red Light!

Some localities have created legislation that requires a property owner to use his or her properties or suffer fines and criminal prosecution. This type of legislation is often masked as a "blight ordinance" or a "property maintenance code" designed to keep properties looking nice. However, there are usually clauses within such legislation that limit the amount of time a property can sit vacant and boarded. The principal here is to "use it or lose it," and it has come under much scrutiny in areas where it exists.

What You Don't Have the Right to Do!

Now for the "cannots" of the landlord business. There are several things landlords must not do; otherwise, they risk getting into trouble. Many of the following rules already have been mentioned in this book, but they certainly bear repeating. The penalties for violation of these rules differ by state and municipality, but all are certainly punishable by fine or imprisonment:

♦ You do not have the right to discriminate against people while renting your property. As discussed in Chapter 8, there are specific federal and state guidelines that landlords must be careful to follow or risk serious penalties.

♦ You do not have the right to remove tenants or their belongings physically from a unit without following the specific court procedures and obtaining the appropriate court approvals. State legislation regarding eviction will differ, and some are more lenient than others.

♦ You do not have the right to change the locks on a unit, often called "lockout" in many states, to force a tenant out.

♦ You do not have the right to enter a unit that is occupied without the tenant's approval unless a dangerous emergency exists. For example, if a gas leak is noticed and the source appears to be inside a tenant's unit, you are allowed to enter or permit emergency services to enter to investigate the problem. Otherwise, typically 24- or 48-hours' notice is required before entering a unit. For required notice and landlord access statutes, see Appendix B.

♦ You do not have the right to shut off utilities that either you or the tenant is supplying as a way to force the tenant out of a unit.

♦ You do not have the right to remove personal property, such as furniture, automobiles, or pets, without first obtaining the tenant's permission. Charges of theft could be brought against you in these instances.

♦ You do not have the right, in many areas, to make improvements to a property that would otherwise require someone to have a license, such as an electrician.

♦ You do not have the right to willfully destroy your property without the proper permissions from local authorities.

♦ You do not have the right to make changes to your property if it is protected by local or state historical societies unless proper permission is obtained.

♦ You do not have the right, in some areas, to use your property any way you see fit without proper approvals from zoning boards and other local authorities.

♦ You do not have the right to force a tenant to obey the law or clean the unit.

♦ You do not have the right to shift the responsibility to the tenant for making important repairs to the unit or building unless both parties specifically agree to those terms.

♦ You do not have the right to quit! Many areas have created legislation such as "blight ordinances" and "property maintenance codes" that force you to sell your property if you decide to no longer rent the units. This, in effect, does not allow you to quit, especially if the housing market does not ensure a speedy sale. The only other option may be to give the property away or go bankrupt. Leaving a property empty, however, is not an option in these areas.

As you can see, the "cannots" outnumber the "cans." Once again, we must remind you that it is beyond the scope of this book to mention every right you may or may not have. Every state differs regarding landlord-tenant legislation and the rights that are guaranteed to each. Unfortunately, one thing remains true: Landlords really don't have many rights other than to pay their property taxes and maintain their property or suffer the consequences.

The Tenant's Rights

Volumes of books have been written regarding tenant rights. This is because in the last 30 years sympathetic courts, legislators, and tenant-advocacy groups have catered to tenants. We hope that our method of listing tenant rights can be translated in such a way that you can easily understand how to handle certain situations. The tenant has the right to the following:

♦ To see any rental unit you have advertised for rent. This includes any unit you advertise anywhere in the community.

♦ To apply for any rental unit he or she wants.

♦ To retain privacy and confidentiality regarding any personal information released to the property owner.

♦ To the use and quiet enjoyment of the property rented. This includes being able to make reasonable modifications to the unit to help provide enjoyment to occupants (such as handicapped-accessible bathrooms).

♦ To a property that is safe and sanitary. This includes having the property meet and satisfy all state and local building, housing, and fire codes.

♦ To a hearing when a dispute arises from landlord complaints. This includes the right to hire a defense attorney to represent him or her in such a dispute.

♦ To the interest accruing on security deposits held by the landlord in escrow. Some states do not require that interest be paid to the tenant; others require that security deposits be kept in a bank account. (For your state statutes on security deposits, see Chapter 10.)

♦ To be protected from environmental conditions arising at the property such as radon and lead hazards.

♦ To withhold rent when an owner does not make repairs or to make the repairs and deduct the cost from the rent owed. (For more details, see Appendix B.)

♦ To receive proper notice regarding late rent, eviction, entry, and inspections.

♦ To participate in rental assistance programs without the owner's permission.

♦ To receive security deposit money paid back in full if the unit is left in good condition. If the landlord deducts unpaid rent or damages from a security deposit, he or she is required (in most states) to provide tenants with an itemized list of the damages and the amount he or she will or won't receive. (For more details on your state laws, see Chapter 10.)

The tenant does *not* have the right to the following:

♦ To damage the unit or to receive security deposit money back if he or she does damage the unit.

♦ To breach the lease or rental agreement.

♦ To not pay rent while using the unit (unless allowed by city or state laws and properly justified).

♦ To not comply with all state and local laws, codes, and regulations.

♦ To use the rented unit for any purpose other than what it was rented for.

♦ To allow persons not on the lease or agreement to live in the unit unless granted permission by the landlord.

♦ To abandon the unit. If tenants take an extended absence, they are required to notify the landlord.

The Right of Entry vs. the Right to Privacy

The right of entry versus the tenant's right to privacy is a very popular topic of discussion among landlords. Both have specific rules and regulations that should be followed to preserve and protect the rights of both the tenant and the landlord.

> ### Rental Red Light!
>
> Many states allow a landlord to legally enter an occupied rental unit if a tenant is absent for an extended period of time. The typical time period is seven days or more. In cold weather climates, pipes may need to be checked for breaks while the tenant is away on vacation. Some states with harsh winters even require that tenants notify landlords of any extended absence during certain months of the year. To even better protect yourself, require tenants to notify you if they expect to be away for extended periods.

Let Me In!

Most states have laws regarding the landlord's right of entry to an occupied rental unit. Most states also recognize the importance of allowing landlords the right of entry to maintain the condition of the rental units and to make repairs.

Rental Red Light!

Most states allow landlords to enter a unit to show it to prospective tenants or buyers, but some do not. Of course, you should follow the proper notice requirements and be sure to authorize this right of entry in your lease or rental agreement.

Most states, however, call for certain requirements to be adhered to before entry can be permitted. Although requirements differ by state, typically a written notice is required 24 or 48 hours before a landlord or designated representative can enter unless there is an immediate emergency that threatens other occupants and/or the property. Notice should be mailed, handed to the tenant, placed in his or her mailbox, or posted on the front door of the tenant's unit. Some states specify what hours are permitted for entry, but they usually allow for entry at times considered "reasonable." (See Appendix B for specifics in your state.)

If your state does not specify how access to the tenant's unit should be gained, then we recommend that you do not simply enter. Instead, try to give the tenant as much notice, in writing, as possible and set up a time that is mutually convenient for both you and your tenant. You must try to give the tenant a reasonable amount of time before entering. If, however, a service person is only available to make repairs to a unit during the next morning, certain exceptions may be made. Only a few hours' notice is not considered reasonable, however, unless there is an emergency. It is in your best interest to be considerate of your tenants' privacy and to do your best to accommodate their schedules. It will make for better relationships between you and your tenants.

If you can, get the tenant to agree to give you access to the rental unit whenever you need it. This will help save you time by not having to contact the tenant and set up appointments every time there is a repair to be done. This may be especially handy if, for instance, there is a mechanical room in a building that can only be accessed through the tenant's unit.

Every state allows landlords to gain immediate access in the event of an emergency. Some emergency situations that would warrant immediate access to a tenant's unit are …

- Smoke pouring from or smoke alarms sounding from a tenant's unit. If no one answers the door, call the fire department and use a key or even break in to try to deal with the fire.

- The smell of gas from a tenant's unit.

- Water pouring from a tenant's unit. It's perfectly all right to investigate a water leak.

◆ The sound of screams from a tenant's unit if no one answers the door upon investigation. In this situation, you or your superintendent should summon and wait for the police before entering the unit.

You can enter a tenant's unit as long as proper notice is given *and* you have a reason. Not all reasons are allowed in every state. And, of course, not every state has a provision for landlord access. We've only listed the states with laws regarding unit access. This means that you should set up your own rules with your tenants, preferably in your lease or agreement, but make sure to have it in writing. Unless noted, a landlord can enter only in an emergency, to inspect the property/unit, for repairs and improvements, to show the unit to prospective tenants or buyers, and during a tenant's extended absence. (See Appendix A for an example of a form requesting entry into a unit.)

Notice Required To Enter a Unit

States	Notice Required to Enter	Any Reason Landlord Cannot Enter
Alaska	24 hours	---
Arizona	2 days	During tenant's extended absence
California	24 hours	To inspect property or during tenant's extended absence
Connecticut	Reasonable notice	---
Delaware	48 hours	During tenant's extended absence
Florida	12 hours	---
Hawaii	48 hours	---
Iowa	24 hours	---
Kansas	Reasonable notice	---
Kentucky	2 days	---
Maine	24 hours	During tenant's extended absence
Massachusetts	Determined by LL-T agreement	During tenant's extended absence
Minnesota	Reasonable notice	During tenant's extended absence
Montana	24 hours	---
Nebraska	1 day	---
Nevada	24 hours	During tenant's extended absence

continues

Notice Required To Enter a Unit (continued)

States	Notice Required to Enter	Any Reason Landlord Cannot Enter
New Hampshire	Adequate notice	Need tenant's prior consent except in an emergency
New Mexico	24 hours	During tenant's extended absence
North Dakota	Reasonable notice	During tenant's extended absence
Ohio	24 hours	During tenant's extended absence
Oklahoma	1 day	During tenant's extended absence
Oregon	24 hours	During tenant's extended absence
Rhode Island	2 days	---
South Carolina	24 hours	---
Tennessee	Time of notice not specified	---
Utah	Not specified	To inspect premises, to show property to prospective tenants or buyers, or during tenant's extended absence
Vermont	48 hours between 9 A.M. and 9 P.M.	During tenant's extended absence
Virginia	Reasonable notice; if entering for pesticide reasons, must give 48 hours' written notice	---
Washington	2 days; 1 day to show unit to prospective tenant or buyer	During tenant's extended absence
Wisconsin	Reasonable notice	During tenant's extended absence

What if the Tenant Denies Entry?

Of course, some tenants cannot be made happy no matter how accommodating you try to be. Even though the tenant may want the repair done, he or she also remains uncooperative regarding your gaining access. If you are confronted with this type of situation, it becomes very important to carefully document and record your conversation regarding the repair and to meet any and all state and local requirements regarding notices to better cover yourself from later being sued for the invasion of the tenant's privacy. Many states will allow you to enter an occupied rental unit even if the tenant is uncooperative as long as you have a justifiable reason for entering. However, never push or force your way into a tenant's unit, or you will risk being held liable. It is also never a good idea to enter alone. Bring someone with you as a witness in case the tenant claims that personal property is missing.

> **Rental Red Light!**
>
> Sometimes a tenant will change the locks on the rental unit. This is illegal in many states because it bars entry to you in the case of an emergency. Tenants are required to give a copy of any keys needed to enter the unit to the landlord or management company. Otherwise, the tenant can be held liable.

Who Else Can Enter?

One common question among landlords is, "Can I allow anyone else to enter a tenant's unit?" The answer is "No!" unless the tenant has been properly notified or there is an emergency.

Local and state inspectors will sometimes want to inspect rental units that they suspect are not in compliance with certain housing codes. Unless the tenant agrees to allow them entry, they don't have the right to enter. If neither the tenant nor you want to allow the inspectors entry, they will have to obtain a search warrant from a judge to allow them to inspect the premises. The same holds true for police officers who seek entry to rental units. However, police officers do not need a search warrant if there is an emergency or they are in pursuit of a criminal.

Other people, regardless of their relationship to your tenant, should never be allowed to gain access to the tenant's unit in the absence of the tenant. If the tenant can be contacted and asked whether it is okay to allow this individual to enter, then you should make an effort to do so, but do not allow someone to enter the tenant's unit without first getting the tenant's approval. And if you do receive the tenant's approval, be sure to verify the identity of the stranger before allowing entry.

Don't risk being held liable for unauthorized entry to the tenant's rental unit. Even if a person's story as to why he or she should be allowed to enter sounds reasonable, do not permit it without the proper approval from your tenant.

Invasion of Privacy

When renting or selling a property to prospective tenants or buyers, certain details regarding the right of entry for the purposes of showing the property must be obeyed. Even though most states may give you the right to show the property, they also protect the tenant's right to privacy. Once again, common sense should be your guide in these kinds of matters.

> **CAUTION**
>
> **Rental Red Light!**
>
> For-sale signs and for-rent signs can be construed as an invasion of privacy if they result in unwelcome inquiries about the property that aggravate the tenant.

If you do not intend to renew an existing tenant's lease or rental agreement, try to work out the particulars before showing the rented premises to a new tenant. If the existing tenant does not leave or a dispute arises, it could alter the new tenant's plan for moving in and could cause all kinds of trouble. Special care should be placed in the lease or rental agreement to help limit your liability in the event that the new tenant's move-in date is delayed.

When attempting to sell your rental property, the same kind of care should be considered. Give your tenants as much notice regarding showings as possible. Problems may occur when a tenant is being bothered by an agent's constant presence and eagerness to make a sale. Tenants usually become uncomfortable about the possibility of having a new landlord for fear that it may lead to a higher rental rate down the road. By trying to accommodate the tenant as much as possible, you may actually help eventuate the sale of your building and reduce the chance of being sued for an invasion of privacy.

Landlords must remain sensible regarding how they treat their tenants. You may own the property, maintain the property, and pay the taxes on the property, but this does not give you the right to be a pain in the neck to your tenants. Smart landlords will not become involved in the day-to-day activities of their tenants. Certain practices could be perceived as an invasion of the tenant's right to privacy, and landlords could wind up in court defending against a lawsuit.

Contacting the Tenant at Work

There are certain situations that may warrant contacting the tenant at work. However, this privilege should be used wisely. Remember that the tenant's place of employment is also a business, and you need to respect that. No matter how you feel about a tenant, never call the tenant's place of employment to criticize the tenant to his or her employer. And if the tenant asks you to please stop calling him or her at work, you should respect those wishes. It is also in poor taste to haunt the tenant at his or her job while chasing after rent that might be owed unless the tenant agrees to meet you at his or her place of work. On the other hand, you may need to visit the tenant at work if he or she has disappeared from the unit, and you need to serve a notice such as an eviction notice.

I Spy a Tenant

Even though you may feel like it sometimes, you're not James Bond (unless that really is your name). Spying on your tenant is an invasion of his or her privacy, and a landlord should be careful not to do so. This situation usually happens when a landlord notices that a tenant seems to have several visitors who stay for extended periods of time. Some landlords then feel obligated to interrogate the tenant's visitors, peek through windows, or knock on the tenant's doors at odd hours of the evening to try to find out who is staying in the unit.

Landlords are not allowed to control the social life of their tenants and should be careful not to harass either the tenant or the visitors. Keep your conversation with visitors to casual hellos and other small talk. Visitors who stay for only a day or two should be of no real concern to you. Visitors who stay for extended periods of 10 days or more, on the other hand, will have to be dealt with. Your lease or rental agreement should specifically address this situation, and upon noticing new occupants, the tenant should be contacted in a nonthreatening manner.

The Least You Need to Know

- ◆ The ultimate responsibility for every property lies in the hands of the owner.

- ◆ The implied warranty of habitability is a legal doctrine recognized by most states that requires the rental owner to take appropriate measures for carrying out repair and maintenance of a building.

- ◆ Some properties are considered exempt from certain types of housing-code regulations due to the age of the building and the scope of renovation required to meet codes.

- ◆ Tenants do have certain basic responsibilities regarding the maintenance of their rental unit.

- ◆ Landlords must be careful to respect the tenant's right to privacy at a property, especially with regard to gaining access to the rental unit.

Part 5

Protecting Your Investment

Throughout the life of your investment, you need to protect the investment. This doesn't necessarily mean that you need to install security alarms. Initiating certain policies, such as one for screening tenants and one for promptly servicing tenant complaints, will help preserve the condition of your investment. It is important for a smart landlord to understand and protect landlord and tenant rights and to carefully insure and improve the property.

This all helps to protect the investment, keep the property nice, and maximize its return either from rent or sale.

Chapter 19

The Manager, the Super, and the Landlord

In This Chapter

- ◆ Getting what you pay for in a management company
- ◆ Hiring a property manager, on and off site
- ◆ What you're liable for as an employer
- ◆ Firing employees

Who is going to handle the day-to-day activities at the property if you decide not to? Who is going to show the apartments for rent, screen the new tenants, handle the leases, make the repairs, collect the rent, and protect your investment if you can't?

Some state laws actually require property owners to hire a manager if they own several units. Fortunately, there are some options available to you. In Chapter 1, we discussed some of the primary characteristics of hiring a management company to handle rental property affairs, but that was not the only option. There are other types of employees who can be hired to help run your rental property. Hiring a property manager or a maintenance man may free up time for the residential landlord who does not want to be bothered with the sometimes tiresome details associated with rental-property management. Of course the smart investor will have factored in the cost of such types of services, so that hopefully there is enough money in the property to cover this kind of expense.

The Management Company

If you plan to own property out of state or a great distance away from where you live, hiring a management company may be a good idea. A property manager is a real-estate professional who can be hired to ensure the profitability of an owner's investment. In other words, it is the function of a property manager to act for the owners regarding the daily activities at the property. A management company should have a broad understanding of certain real-estate aspects as well as some important qualifications. Property managers should have knowledge of business and business administration, including a general understanding of urban and economic forces and how they affect rental property.

Facts for Rent _____

The Certified Property Manager (CPM) is a designation available to members of the National Association of Realtors who specialize in property management and who want to further their professional qualifications. Available from the Institute of Real Estate Management (IREM) are designations for onsite managers called Accredited Resident Managers (ARMs), and firms that qualify can receive the Accredited Management Organization (AMO) designation. If you are interested in this qualification, contact IREM at 1-800-837-0706 or visit their website at www.irem.org.

Property management companies also have to know how to set market rents by considering market conditions and space availability. They should have an understanding of the financial aspects of operating the property to better ensure that a profit will be made after all expenses and overhead are paid for.

A good property-management company will familiarize itself with the local area in which the property is located and will develop business contacts such as banks, service technicians, and other professional associations that will benefit its clients.

The Management Contract

If you hire a property-management company to look after your property, you will have to sign a contract. This contract is between you (the property owner) and the company hired as the property manager. The contract should describe the rights and duties of both the manager and the owner. The following items should be carefully covered in the management contract:

- The exact description and address of the property to be managed.

- The names of the owner and the manager. Normally, the manager will act as an agent for the owner and can act on the owner's behalf.

- The term for which the contract will run, including the start and finish dates of the contact.

- The duties and responsibilities required of the manager.

- Compensation paid to the manager, usually based on a percentage of gross collections (typically, 5 to 8 percent).

- The extent to which a manager can spend funds without the owner's consent.

- Reports regarding the property that should be furnished to the owner upon request or on a predetermined schedule.

- The obligations of the owner to furnish documents and funds as needed.

Before signing anything, be sure to check out the management company's reputation and references. Find a company that has been in business for a few years and that has a low turnover rate with clients. Don't stop there, though. Be sure to call those clients and get the real scoop.

Rental Red Light!

The duties and responsibilities of a property manager should be carefully detailed. For instance, the hiring of employees, the handling of tenant complaints, the collection and distribution of revenue, and an explanation of what happens if funds are not sufficient to cover expenditures should all be included. In some states, property managers and/or leasing agents must hold a real-estate license to negotiate leases, show properties, or act as an owner's agent. Check with your state's real-estate commission.

Measuring a Manager's Success

A good property-management company will set goals and objectives for a property that the company will strive to achieve. Some examples of rental property–related goals are as follows:

- Increased profits to the owner

- Fewer vacancies

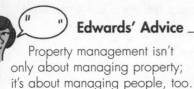

Edwards' Advice

Property management isn't only about managing property; it's about managing people, too.

- ◆ Lower delinquencies
- ◆ Lower rates of unit turnover
- ◆ Good relationships between owners and tenants
- ◆ Property improvements
- ◆ Fewer complaints and repairs

The Resident Manager

Some landlords look to hire a resident manager to handle the daily activities at a property instead of a fully equipped property-management company. A resident manager is an individual who can be hired to be an onsite manager at a rental complex. This individual can either live on the premises or just maintain a rental office at the property. There are several questions an owner must have answered before hiring a resident manager:

- ◆ **What will the resident manager's duties be?** Will the manger be responsible for selecting tenants, collecting rents, making repairs, or hiring and firing employees? The duties and responsibilities should be spelled out in the contract for hire, much as they would be for hiring a management company.

- ◆ **How much do you intend to pay the manager?** Will the payment be an hourly wage or a flat salary? This will, of course, depend on the scope of duties with which the manager will be faced.

- ◆ **Is the job full or part time?** How many hours do you expect the manager to be available either at the property or by pager? If you want the manager on call at certain hours to respond to emergencies, you may have to increase the pay.

- ◆ **Will this manager live on or off the property?** This will depend heavily on the scope of responsibility the manager will have.

Rental Red Light!

Be wary of giving a manager who lives at your property reduced rent. This form of payment can sometimes be taken for granted. Also, a reduced rent alone is often not sufficient payment for a full-time manager. This type of arrangement can pose additional problems in areas governed by rent control. Keep in mind that, if you do plan to make payment in the form of a reduced rental amount, you're still obligated to pay social security and payroll taxes.

The position of resident manager can be advertised in the newspaper, or you can hire a headhunter to find the best candidate. Have all potential candidates fill out an application. A smart landlord will take precautions to thoroughly check an employee applicant's qualifications. Find out the amount of education the applicants possess, their experience, and whether they are licensed to lease or manage rental units, as this is required in some states. Owners also should check references as well as credit, criminal, and driving histories.

Past experience will help dictate what you are looking for in a manager and how much you want to pay. If you are looking for a manager who can do handiwork ranging from painting to plumbing and electrical and who can also deal directly with the tenants, you are looking for a more experienced candidate. If you know what you need before interviewing, you'll know the right Joe or Sally before he or she walks through the door.

Facts for Rent

The Building Owners and Managers Association (BOMA) offers a professional designation of Real Property Administrator (RPA) for individuals in the field of property management. Professionals interested in this designation should contact the Building Owners and Managers Association at 202-408-2662 or check out the website at www.boma.org.

Welcome the New Guy

Upon hiring a property manager, you should make an effort to introduce the person to the tenants in the building. Many states require that you give the tenants the manager's name and address. Many states also require that you notify the tenants to let them know that the manager is authorized to deliver legal documents on your behalf such as eviction notices. It's a good idea to notify the tenants about the new manager in writing, even if the state does not require this. Walk the new manager around the property, personally introduce him or her to as many tenants as you can, and explain certain policies and mechanical aspects while you tour the building.

The Super

We all remember the lovable character Schneider on the hit TV show *One Day at a Time* during the 1970s. He was the greasy guy in the blue jeans, T-shirt, and tool belt, whom all the tenants loved. We even had a fellow (only his name was "Spider") who

Edwards' Advice

Make sure that your insurance covers any illegal acts committed by your employees.

Landlord's Toolbox

Obtain two copies of any landlord-tenant handbooks and state statutes regarding landlord-tenant laws and eviction laws in the state you do business in. Supply one copy of each to your manager and keep one for yourself. You'll most certainly need them as reference guides.

worked on our properties for years as a superintendent, and the resemblance was uncanny.

Many landlords find it handy to employ the services of an individual who can handle certain repairs and property upkeep such as fixing a water leak, mowing the grass, and removing garbage. Sometimes these handymen are called on to make ready vacant rental units or to look after emergencies during late hours. Many times, these individuals live on the premises and know tenants on a more personal basis because they are neighbors. Often owners will reduce the rent for these individuals who agree to help out around and keep an eye on the property. This works out well when the owner is looking for an extra set of hands and eyes on a property. However, it can also be the source of problems with your other tenants if the individual touches the wrong thing or says something he or she should not.

The Management and Liability

When you hire people to work for you, you become an employer. Suddenly, you are in a whole new arena of liability. The actions of your employees can get you into trouble if they are not careful. Remember that a manager is hired to act for the owner in situations pertaining to the rental property. An owner could be sued if it is found that the manager acted irresponsibly or negligently in certain circumstances. For instance, an owner could be found liable and be subject to a penalty if the manager or management company does any of the following:

♦ Discriminates with advertising, leasing, and other business policies

♦ Does not attend to dangerous conditions resulting in injury at the property

♦ Commits a criminal act at the property or while representing the owner

♦ Violates tenants' rights to privacy

♦ Violates state and local laws governing leasing, security deposits, evictions, or any other facet of the rental industry regulated by law

It's important for a landlord not only to know the law but to select a property manager who is familiar with it as well. Otherwise, the landlord risks being sued.

The Landlord or the Employer

When a landlord hires someone such as a resident property manager or a superintendent to handle business at a rental property, the landlord becomes an employer. Because you are now someone's boss, you have certain obligations to be performed for the government. Whether you compensate an employee with a salary or a reduced rent, you are required to pay income tax, pay Social Security and Medicare taxes, and follow certain other obligations such as minimum wage and overtime regulations. If you do not, you could face substantial penalties. In addition to these obligations, there are also unemployment taxes and workers compensation to contend with.

Rental Red Light!

Make sure to pay payroll taxes on time. Otherwise, the IRS will find you and level large fines against you, complete with interest charges if the bill becomes delinquent. Unlike most other debts, payroll taxes must be paid back even if you file bankruptcy.

Many landlords attempt to bypass these types of obligations by paying employees as independent contractors. Independent contractors are typically considered to be in business for themselves and are not guaranteed the same rights as employees.

The IRS, however, clearly defines independent contractors as individuals who provide services for the public as a whole and control the project at task exclusively. Resident property managers could be considered employees because they would have been hired by the property owners who, at the same time, would have set the hours and responsibilities of the managers. If, however, the manager works for several different rental owners, the argument could be made that the manager is an independent contractor.

For more information regarding legal obligations of employers, contact the Internal Revenue Service at 1-800-829-3676.

For more information regarding minimum wage and overtime laws and regulations, contact your nearest office of the U.S. Labor Department's Wage and Hour Division or your state's labor department.

You're Fired!

If a property manager is not working out, you may have the unfortunate task of firing the person. The contract can be terminated at any time as long as it wasn't set to run for a specific period of time. You can only terminate someone's contract for just cause such as if the manager performs poorly; does not follow instructions; violates federal, state, and local laws; or endangers and threatens the safety of tenants.

You cannot fire someone, however, if he or she refuses to carry out an illegal act such as dumping hazardous waste in a state forest. You also cannot discriminate against the employee and fire him or her based on race, age, or gender.

If things go bad with a resident manager or superintendent who happens to live at the property, you may also have to eventually evict the individual. To better protect against this type of situation, it is a good idea to have a manager sign separate management and month-to-month rental agreements. That way, if the manager is fired, it will not affect the tenancy. As a tenant, the ex-employee will have to continue paying rent or risk being evicted just like any other tenant. The month-to-month agreement gives you the opportunity to evict the tenant after proper notice has been given. If the ex-employee is locked into a fixed lease, you will have to wait either for the individual to neglect paying rent (to evict) or for the term of the lease to expire (to refuse a renewal).

The Least You Need to Know

- Before signing a contract with a property-management company, be sure that it can perform what you ask. Check out its current clientele, references, and experience.

- Determine the duties, responsibilities, and pay of your property manager before hiring.

- Protect your business against employees' actions by ensuring that managers know all local, state, and federal laws as well as your own rules.

- Firing a resident property manager can be tricky. A good option is to have a month-to-month rental agreement separate from the work agreement.

Chapter 20

Keeping a Clean House

In This Chapter

◆ Making vacant apartments ready to rent

◆ Going beneath the surface to get your property in top shape

◆ Determining whether to fix it or replace it

◆ Keeping the building up to code

◆ Keeping up a property's outside appearances

Over the years, we've purchased more mops and brooms than we care to remember, and sometimes we've even used them. The truth is, however, that in today's world, a landlord has to do more than occasionally sweep the building's halls. To keep the investment in tiptop shape and to maximize returns, a property not only must be kept clean, it must also be improved upon. New siding, windows, and doors are improvements that will pay off in the long run for the property. Painting the exterior trim, interior halls, decks, and staircases every few years will keep the property looking nice. Removing garbage and debris that pile up on a property will keep it clean and safe. This kind of property care all adds to the life of your investment, both while you're renting it and when the time comes to sell it. A nice, well-kept property is not only more valuable but also a symbol of an owner who takes pride in owning it.

Maintaining the Property

When you purchase and own investment property, you also acquire the responsibility to maintain the property in an orderly fashion. Maintaining the property can have many different meanings.

Edwards' Advice

Remember the old cliché, "Handsome buildings attract handsome tenants."

First of all, the units that are rented must be made clean, safe, and habitable for renters to occupy. Units available for rent should be painted. Bathroom and kitchen fixtures, tile, linoleum and wood floors, appliances, and windows should all be cleaned before a tenant moves in.

The exterior should be made presentable to the public to attract new tenants. Trim around exterior doors and windows should be painted. Decks and staircases may need to be painted. Garbage, debris, and junk cars need to be removed.

Of course, maintenance also means repairing units after the tenants have occupied the structure. Unit repairs are very common and must be handled in a timely fashion. Leaks, drafts, and broken fixtures in a unit should be attended to quickly to preserve good relations between you and your tenant. The result will be a steady rent payment.

Smart landlords also make an effort to improve the property. New siding, windows, and doors will improve on the life of your investment. Adding items such as brass house numbers and mailboxes not only improves the appearance of your building but also attracts better tenants.

Preparing the Rentals

In Chapter 6, we mentioned the importance of vacancy make-ready for attracting new tenants to your building. Certain standards have been viewed as acceptable to tenant advocacy groups, housing and building-code inspectors, and the rest of society. Even though law requires some standards, others can be set at the discretion of the landlord.

When preparing units, you will have to deal with a cleanup job before a cleanup job. Tenants rarely completely remove everything from a unit, and you will be the one to dispose of their broken chairs, stacks of papers, and the worn-out three-piece couch set they didn't want to lift into their moving van. Every state has laws about how long you must hold on to a past tenant's belongings. Your best bet is to get a tenant's forwarding address or phone number if possible, so that you can contact the tenant after he or she moves. If the tenant does not remove his or her items in a timely manner and you are required by law to hold on to the stuff for, say, another few weeks, it's best to move the left-behinds to a storage area before showing the unit to new tenants.

Some basic preparations need to be done to every unit. To keep track of what needs to be done to a unit or what already has been completed, type or write up a checklist of items and make several blank copies to keep handy.

Using this checklist will accomplish three things: It will make the task of make-ready seem less overwhelming, it will help move you along to finish the make-ready, and by keeping a history of what has been fixed and replaced in the units, it will help you determine whether the units are financially worth it. If you're investing more and more money into a property that keeps deteriorating faster and faster, it might be time to sell.

> **Landlord's Toolbox**
>
> Use caulking to fill cracks, especially along the ceiling edges in a unit. Caulking is inexpensive to purchase, is simple to use, and helps provide a clean, tight appearance to the unit.

For the remainder of this chapter, we will discuss the make-ready project of a rental unit in more detail.

Cleanliness Is Next to Godliness

As mentioned in Chapter 6, landlords must present a product that is clean and sanitary to new potential tenants. In addition to the obvious cleaning involved such as removing garbage, sweeping, mopping, and vacuuming floors, one big factor that lends itself to the image of cleanliness is applying new paint to walls, ceilings, windows, and doors. Handprints show on walls; smoke stains discolor the ceilings; paint chips around doors and windows. Anything that originally was painted may very well need a new coat before a unit is re-rented. The new paint will help give the appearance of cleanliness.

Wipe down appliances inside and out. Clean off grease and mildew that builds up on stoves and refrigerators. New tenants will view the new apartment as special until they discover that they have to clean dirty appliances. Floors that are covered in hardwood or vinyl may need to be mopped and/or waxed. Windows and storm windows should all be cleaned.

It is important to try to make a rental unit gleam before you show it to prospective tenants; this will help sell the unit and will shorten the amount of time the unit remains vacant.

Rental Red Light! _____

When preparing a unit to show to possible renters, it's best to have the unit as close to being ready as possible. When renters look at a unit, it's difficult for them to see past a dirty carpet or marks on the walls, even if you describe to them what will be fixed and replaced. This doesn't mean you should wait to advertise the unit until it is completely finished, but you will rent the unit faster by showing it in its best condition. This also will save you from showing the unit six or seven times when you could rent it to the first or second prospect.

Safe and Secure

The entrance to the rental unit is very important. The front door should be solid, weather tight, and have sufficient locks. Entrance doors that share a common hallway often are required by state fire codes to be fire rated, which means that the door must be able to sustain fire for a specific period of time. If your building requires fire-rated doors in your common entrances and you do not have them, you could face severe penalties. Heaven help you if a fire occurs and someone gets hurt or perishes— Call your lawyer.

Rental Red Light! _____

Water leaks can cost a property owner a lot of money. Not only is the water usage expensive, it also causes damage to floors and ceilings in the form of rot and decay. Look for and repair water leaks as quickly as possible to help prevent this kind of damage.

The condition of the floors is very important. Whatever kind of floors the unit has, they should be impervious to water. This means that any wood- or vinyl-covered floor should be sealed properly to keep water that might spill from seeping through and causing damage below the unit.

Rental Red Light! _____

Laws, codes, and ordinances will differ by state and town. Be sure to check with your state and local building and fire officials regarding the requirements and placements of smoke and carbon monoxide detectors.

Outlets in the vicinity of sinks should be ground-faulted for safety reasons. Bathrooms should be properly vented per your state and local building codes. Light fixtures should have working bulbs and switches. Smoke detectors and/or carbon monoxide detectors, if your state requires them, should be in good working condition and should be properly placed throughout the unit per your state and local fire codes.

Make sure that bedroom, bathroom, and closet doors have working handles and open and close properly. Windows also should open and close properly and should be complete with working locks.

Just Throw Some Paint on It!

One of our favorite phrases is to hear someone say, "Just throw some paint on the building." Some other favorites are, "Why don't you pop some new windows in there?" or "Just toss a new roof on that building!" Usually, people who have never painted a wall in their life let alone replaced a window or roof make these statements. Regardless, we thought it was a good way to start discussing the kinds of property maintenance and improvements that a rental owner should consider while renting a building.

 Edwards' Advice

If a property looks good to an insurance company, it may be assigned a lower premium, which translates into money in your pocket.

Beauty Is Skin Deep

It is important for a building to have eye appeal to the average passerby. After all, this person may be the individual who ends up renting from you. If the exterior of a building is in nice condition, it will help you in your quest to get insurance coverage because most companies will send an inspector to look at the outside of your building before agreeing to insure the property. An aesthetically attractive building will also help relieve pressure from building officials about the condition of your building.

Maybe the building needs a paint job and maybe it needs siding. The decision is, of course, yours to make and will most likely be based on your financial capability. Don't be duped, however, into thinking that paint is less expensive than siding. You should carefully look into both possibilities and weigh the benefits of both before deciding.

Here is a list of things to keep an eye on:

♦ **A good foundation.** Look over the foundation from the outside and fill any cracks or holes you find with cement or concrete. Many times, it is a good idea to paint the exterior foundation with a concrete paint that can be color coordinated to the building and that helps seal the foundation from exterior elements.

Rental Red Light!

Siding may not always conform to the style of other buildings in an area, but if local codes allow for it, you may find that siding will have a longer life expectancy as well as looking really nice.

Rental Red Light! _____

Replace gutters that are either missing or broken. Gutters are essential for directing and removing rainwater; without properly working gutters, you risk allowing water damage to the building.

If you plan to replace exterior porches, decks, or staircases, make sure to review your state and local building codes for legal spec requirements.

- **Let the sun shine in.** Old windows are the pits and should be replaced every 100 years or so. New plastic replacement windows are easy to install and look very nice. If old fashioned is more your style, newer windows that resemble older styles are available. You can go through the task of rehabbing existing windows by removing the old paint and refinishing them, but a project like this can be painstaking and very time consuming.

- **Nesting places.** Look over the *soffit* and *fascia* boards on the building. These are the areas around the top of the exterior wall of the building that separate the walls from the roof. This is the part that the squirrel chewed through and the birds have nested in. These areas should be repaired so that animals are kept out and it looks nice. While you're up there, you should make sure the gutters are connected and clean.

- **Top it off.** A roof is one of the most important aspects of a building and is one of the most expensive to replace. Roofs are designed to last for specific periods of time, normally 15 years, and then they need to be replaced. Many property owners will not replace the roof until it leaks, sometimes waiting too long and increasing the cost due to water damage.

- **Chimneys.** Check out the chimney for loose or missing mortar and bricks. Chimneys should also be cleaned every few years. Professional chimney sweeps are available to provide this kind of service.

- **Extra exteriors.** Exterior porches and decks, stairs, and railings may need to be power washed and properly surface coated to help prevent deterioration and to beautify the property.

You Can't Judge a Book by Its Cover

We hope you feel the same way about this book and have so far enjoyed our perspectives. Let's continue with the same idea being applied to the inside of your building.

If there is a common hallway or staircase shared by tenants, its walls and ceilings should be clean with paint intact. Make sure the floors and stairways are clean and well lit to add to the nice appearance and to prevent injury. Make sure railings on staircases are secure and stair treads properly tacked down.

The mechanical room, basement, or cellar, as some of us like to call it, may very well be the most important room in the building. This is usually where the heating systems, water heaters, and electrical panel boxes are located. Here you will very often find gas meters, oil tanks, water-supply valves, and sewer lines. All these items should, of course, be checked and maintained on a routine basis to be certain that they are working properly.

Edwards' Advice

Do yourself a favor and label the boilers, water heaters, gas meters, electrical boxes, and water pipes to correspond to the rental units to which they belong.

There is also a host of other things to check for while down in the basement. For instance, you should check the basement stairs for sturdiness and safety. Make sure the basement is well lit in case you, a serviceman, or your tenant needs to enter for some reason. Check the inside foundation walls for cracks and loose mortar.

Most basement ceilings are decorated with a number of water-supply lines that carry the water up to the units. These pipes should be checked for leaks and then insulated accordingly to protect the pipes from water freeze-ups. Also check for unwanted guests such as pests and rodents that usually start from underground and work their way up. Filling in any cracks in the foundation will help keep the bigger critters out, but the smallest ones will need professional help, also known as your friendly exterminator.

"Hey, Can I Show You Something?"

Okay, you can't very well keep a clean house without repairing and maintaining rental units currently being rented. We mentioned the importance of servicing tenants in Chapter 15. Here we reiterate this importance but also express the benefit to the building when repairs are dealt with promptly. A timely repair can save tons of money in damage done to the unit and the building.

If the tenant complains that the toilet is rocking from side to side on the floor, and it is not responded to quickly, the result will eventually be a damaged wax ring at the base of the toilet, which will then allow for water to seep from the base of the toilet onto the floor. Eventually, rot will occur to the floor around the bottom of the toilet, which will lead to even bigger problems and repairs. The toilet may even break if it

Edwards' Advice

Beware you do not fall victim to the old cliché, "10 percent of my properties are taking up 100 percent of my time." If this is something you are saying to yourself then its time to analyze all your property and determine which ones make up the troubling 10 percent then get rid of them.

Edwards' Advice

Call the public works department in your area to find out the days that garbage is picked up on each street where your properties are located. Find out what is required from owners as far as garbage bins and what items are acceptable for placement at the curb. This information is useful to tenants and superintendents whom you expect to keep the building clean.

continues to be used and is rocked back and forth. For the price of a few new toilet bolts and a little effort to better secure the toilet to the floor, all of this damage and repair could have been avoided.

Taking Out the Trash

It is difficult to keep a clean house when garbage and debris builds up at the property. In many states and localities, there are laws and ordinances that restrict garbage buildup at properties. In these areas, the owner will usually be held accountable for the removal of the garbage, and violations are punishable by fine and/or imprisonment. If you own several properties and maintain them yourself, garbage removal can seem like a full-time job. Even if you own just one property, garbage buildup can be considerable if it is not removed daily. As mentioned in Chapter 15, you should send a city truck pickup notice to all new tenants regarding the day garbage is picked up if this service is available in your building area. If not, a plan and system for removal should be designed, and tenants should be alerted to the policy for garbage removal. This may require the use of a dumpster service at the property for tenants to dispose of garbage.

Your Property, Not a Used Car Lot

Many state and local laws forbid the existence of junk and unregistered cars at properties. Again, owners will be held accountable for this and can be punished by fines and imprisonment if the situation is not remedied. Smart landlords do not permit junk and unregistered cars to remain at a property because when one shows up, it usually isn't long before more will. Not to mention the fact that the parking area will begin to resemble a car yard instead of a rental building. Often, there are towing services available to help remove these automobiles when they either are not moved by the owner or are abandoned. Contact your state and local authorities regarding the removal of such automobiles and be sure it is done properly so that you are not held liable for tampering with someone's personal property.

Keeping Up Appearances

Let's face it. When you're in business, it's important to dress for success. In addition to putting on nice clothes, you must also wash your face and hands, brush your teeth, and comb your hair. Your physical hygiene is as important as the clothes you wear. Think of the land that your properties sit on as personal hygiene. Nice-looking grounds are as important to the building as how the building is dressed.

High grass and tall, unruly weeds and bushes make a property look unkempt and shabby. Keeping the grass cut during the spring and summer months will portray an image of a responsible property owner who cares about the image of his or her building. Trimming bushes and hedges also lends to a more positive image. Planting flowers around the grounds gives the appearance of not only a well-kept property but also serenity and charm. This will attract potential new tenants and keep you in business.

The Least You Need to Know

- There are several different ways to handle maintenance at a property such as deciding whether to replace something or fix it.

- When you purchase rental property, you inherit the responsibility to maintain that property.

- Cleanliness is next to godliness when preparing a unit for rent.

- Water damage is one of the most expensive forms of damage that can occur in rental units.

- Many states and localities have laws and ordinances that require property owners to keep the buildings up to fire and safety codes and to remove garbage and/or junk cars.

21

Running the Rental Office

In This Chapter

- ◆ Getting the startup supplies you need
- ◆ Managing your time and organizing your records
- ◆ Running the home office
- ◆ Setting up shop outside the home

In a corporate, middle-size, or even small company, you'll find that everyone has a job to do. The bookkeeper keeps the books, the office manager manages the office, the middlemen and women keep the papers shuffled in the right places, and the president tells everyone what to do. For a do-it-yourself landlord, the level of corporate management is simple. The landlord is the bookkeeper, the office manager, the sales staff, the mail clerk, the receptionist, and the cleanup crew, just to name a few. You also are president, of course, and being president means that you get to tell yourself what to do. That's what being in business for yourself is all about!

Being in business for yourself also means that you need to learn how to run your operation smoothly. As your business grows, so will your need for organization and efficiency. If you're just starting out, you might be able to get by without a computer because your paper load will be minimal. As you acquire more rental properties, however, you will acquire more of a workload. Keeping track of everything from your tenants to paying your bills will seem time consuming, but not making an effort to do so will prove costly. Investing in the right tools can help you to manage the investment and maximize its performance.

Office Setup

Landlording is a business like any other, and running it as a business is the best way to stay in business. When starting up, you will need the basic supplies. Among the usual suspects of a stapler, a phone, pens, file folders, and a desk to put them on are other basic and not-so-basic supplies that will make your office run smoothly.

Paper Clips and Then Some

If you think you can run a business without the basic supplies, think again. While you're picking up your desk lamp and paper clips, include the following on your office-supply shopping list:

◆ **Business phone with speaker feature.** Having your hands free while you're on hold and handling a few things at once will save you money on physical-therapy bills for neck strains. If you're running a home office and want a home life, a separate phone line is your best bet.

◆ **Answering machine or voicemail.** You will get calls 24/7. If people can't leave a message, count on them not calling back or calling back angry. Get a good answering machine, one that saves the date and time of your messages, or sign up for voicemail through your local phone company.

◆ **Fax machine.** You will need to receive credit reports and other info over the fax, and you will need to fax out info as well. Contrary to popular contemporary belief, not everything is done by e-mail. Well, not yet.

Landlord's Toolbox

Voicemail can be a great option. Calls are never missed because, whether you're on the phone or away from the office, messages are left with the voicemail service. Voicemail messages also are easy to retrieve and save from wherever you are. This is especially handy if you work from home and live with others who will be occupying the phone. You can get voicemail through your local phone company, and it usually costs under $10 per month.

◆ **Photocopier.** They're not as expensive as you might think, and you will use this constantly. In the long run, it's less expensive than getting 25¢ copies at the gas station. And it's time-saving.

Landlord's Tool Box

As most of you know, once you have a cell phone, you won't know how you lived without one. Checking and returning messages from your cell phone will save time. You can have tenants use the main office number to leave messages, and you can choose to whom you give the cell number. Beware of caller ID, though; many tenants have the service and will soon have your cell number if you call them from your cell phone. This could prove to be an aggravation as well as an expense in phone bills.

If your property managers or maintenance staff also have cell phones or pagers, this could be a great benefit. If you have staff members, you might want to request that they each buy their own phones or pagers and then reimburse them for work calls. You could also buy phones or pagers for the staff to pick up and leave at the office each day, but this route leaves you wide open for costly equipment to take a walk.

◆ **Printing calculator.** For accounting reasons, there's no sense in getting a calculator that doesn't print out.

◆ **File cabinets and plenty of file folders.** Stacks of files on the floor get lost and coffee-stained. There are a lot of cheap file cabinets out there now—plastic, on wheels, and your standard gray metal.

◆ **Paper shredder.** We'll presume that you're not recreating Watergate, but it's still a good idea to get rid of unwanted documents this way.

◆ **Scanner.** You might find a scanner useful because you can scan paper copies of leases, bills, or other documents not requiring a personal signature into a filing cabinet inside your computer. A scanner also saves you from retyping documents that, once scanned in, can be edited on your computer.

◆ **Cork and marker boards.** "Out of sight, out of mind" really applies to office organization. Whichever system works best for you, be sure to post the important things: duplicate keys to all your units, vacancies, repairs, a calendar for showings, or anything that you'll need to refer to often.

◆ **For-rent signs.** Big and small, for-rent signs on windows and lawns with your telephone number will be your best advertisement.

◆ **Store it.** If you don't have a place just for storing your tools, plumbing and electrical parts, smoke detectors, mailboxes, toilet seats, light bulbs, trash bags, cleanup supplies, for-rent signs, and more, you will soon need one. Set aside room on your home property or on one of your rental properties.

Enter the Twenty-First Century

There's no doubt about it these days, getting the right computer and software will organize things you didn't even know needed organizing. As your business grows, everything from finances to eviction notices will seem like a breeze when you have a machine to take care of it. For accounting purposes, a computer can't be beat. Think of tax time. What's easier, rummaging through shoeboxes of receipts to calculate what you've earned and spent over the year or printing out a report from your computer?

If you currently own only one or two properties, you can get by without a computer. Keeping records by hand or by typewriter probably won't be that cumbersome. On the flip side, this might be the perfect time to get technical, especially if you are computer illiterate. If you wait until your business grows even more before purchasing a computer, you will have to stop and set aside even more time to transfer the piles of growing files onto your new machine. Not to mention learning how to work the thing in the first place. The bottom line is this: Don't be afraid; user-friendly computers do exist, and they will help in your quest to run an efficient business.

If you don't already own a personal computer, check around before leaping at the first one you see. Ask your fellow landlords and friends what they have. Go to their houses and test drive some of their computers and software. Now that computers are a common home-office tool, there are bargains to be had. There are also a lot of bad deals out there, so beware of the slick computer salesperson. Everyone's needs are different, but make sure you choose a computer with a good amount of memory (128 megabytes of RAM or more), modem speed (56K or more), and the right software including a good word-processing program, an easy-to-use accounting program, such as Quicken or Microsoft Money, and Internet software.

Let Your Computer Manage the Property

Living in the twenty-first century means learning new effective ways to manage your property such as with computer software. There are several types of management- and landlord-oriented software products available for purchase, which may lend the kind of management support that you need to effectively operate your property. Each of the ones we researched had similar features such as a tenant, rent roll, bill paying, and property data, but there were some differences. Each user format slightly differed. Some offered legal databases, office forms, and advice on the software. Others offered online web support and access to other website material.

The costs of applicable software varied from $40 to $1,000, depending on the features and the number of units to which it was to be applied. We suggest that you research multiple software products and weigh the features they offer against the price you pay. A good software package should incorporate the basic features mentioned and combine it with an accounting program complete with check ledger, multiple accounts, and account report capabilities. A software product with these features, coupled with this book, is perfect! We took the liberty of listing some popular management-software products in Appendix C.

> **Landlord's Tool Box**
>
> E-mail is not a necessity, but it's a great tool. The Internet and e-mail are great ways to get connected with other landlords, provided that you have a computer to get connected in the first place. (See Chapter 22 for more on finding your local landlord community on the web.)

Whatever configuration of wires and plastic you invest in, it will be worth your money when it gets the job done. Be sure, however, not to rely solely on the machine. Back up all your files and print hard copies of all accounting reports, forms, and anything else you create on the computer. Home computers these days are pretty reliable, but they're not always a sure bet. Always have a backup when it comes to computer files.

Making Connections

When setting up shop as a landlord, make your presence known. Get references from other landlords as to which electrician, plumber, roofer, sider, lawn care, and snow-removal contractors have the best reputations. Call your local housing authority to let them know you have vacancies and to pass the word on to those in subsidized housing programs. Pick up the local papers and skim through to find out which ones list the most rentals. Then call the papers and get their ad rates. Print up business cards and post them at local restaurants, stores, and college campuses if any are nearby.

As a landlord, you may think that networking is not really a necessity. Just stick to taking care of your buildings and renting them, right? Networking can only help your business. People talk and, especially in smaller communities, reputations get around fast. If people in town get to know you and know you are looking to increase your investments, you will get inside info on buildings before they go on the market.

The Daily Grind: Prioritize, Prioritize, Prioritize

It's Monday. You've just come back from a quiet and restful weekend with no emergencies and lots of time doing nothing. Your answering machine is blinking—you have 42 messages. You've got bills to pay and rents to chase down. What do you do first? First, you take a deep breath and make a cup of tea. In any business, time management—known technically as "what the heck do I do first?"—is important.

Keep it in perspective, though, and try not to let managing your time take over your time. If you have hired office and/or maintenance staff, you should all be working together to divvy up the responsibilities. If you're on your own, then managing your time the right way will make all the difference in getting the job done.

Managing Your Time

Let's go back to Monday and the 42 callbacks to make, half-dozen bills to pay, and half-dozen more rents to track down. Checking your messages is priority number one. Emergency repairs should be taken care of right away, especially if this is wintertime (provided that you live where there is a wintertime) and frozen pipes are a concern. Calling back people who are looking to rent is also a top concern. Paying your bills heads the list, too. What the heck do you do first?

Rental Red Light!

When people are looking for a place to live, they usually respond to several ads at once and, especially if they work nine-to-five jobs, will want to set up appointments that do not interfere with work. If you own property in a tight market in which housing is scarce, first looks are often first taken.

After you get all your messages from the answering machine or voicemail and have checked the fax machine, you're ready to set your priorities. Don't start making callbacks until you've organized what you'll do first. If you try to call back all 42 people, including your Aunt Frieda who just called to say hi, pretty soon it will be lunchtime, and some priorities that should have been taken care of in the morning have gone right out the window.

When organizing your to-do list, make two categories:

◆ **Category #1, a.k.a., The Now Category.** Emergencies and time-sensitive projects, such as repairs and meeting the building or health inspector, are top priority. Some repairs such as a running toilet will take a back seat to busted pipes or broken steps, but any repair should be considered a priority over Category #2.

◆ **Category #2, a.k.a., Pencil It In.** Don't just list everything else that needs to get done, schedule a time for getting it done. Your bills can be taken care of during quiet times such as late afternoon when it's difficult to get people on the phone. If you know your late-paying tenant gets home from third shift at 10:30 A.M. and then goes right to sleep before getting up for work again in the evening, make sure you're on his or her doorstep at 10:30 A.M. sharp.

Facts for Rent

When talking to prospective tenants on the phone about your vacancies, tell them as much as possible about your units. Relate their size, layout, amenities, school district, closest bus lines and stores, age and style, and location. The more info you can give over the phone, the less disappointed tenants will be when they see the unit. This will save you from showing the unit over and over again.

The trick to time management is not to over-manage. Write things down on a to-do list, your calendar, or whatever system you've created, and just do them. If you're not careful, you might spend too much time scheduling everything, and then you'll have to move it around again when it doesn't get done because you've spent too much time scheduling. Things will come up during the day that you haven't planned for—that's a certainty.

Landlording is not your ordinary desk job, that's for sure. You will probably spend less time at your desk than you even imagined. Make the most of the time you do spend at your desk and plan your day as best you can. You can't beat the clock and build Rome in a day; know your limits. You can work out a schedule that uses your time wisely and that wrestles the concept of time into submission. At least for the time being.

Stick It on the Wall

Files are great for filing things that have been completed, but they're not the best for staying on top of things. If something is out of sight, it will be out of mind. The best thing to do when you need to refer to something often is to stick it on the wall. Put it in plain view and it will stay fresh in your mind. Things to put on the wall include ...

◆ **Repairs.** Keeping on top of repairs to be done in each unit is easier when you have a way to post them. Whichever way works best, on a cork board or hanging from clips or small containers, be sure it's close at hand and eye.

- **Keys.** Always keep a duplicate set of keys for every unit and every door on every property. Hang them on the wall with each one labeled. Know that you will not remember which key goes to which door. Always remember to return the keys to the right spot. When you're running out for a repair, the last thing you want to do is spend a half-hour looking for the basement key.

- **Vacancies.** Keep an erasable marker board updated with all vacancies. This not only is a quick reference for you, but if it's also visible to people who enter your office, then it's another way to advertise to prospective tenants.

- **Schedules.** If you don't keep a planner or desk calendar to schedule showings, buy a wall calendar and keep it close to your desk.

- **Anything important.** Hang up garbage-day pickup schedules for all your properties, put rental applications on a clipboard, and keep close anything you need to get to quickly.

Keep It Safe: Stash Your Cash

If you or your property management staff collect some rents in person, take extra caution:

- If you collect five, six, or more cash rents at a time, suddenly you are carrying around a whole lot of money.

- If you have to chase tenants down for rents and they pay in cash, try to bring someone with you on your route.

- If you're collecting a lot of cash rents at once, try to vary the route from month to month.

- If possible, try not to carry a lot of cash on you at once. Break up the rent-collecting by bringing back cash to the office.

- If you collect a lot of cash rents, deposit the money quickly.

- If you find that you cannot get to the bank quickly enough, consider buying a safe. Get one that either bolts down or is ironclad heavy.

Keeping Records

Although you will use your computer to create records needed in daily operations, you won't have everything on the computer. Probably the most important thing you can do to run a tight ship is to keep thorough and efficient records. Realistically, it is nearly impossible to keep track of every single possible thing you do in a day. And every single thing doesn't need to be recorded. Just every single important thing such as conversations with tenants, conversations with past landlords about tenants, repairs made, credit checks, copies of rental agreements, money exchanges, and expenses and income for each property. Keep a copy of anything you give to a tenant including his or her rental agreement, rent receipts, credit checks, and any notices or letters sent to the tenant. It's best to create labeled tenant folders to keep the copies in, and protect each in a fire-safe filing cabinet.

Landlord's Toolbox

Banking on the Internet is becoming increasingly popular. You can also set up bill payments online. If you go this route, make sure you keep constant track of where your money is being divvied up, especially if automatic withdrawals are being taken out of your account. If one month you do not receive the rent payments needed to cover the bills, you're stuck. Some bill-paying sites and banks have features that enable you to see what is being paid before the money gets removed. Before signing on, make sure you know where and when your money is taken out of your hands.

All Accounted For

Keeping good accounting records means keeping up with them. Some landlords accept monthly and weekly rent payments. Keeping track of income on a monthly basis is probably the easiest route. To keep up with incoming rent payments, record the payments as they come in. When accounting for income and expenses, before you remove your profit, try this method (provided that rent payments are paid on the first of the month):

◆ On the tenth of the month, review all rent payments received and recorded. Make a list of who still owes you and who has received late rent notices. Make calls or visit tenants as soon as you can to collect overdue rent. Prepare eviction notices for delinquent payers.

◆ On the twentieth, tally up late rents again. Make more calls and more visits to tenants if necessary. Check on eviction paperwork status.

 Rental Red Light!

Always pay yourself last! The best way to lose your business is to take out your own income before paying your bills.

♦ On the thirtieth, distribute the income. Make sure all expenses for all buildings have been accounted for and then organize the leftovers. Move the allocated amounts to the escrow accounts you have set up. Then pay yourself. If you have staff, consider setting up a separate checking account to cover this expense if you decide to pay them weekly or bi-weekly.

Here's Your Receipt

Always give out receipts and keep a copy for yourself when receiving payment for anything. You can pick up an inexpensive carbon-copy receipt book at any office-supply store. When you fill out a receipt for payment, make sure that you include the date, the amount, what the payment is for, who it's from, and any balance due. Always remember to sign your receipts.

Some landlords, especially if they receive most rent payments by mail, send a computer-generated slip to tenants before rent is due. This serves as both a reminder and a record of rent due. You can also include a self-addressed envelope to make it even easier for a tenant to drop that payment in the mailbox. With this type of slip, you can have the tenant keep one part that itemizes when rent is due, how much is due, the late fee (if any), and when he or she will be charged a late fee. The tenant sends the other part, your copy, with payment. This can be either handwritten or typed out; what matters is that both you and the tenant have a written record of payment.

Tenant Logging

Have a separate notebook, binder, or computer file to record each tenant's history. Be sure to include the tenant's name (and the names of anyone else living in the unit), address, day and nighttime phone numbers, lease renewal date or when the month-to-month or week-to-week occupancy began, amount of security deposit paid, when rent is due, work pay schedule, and history of rent payments.

Make sure that you also have a place to record any conversations, repairs made, repairs needed, repair costs, disputes, or understandings made with the tenant not detailed in the written agreement. Anything that will help protect against claims of noncompliance or retaliation or that will help in an eviction case should be written down. Better to take a few minutes to record, and even photograph, a repaired broken step than to try and defend yourself in court without any proof.

In addition to a log book (or instead of, whichever works better for you), keep a separate file folder for each tenant. In the folder, keep a copy of the rental application, rental agreement, credit-check report, any other info from when the tenant moved in, and all info to come.

Recording Your Handiwork

Floating sticky notes and loose pieces of paper get lost. A loose note with a repair on it will also get lost and will never be taken care of until the tenant calls the health department to complain. Pick up a tear-out blank book with duplicate sheets that you can use to write down repairs.

Rental Red Light! _____

Don't make exceptions to your rules. If you don't accept pets, stick to the no-pet rule with everyone. If you limit the number of cars allowed on a property, stick to your guns. Once you break a rule, you'll break another and then another and soon trouble will follow—if not in cost then in disputes with your other tenants. If you knowingly decide to break a rule with a tenant, make a note of it. Then, when you forget next month that you allowed a tenant to start a bird sanctuary in the backyard, you'll have a written record before confronting the tenant.

Now, when you tear off the top sheet, you're back to square one with floating paper bits, right? For you and/or your maintenance staff to keep track of the repairs, your best bet is to avoid stacking the repair notes on the desk or putting them in a file where you can't see them. Instead, put them where you can see them. Buy a corkboard, clips, hanging see-through containers, or some other way to post the repairs in plain view. When you post them, however, make sure that you have a spot for each unit. When the repair has been completed, use the same slip to make a note of what was taken care of and when and if you spoke to the tenant about the repair. File this copy in the tenant's folder as a record.

You might also want to keep an extra copy of the repair and file it in a separate file for the unit. Keeping a history of repairs for each unit can help determine whether your properties are worth the upkeep. Of course, this is provided that the repairs are due to a faltering building and not tenant misuse.

Landlording from Your Den

You've just signed the papers to own your second rental unit, a four-family. Your first venture into the world of landlording, a five-family, has brought in a steady income with few hassles. You're looking forward to overseeing nine units and will soon quit your day job. So where do you do business? You don't have commercial space in either building, but you could rent a small office space from Sharon, another landlord down the street. The rent Sharon is asking for is higher than two of your units combined, and there is almost too much space for your small office. What do you do? Is it time to move your office out of the home? In this situation, it doesn't seem like the right time. For now, you need to learn how to work and manage your business from home.

Managing from home means that your fax is next to the fridge, your files are on top of the fridge, and your water cooler is the kitchen tap. Getting organized at home can be tough, especially if you're low on space. And depending on where your rental buildings are located compared to your home, going back and forth between the units and home can be headache inducing. Here are some of the cons to working from home:

◆ **No professional space to conduct business.** You will find yourself conducting business from the parking lot, the units, and even the gas station. You might spend more time setting up meetings with tenants or contractors outside an office space than actually conducting business within one. For obvious reasons, it is not wise to invite strangers, especially tenants, into your home. Theft is not your only concern here; there is also a lot of resentment in the world that could come back to haunt you when rent is due!

Edwards' Advice

Working out of your home as a landlord means that you will need to meet tenants at the properties for showings, and this could mean a lot of wasted time. Instead of meeting prospective tenants in the office first, having them fill out an application form, and then showing a unit, you've done it in reverse. If you show someone one or more rental units and then have the person fill out an application form only to find out that he or she cannot afford to rent from you, you have just wasted an afternoon.

◆ **More running around.** Depending on how close your home is to your rental units, you might find yourself lugging around things such as rental applications, rent money, and files. Working from home can be convenient because it cuts down on rush-hour commute time. But because landlording requires as much if not more time in the field as behind a desk, back-and-forth commute time can be increased.

◆ **No place for tenants to bring rent.** If you have tenants who do not mail in their rent, you'll be doing a lot of rent chasing every month.

◆ **Choose: no peace or no quiet.** Having a home office means you will never get away from it. Getting a separate phone line will help, as will using a separate room, door included.

The benefit of working from home is that you're home. Taking care of some paperwork after dinner is easy because it's right down the hall or on the other side of the table. You can also save money on renting from someone else if you do not own commercial space to have your office in. Your home office is also a tax deduction. And, in the meantime, you can save a little money on supplies. Let's say you own a personal computer that you use for both personal and business record keeping. Moving out means that you'll need to invest in a computer just for the office as well as several other types of office tools.

Leaving the Den: Setting Up Shop Elsewhere

So how will you know the right time to move from the kitchen table to "real" office space? A good indication that the time is right to move your office out of the attic is when you are financially ready. Let's say your business is growing at a steady pace. Your units are all rented, and you're just about to invest in more properties. Your home office space is overflowing and spilling into the hallway. It sounds like you're ready for a move. The key here is management. If you find that you are unable to manage from your home and that you are financially stable enough to rent office space or you have the opportunity to use one of your own commercial spaces, then the time is right. Pack up those files and have some signs created for your new office front door.

Planning for business growth can be tricky, however. Ideally, you should aim for steady growth. While you're still a small-time landlord and own a small number of units, sit down and create a business plan. Decide what types of rental property you want to acquire and when. Set an office-moving goal for yourself. Tell yourself that you will move into office space after you, for example, have bought five buildings or have income from a minimum of 20 units. No business plan is ever followed to the letter, but setting your goals and knowing what you want to accomplish will make it easier to get there.

When you do make the move, make a smart move. Find an office space that is close to your properties or the main bulk of your properties. Tenants and everyone else you do business with will be more inclined to conduct business with you if you're easy to find. Pick a location on a busy street. Have your business name in big, bold letters on a sign outside the office. Right next to that sign, have another sign that says "Vacancies" or "No appointment necessary" or anything that will draw people into your office. When looking for apartments, people will scan newspaper ads, but they will also be inclined to talk with a property owner who might have several vacancies from which to choose.

Rental Red Light!

When creating a business plan, don't forget to keep your eyes peeled to your local real-estate market. Landlords are in the investment business, and smart investing landlords make a good living only when they sell at the right time. Let's say you plan to move your office space next week because you've just bought rental property #5, and according to your business plan, the time is right. But you also have the opportunity to sell property #3, your lowest moneymaker. Should you hold on to #3 just because you've set a goal to only move when you own five buildings? No! A business plan is smart because it gives you direction, but it shouldn't guide your every move. Be flexible and do what's right for your investments. The "where" of managing your investments will fall into place when the time is right.

Taking the leap from your den to a "real" office will be scary and exciting at the same time. You will now be looked upon as having a "real" business. Like it or not, people who work from home get the shaft when it comes to respect. And you, too, might even feel that you are now "really in business" once you have a sign on the door and a waiting area with a cushy chair or two. Whether you decide to work from home or relocate outside the home, the important thing is that you stay in business in the first place! Be proud of your business, wherever it is. As the old saying goes, "Wherever you go, there you are."

The Least You Need to Know

- Acquire the basic supplies and more, such as a speakerphone, record-keeping files, and an easy-to-use computer, for an efficient office.

- Keep important records that pertain to your tenants, repairs, and anything that will protect you in court or from going to court. Keeping efficient accounting records will make tax time easier.

- A home office is manageable if you can set aside an area just for office space, can handle the extra hassles of not having an office space outside the home, and can preserve your home life.

- Create a business plan to help determine when to move out of your home office.

Chapter 22

Stay Informed and Get Involved!

In This Chapter

- ◆ The importance of rental organizations
- ◆ Advocating law revisions
- ◆ Joining a landlord organization
- ◆ Starting your own landlord organization

One of the most common comments from landlords is that they feel as if the laws and legislation governing the rental business affect them alone. Has anyone else suffered from a loss of income due to a long, drawn-out eviction? Has anyone else ever had his or her property destroyed? The answer to these and other questions is a resounding yes!

If you're just starting out, you might feel somewhat alone. A lone wolf, perhaps. Day to day, you'll have contact with your tenants, contractors, and employees (if you have any), but chances are you won't stumble across other landlords unless you find them in a group, perhaps waiting for their case to be heard in court. Groups of landlords do exist, however; it's just a matter of sniffing them out.

If you decide to take your involvement up a notch by advocating for law changes, you may find more than just safety in numbers. You will hopefully learn a thing or two and share your experiences with others. You also may find pride and satisfaction in the fact that you've made a difference (or tried to) in your profession. Perhaps you may even help to create ways in which to better enhance the return on your rental property investment.

Advocating Law Revisions

Don't have time to get involved? You won't think so the day a tenant beats you in court on a technicality that you overlooked in the eviction process. You won't think so the day you find your rental unit heavily damaged by the last tenant, and you aren't able to have the tenant arrested. It's easy to get angry about the legal system on the days when things aren't going your way. But what can you do about it? Join a landlord organization! Call your legislator! Why not? Tenants often have their own organizations, and sometimes these organizations can be quite influential with area legislators who have the power to change and create legislation that seriously affects rental owners.

Often, landlord organizations work to create changes in legislation affecting rental owners. Sometimes organizations like this physically testify at their respective state capitals about a particular piece of legislation, or they hire a lobbyist to work the floors of the legislature and help make changes.

Change doesn't usually come without a price. The price you can expect to pay might be nothing more than the annual dues paid to belong to a landlord organization, or it might be your welcomed volunteer efforts in support and leadership of a landlord organization.

Facts for Rent _____

Founded in 1978, the Washington, D.C.–based National Multi Housing Council (NMHC) is an advocacy and consulting organization for large apartment firms. NMHC is also a partner to the National Apartment Association (NAA) and works with branches of the U.S. government to promote favorable rental housing policies. The organization conducts research on housing trends and also releases the annual NMHC 50, a ranking of the 50 largest apartment owners and 50 largest apartment managers. There is some freebie content available on the NMHC website (www.nmhc.org), but most is reserved for paying members.

The important thing to understand, regardless of your decision, is that change doesn't happen overnight. Typically, much effort is required to make even the most miniscule of changes in existing legislation. Try not to become frustrated by an apparent lack of progress. Remember that it took several years to create the kind of lopsided legislation that many rental owners face, and it will take several more years to balance the scale.

Join a Local Property-Owner Organization

If you do know some other landlords, call them and find out if any organizations exist in your area. There might be a state organization or one organized by county or city. You might have to latch onto an organization that's a bit out of your area, such as in another county.

No matter where your organization is located, it can still be worth the drive. Most landlords have the same concerns about tenants, laws, and rights. These groups provide a place for landlords to share basic office gossip and talk shop. Joining with others of your kind will make your job easier because you can talk with people who go through the same thing you do every day. Many landlords joke that belonging to a landlord organization is much like belonging to a support group. It's a great place to share your war stories and gain support from people who truly understand your pain.

The best part of belonging to such a group is having the capability to access a wealth of information regarding the rental industry. Landlords who come together will share important tips about rental techniques, tenants, and rental market and sale information. A landlord who attends these types of groups should listen and take notes because the information will prove invaluable.

If you are not friendly with other landlords in your area, you should ask town employees, such as a building or housing inspector, about the existence of such organizations. The secretary of state may be able to tell you whether any such organizations are registered with the state

Edwards' Advice

When checking out landlord organizations, try to stick to the state in which your property is located (unless you join an organization on the web). A lot of discussion among the members will revolve around state and local statutes.

Edwards' Advice

A smart landlord never stops learning! Landlord organizations help educate rental owners so that they can make only the best decisions regarding their rental properties. Join one and learn new ways to help yourself.

and where they are located. Most states have a rental housing or landlord organization that may be affiliated with local chapters, perhaps even in your area. Appendix C lists some of the many organizations across the country, including some with websites.

Nothing to Join? Start Your Own!

Starting your own organization takes a lot of time and effort. A lot of "good idea organizations" fall flat even though starting up and getting that first meeting on the calendar is easy. Keeping the organization and the attendance record going is another story. Be sure you really can devote time to the cause so that you're not disappointed in yourself or others further down the road.

Edwards' Advice

When deciding on a dues structure, try to keep dues fairly low. Make sure your members get a real bang for their buck. Most landlords are happy to pay as much as $50 a year if they are getting something in return such as a newsletter, monthly meetings, or lobbyist representation at the state capital.

Rental Red Light!

Decisions will have to be made regarding your landlord organization. You might need to incorporate as either a for-profit or nonprofit organization. Speak with an attorney regarding the incorporation and tax requirements for certain types of corporations.

When considering the startup of an organization, ask yourself the following questions before making any calls:

- **What kind of an organization do I want it to be?** Do you want to produce a newsletter? Do you want to just meet socially? Do you want to fight legislation? Do you want to meet just to share info? If you have a few ideas but are not sure, take a survey. Call other landlords and ask them what kind of organization they'd like to join, if they were to join one.

- **Who do I know?** Make a list of people who might be interested in joining. Not just property owners but town officials who have been heard saying, "It would be great to talk with several landlords in one group setting." Okay, so you probably won't hear that, but if you go to enough town meetings, you'll know who might be interested. If you don't go to town meetings, you should start. Sometimes local officials such as assessors or economic developers keep lists of rental owners who own property in the town, and they might permit you to have a copy of the list.

♦ **Will anyone come?** Don't go back to the second question just yet to revise the list from "people you know" to "people you know who will really show up." Call everyone, but if you're getting lukewarm responses and only you and your friend Bart actually show up to the first meeting, don't get discouraged. Try a different approach or call everyone who didn't show. Remain persistent. Send a newsletter or a flier describing the last meeting as well as future ones. Put together a calendar of events and be sure to list future meeting dates.

♦ **Is there a concern or recent law that will get people involved?** People are most often called to action when something really irks them, especially if that something has really affected their business. If there is a local concern or something that unaware landlords should be concerned about, you should mention it to as many of them as possible. Put this information in the newsletter.

♦ **Do you have a place to go?** Think twice about holding meetings in your basement. This might be good for starters, but home meetings have two strikes against them: (1) It's hard to get rid of people, and you can't leave to go home because you already are; and (2) Conducting meetings in a home setting leads to very casual talk. A laid-back and comfortable organization is fine (there's no need to be militant), but if you're meeting to actually accomplish something, it won't happen on a couch. Find a school classroom or a place in the town hall, community center, or any local gathering place.

Starting an organization takes a lot of time, but it is worth it. If you can enlist the help of other property owners, the organization has a better chance of getting off the ground—and staying there.

Stay Informed Through the Internet

Several different websites are devoted to the rental industry. These websites offer a wealth of information including rental tips, legal advice, advertisements, referrals, and state statute information. Some require that you join for a small fee, but all provide valuable sources of information. Here are some of the popular sites we were able to find:

www.mrlandlord.com

www.rhol.com (Rental Housing On Line)

www.nmhc.org (National Multi Housing Council)

www.aptbiz.com

www.landlord.com

www.landlordportal.com

The Least You Need to Know

◆ Rental owners who feel they are the only ones having a hard time must understand that they are not alone. There are others who have come together to share ideas and thoughts, and these people can be of help.

◆ Landlords must be cautious and not become discouraged when attempting to make changes in legislation affecting their industry.

◆ Starting your own organization takes time, patience, and organization.

◆ Landlord organizations work to educate, share ideas, and make changes that will have a positive effect on both their state and local communities.

Useful Forms

The following are sample forms that may be used by landlords and property managers in the operation of their rental business. Please read the forms carefully before using and make sure that each will fit your needs.

Rental Application

_____

Full Name

_____

Co-Applicant Name

_____

Your Date of Birth

_____

Co-Applicant's Date of Birth

Present Address (# Street, City, State, Zip Code)

_____

_____

_____

Present Monthly Rent $_____

Present Tel# _____

How Long at This Address?_____

Soc. Security# _____/____/_____

Drivers License# _____

Co-App. Soc. Sec.# _____/____/_____

Drivers License# _____

Co-Applicant Tel# _____

OTHER MEMBERS OF HOUSEHOLD LIVING WITH YOU, VEHICLES:
Make, Model, ID#

_____

_____

_____

Full Name, Age, Soc. Sec.#, and Gender:

_____

_____

_____

Closest Relative (Name, Address, Phone#, Relationship)

_____

_____

_____

List any pets you may have and describe them:

_____

_____

_____

Have you ever been evicted?   YES   NO (Describe circumstances)

_____

_____

_____

Present Landlord's Name and Telephone#

_____

_____

_____

Present Landlord's Address   (Street#, City, State, Zip Code)

_____

_____

_____

Previous Address and Telephone#

_____

_____

_____

Present Landlord's Address   (Street#, City, State, Zip Code)

_____

_____

_____

APPLICATION FORM PAGE 2 OF 2

LAWFUL SOURCE OF INCOME INFORMATION (YOU) INCOME

_____

_____

_____

Your Source of Income   How Long?   Telephone#

_____

_____

Co-Applicant's Employer Name and Address   How Long?   Telephone#

_____

_____

Co-Applicant's Source of Income   How Long?   Telephone#   Other

_____

_____

Co-Applicant's Employer Name and Address   How Long?   Telephone#
Total Income

_____

_____

_____

YOUR MONTHLY RENT CANNOT EXCEED ___% OF YOUR MONTHLY SPENDABLE INCOME TO QUALIFY.

Banks you use:

_____

Name: Location: Account#

The applicant warrants that all information contained herein is true, and hereby authorizes the release of this information for the purpose of a credit check.

_____

Applicant Signature: Date:

Credit Check Release

I/We hereby apply for the apartment listed above, with my/our signature(s) below, I/We hereby authorize and request all credit reporting agencies, employers, credit and personal references release all pertinent information about me/us. A photocopy of this shall be as valid as the original. I/We understand that the credit report (rental history, arrest and/or conviction records, and retail credit history) will be done at the facilities of Company Name, Address, Consumer Telephone Number_____. Credit.

Signed: _____   Date: _____

Signed: _____   Date: _____

Signed: _____   Date: _____

*THE CREDIT CHECK FEE IS $_____ PER ADULT {Out of State $_____} AND THE COST OF THIS CREDIT CHECK IS THE RESPONSIBILITY OF THE APPLICANT. **THIS FEE IS NOT REFUNDABLE.**

Deposit Agreement

Deposit $ _____   Applicant Signature: _____

Unit Address: _____

Deposits are not refundable and will hold
the apartment at _____ until _____.

OFFICE USE ONLY   ACCEPTED   Rejected

Lease Agreement

Both the lessor and lessee for and in consideration and covenants hereinafter reserved
and contained, to be paid, kept and fulfilled on the part of the lessee and the lessor
hereby enter into the following agreement:

Date _____

Dated at _____

Lessor _____

Address _____

Owner of Record _____

Agent for Owner _____

Lessee _____

Address: _____

_____

_____

Leased Premises _____

Term of Lease _____

Lease Start Date _____ Lease Stop Date _____

Yearly Amount $ _____ Monthly Amount $ _____

Monthly payments are due on the first day of the month with payments to begin on _____. If not paid by the _____ day a _____% late fee will be charged $ _____.

Payments are to be made to

_____

Address: _____

_____

_____

Security Deposit Paid _____ First Month Paid _____
Last Month Paid _____

Animal Deposit _____

Deposit Agreement_____ See Addendum _____

Unit to Be Used as _____ No. of Occupants _____

Full Name _____

Date of Birth _____ Social Security No. ____-_____-_____

All occupants who will be living in unit:

Name   D-O-B   Social Security No.

1. _____   _____   ____-_____-_____

2. _____   _____   ____-_____-_____

3. _____   _____   ____-_____-_____

4. _____   _____   ____-_____-_____

5. _____   _____   ____-_____-_____

An additional fee of $ _____ pcr month will be charged for each additional occupants not on the lease.

Make of auto and marker number _____

Are you or any occupants now in the U.S. military service?

Yes _____   No _____

Branch _____ Date of Discharge _____ I.D. _____.

If you or any occupant should enlist in the military service while occupying this unit you must notify the lessor in writing.

Signature _____

Appliances in unit _____

Lessor does not take responsibility for the repair or replacement of appliances.

Lessee to pay for: Water _____ Sewer _____ Gas _____ Oil_____ Electricity_____ Telephone _____ Cable T.V. _____

Lessee agrees to provide _____ fuel for the purpose of a steady flow of energy to heat the unit to a temperature of at least ___ degrees and accepts responsibility for any damage caused by lack of sufficient fuel creating damage to the unit or the heating equipment.

Signature _____

Number of smoke detectors in unit _____

Lessee has inspected all smoke detectors in the unit and has found them to be in good working condition and agrees not to tamper with them and if said detectors become in need of repair lessee agrees to contact the lessor in writing of their disrepair.

Signature _____

Lessee understands and covenants that taking occupancy of this leased unit makes them the controlling factor of this unit and does by this action take full responsibility for upkeep and compliance with all state federal and local codes. Lessee agrees to contact the lessor in writing of any noncompliance.

The taking possession of the leased premises shall be conclusive evidence that the lessee has examined the unit and building that the unit is in, with all common areas, and that they were in good condition at the time of occupancy. For the purpose of this clause the word lease shall also include month-to-month tenancy.

Lessee agrees to insure (Tenants Insurance) against all losses that may occur to him- or herself or visitors or occupants, and name the lessor as additional insured on the policy.

In the event environmental conditions are found to exist at the premises and the health and safety of the occupants is determined to be in jeopardy, the lessee agrees to vacate the premises and this lease will become null and void.

Signature _____

Lessee agrees to the following:

1. To make no repairs without the consent of the lessor.

2. To repair at his or her cost all damage made to the unit including glass, heat, air-conditioning, electrical, plumbing, hot water.

3. To keep sidewalks, steps, and parking areas free and clear of ice and snow.

4. To keep grass cut and hedges trimmed adjacent to his or her unit.

5. To allow the lessor access to the unit for the purpose of examining, to show the unit to prospective tenants or buyers, and to make repairs or general inspections.

6. The lessor may enter the unit in the case of an emergency without the lessee's permission.

7. The lessee agrees to obtain rental insurance.

8. At the termination of this lease leave the unit in good condition.

9. To leave behind any fixture added to this unit.

10. Not to leave behind rubbish or furniture when vacated.

11. To remove all rubbish to the curb for town trash pickup or remove to a removal area.

12. To abide by all state, federal, and local codes including fire codes.

13. Not to add to or take from the property without the lessor's permission.

14. Not to keep animals without the lessor's written permission.

15. Not to assign or sell this lease without the lessor's written permission.

16. Not to park cars or apparatus in other leased areas.

Severability Clause: In the event any clause in this lease should be found to be unenforceable then that clause alone shall be deemed defective from this lease and the rest of this lease will remain in force.

In the event that the monthly payment is not received within __ days of the due date for payment, the lessee understands that legal procedures as prescribed by state law can and will begin. All reasonable costs of sheriff, court, lawyer, movers, administration, and collections will be owed by the lessee.

The lessee agrees that this lease is and shall be subject and subordinate to all mortgages now or to be placed on the property. This clause shall be self-operative.

In the event the premises are damaged or destroyed by fire or other disaster or acquired for public use, then this lease, at the option of the lessor, shall cease and terminate and the lessee will have no claim for damages.

In the event the lessee remains or transfers to another unit owned or managed by the lessor during or after the start or stop dates of this lease without signing a new lease, or has his or her lease terminated by a notice to quit, a holdover tenancy will exist and all terms and conditions of this lease will prevail.

Parking is provided by permission only and can be revoked at any time by the lessor or his or her agents. Unregistered cars will be towed at the owner's expense.

All checks returned by the bank unpaid will be subject to a $_____ charge.

HAND AND SEAL

Lessor _____ **Date** _____

Lessee _____ **Date** _____

Lessee _____ **Date** _____

Co-signer Name _____ **Soc. Sec. No.** ____-_____-_____

Address _____

Signature _____ **Date** _____

The co-signer agrees to conform to all aspects of this lease in the event that the lessee defaults on his or her obligations.

ADDENDUM

Move-In Letter

Date _____

Dear _____

May I welcome you to your new home and I wish you and your family an enjoyable stay. The purpose of this letter is to spell out what you can expect from management and what we will expect from you during your stay.

1. Rent:

Your rent will be due on the first day of the month and should be paid to this address:

_____.

2. New Roommates:

If you plan to have someone move into the unit who is not on the lease, he or she will need to fill out an application and be approved for the unit before moving in.

3. Notice to End Tenancy:

We will need from you a 30-day notice to vacate. We will contact you 30 days prior to your lease renewal date to resign a new lease.

4. Deposits:

We will hold your deposit in an interest-bearing account and will return it to you with interest within _____ days after you vacate the unit. In the event that you stay on for another year you can receive the interest earned upon the anniversary of your lease or rental agreement.

5. Manager:

The name of the person who is acting as manager of the unit you occupy is

_____.

6. Landlord-Tenant Checklist:

A checklist of property condition will be recorded at the time of occupancy and the checklist will be updated at the time you leave the unit.

7. Maintenance/Repair Problems:

Please contact _____ at telephone number _____ to report problems at your unit.

8. **Annual Safety and Maintenance Update:**

We will be doing an inspection of the property you live in to determine safety and maintenance regarding smoke detectors and fixtures. We will contact you to make an appointment.

9. **Insurance:**

You will be responsible for your belongings and you might want to obtain renters insurance.

10. **Telephone Number Changes:**

If you have a change in your telephone number, please contact us with the change.

Sincerely,

Please sign and return.

Date _____

Signature _____

Move-Out Letter

Date _____

Dear _____

We have been informed that you plan to vacate the unit you occupy.

Please note our policy regarding vacating units.

All units will be inspected after the tenant leaves the unit and the checklist used when occupied will be updated to note repair.

The cost of repair not considered ordinary wear and tear will be deducted from the security deposit being held by us.

We have included a copy of the checklist you signed at the time of occupancy.

Please look it over and repair or clean as needed all the categories listed on the checklist.

If you have any questions regarding the type of cleaning expected, please call us.

Please don't leave anything behind.

The unit was empty when you took occupancy and we expect it to be empty when you leave.

You should cancel all services ordered by you and change your address with the postal service.

You will need to return the keys to the unit or you will be charged to change the locks.

Please provide us with your new address so that we can return your deposit to you.

If you have any questions, please contact me at telephone number _____.

Sincerely,

Address _____

Telephone _____

Fax _____

Original Tenant and New Tenant Addition to Lease

Date _____

Dear _____

Please be advised that I am the person authorized to lease the premises known as
_____.

I have reviewed the application of _____ and am pleased to inform you that _____ has been accepted.

Please note that before _____ (new tenant) can move in, both you and _____ must sign a new lease for the premises you occupy.

Please contact me at your earliest convenience so that we can arrange a time to meet and sign a new lease.

Sincerely,

Address _____

Telephone _____

Fax _____

_____ (Landlord)

_____ (Address)

_____ (City and state)

_____ (Phone)

Transfer of Ownership Notice

Date _____

To _____

Please be advised that the property that you occupy has transferred ownership.

The new owner is _____.

Please direct all rental payments, inquiries, or questions regarding the property to us at _____.

Sincerely,

Address _____

Telephone _____

Fax _____

Property Management Agreement

Property Location _____

Date _____

Owner of Record _____

Address _____

Telephone _____

Fax _____

Type of Property _____

The _____Co. hereby enters into an agreement for property management services for the above-mentioned property with the above owner of record.

This agreement is for a term of _____ year[s] and will begin on _____ and end on _____.

If at the date of termination a new agreement is not signed but management continues, all the terms and conditions of this agreement will remain in force.

The owner[s] hereby assigns the _____Co. as agents to collect rents, advertise, negotiate, sign leases, coordinate maintenance and repair, hold and disperse monies, and in general act as the owner's representatives in matters regarding the property.

The owner[s] hereby agrees to maintain fire and liability insurance on the property and agrees to hold the _____Co. harmless from any litigation regarding the property.

The _____Co. does not by this agreement assume the owner's responsibility nor liability of ownership:

The _____Co. shall receive a fee based as follows:

_____% of collections.

$_____ per hour rate for general maintenance.

Dollar for dollar for vendor contract services.

One month rent for unit rental or leasing.

All the expense of operation will be extracted from monies collected unless the collections do not cover the cost of operations, whereas it will become the owner's responsibility to subsidize the amount needed to cover the cost.

The owner[s] hereby authorizes the _____Co. to place a management sign on the property for the duration of this agreement.

Owner[s] signature _____

Date _____

Signature _____

Property Manager _____

Date _____

Address _____

LEAD PAINT ADDENDUM TO LEASE

Tenant has received a disclosure form and booklet regarding lead paint.

I/We the undersigned tenant, do hereby acknowledge and agree that the premises that I/We are leasing and that I/We and the above members of my family and or invites are entitled to occupy and use are:

The space within the visible painted/finished surfaces of the walls, floors, and ceiling, including those surfaces of the doors, windows, and other furnished attachments to said surfaces. I further acknowledge and agree that I and the named members of my family and/or invites, have no right, control, or access to any portion of the structure of these premises, above, below, behind, or within said surfaces, which remain the sole possession of the landlord. I further agree and acknowledge that I can not and shall not affect said surfaces in any way including, but not limited to breaking, tearing, piercing, painting, or attaching anything without first requesting permission to do so in writing and delivered to the landlord for his or her approval. No such approval shall be considered valid, or in existence unless expressed in writing, signed and delivered to the tenant.

I/We further expressly agree and warranty as tenant to the landlord, that if any person shall attempt to perform any act, by hand, instrument, or tool affecting any portion of the space, or materials beneath said visible painted/finished surfaces, that I shall inform them of the above restrictions and shall there and then deny them access to said surfaces, until such time as notice has been given to the landlord and he or she has responded in writing, or until such time as a order from the Superior Court, addressed to the landlord has been given to me pursuant to State Law.

If I/We or any person acting on my behalf, or with my permission shall cause violation of the above terms, conditions, or warranty, I/We hereby acknowledge and agree that I/We shall be fully liable and responsible to pay to the landlord all fees, penalties, fines, and or costs of repair and or remediation required within, or without of the leased premises as a result of the breach of the above terms, conditions and/or warranty.

Lessor _____ Date _____

Lessee _____ Date _____

Repair Form

Date _____

Name of tenant: _____

Address: _____

_____

_____

Dear _____

We have received notice that your unit is need of repair.

We will have the problem investigated on _____, at approximately _____ (time of day).

We expect to be able to complete the repair at that time but in the event we cannot we will notify you of the time constraints we will have regarding the completion of the repair.

Sincerely,

Address: _____

_____

_____

Telephone _____

Fax _____

Return of Deposit Form

Date _____

Name of tenant _____

Address: _____

              _____

              _____

Regarding the vacated apartment

Dear _____

Enclosed please find a check in the amount of $_____

Breakdown is as follows:

Security Deposit Paid $_____

Repairs $_____

Total $_____

Interest Earned $_____ Total $_____

Good luck in your new apartment.

Sincerely,

Date _____

Security Deposit Itemization

Date _____

Name of tenant _____

Property address _____

Dear _____

Please be advised that you vacated your apartment on _____.

Our records indicate that you had a security deposit held by us in the amount of
$ _____.

Security Deposit Received: $ _____

Interest on Deposit: $ _____

Total: $ _____

Itemized Repairs

_____

_____

_____

Total Repair Cost: $ _____

Total Cleaning Cost: $ _____

Legal Cost: $ _____

Other Deductions

_____

_____

_____

Total Cost: $ _____

Security Deposit Held: $ _____

Amount Owed by Tenant: $ _____

Amount Owed to Tenant: $_____

Please Remit: $_____

Sincerely,

Address _____

Telephone _____

Fax _____

Termination Notice

Date _____

This notice is to alert you that the lease you entered into on _____ will terminate on _____ for the premises you occupy at _____.

Please note that unless a new lease is signed before the date of termination, you will
have to vacate the premises on or before the termination date.

Please contact us to make arrangements to sign a new lease or schedule a date to vacate
the unit.

Sincerely,

Address _____

Telephone _____

Fax _____

Towing Form

Date _____

Address _____

_____

_____

To Whom It May Concern:

RE: [Description of vehicle]

VIN #_____

Please be advised that in compliance with Town of _____ regulations, unregistered vehicles are not allowed on the property you occupy.

A towing service has been instructed to remove the vehicle.

If you do not wish to have your vehicle towed, please remove it immediately or contact us to make arrangements for the removal.

The cost of removal and storage will be the owner's responsibility.

Sincerely,

Address _____

_____

_____

Telephone _____

Fax _____

Notice of Intent to Enter Dwelling

Date _____

Address _____

Dear _____

This is to inform you that on _____ at _____ (time of day) we will need to enter the unit you occupy for the following reason.

To make repairs to the following:

_____

_____

To show the premises to the following:

_____

Other:

_____

_____

_____

We would like you to be there at the time we need to enter the unit. Please notify us if the date or time is inconvenient or if you object to us entering your unit as scheduled.

Sincerely,

Address _____

_____

_____

Telephone _____

Fax _____

Unit Condition Checklist

Location _____

Move-In Condition _____

Move-Out Condition _____

Heat/Air _____

Electric _____

Yard _____

Deck/Porch/Steps _____

Garage _____

Living Room

Smoke Detector _____

Light Fixtures _____

Shades/Blinds _____

Window _____

Floor/Carpet _____

Walls _____

Ceiling _____

Kitchen

Smoke Detector _____

Refrigerator _____

Stove/Exhaust Fan _____

Cabinets/Counters _____

Sink/Faucet _____

Floors _____

Windows _____

Shades/Blinds _____

Light Fixtures _____

Walls/Ceiling _____

Dining Room

Smoke Detector _____

Walls/Ceiling _____

Floor/Carpet _____

Window _____

Light Fixtures _____

Shades/Blinds _____

Bathroom

Wall/Ceiling _____

Tub/Shower _____

Sink/Faucet _____

Toilet _____

Racks/Cabinets _____

Floors _____

Window/Fan _____

Light Fixtures _____

Blinds/Shades _____

Hallway

Smoke Detector _____

Walls/Ceiling _____

Floor _____

Bedroom

Smoke Detector _____

Walls _____

Ceiling _____

Floor _____

Window _____

Shades/Blinds _____

Light Fixtures _____

Signature_____

Move-In _____ Move-Out _____

Statutes for Landlord-Tenant Laws

The following states have adopted the U.S. federal government's Uniform Residential Landlord & Tenant Act: Alaska, Arizona, Florida, Hawaii, Iowa, Kansas, Kentucky, Montana, Nebraska, New Mexico, Oregon, Rhode Island, South Carolina, Tennessee, and Virginia. The remaining states have written their own laws. Separate laws regarding mobile/manufactured homes, co-ops, condos, or vacation rentals have been noted for each state.

Main Statutes

The following list shows the main statutes for all 50 states plus Washington, D.C. Some states may have amended their landlord-tenants laws, so be sure to get the latest info from your consumer protection agency or check out your local landlord website (see Appendix C).

Alabama

AL Code: Title 35 (§§35-9-1 to –100)
RENT RULES: —-
SECURITY DEPOSIT: —-
NONPAYMENT OF RENT: —-
BREACH OF LEASE: §35-9-6
RENT WITHHOLDING: —-
REPAIR AND DEDUCT: —-
LL ACCESS: —-
LL RETALIATION: —-

Alaska

AS Statute: Title 34/Chapter 3 (§§34.03.010 to .380)
RENT RULES: §34.03.020(c)
SECURITY DEPOSIT: §34.03.070
NONPAYMENT OF RENT: §09.45.105
BREACH OF LEASE: §§09.45.090; 09.50.210; 34.03.220
RENT WITHHOLDING: §34.03.190
REPAIR AND DEDUCT: §34.03.180
LL ACCESS: §§34.03.140; .300 (a)&(b)
LL RETALIATION: § 34.03.310(a)&.360

Arizona

AZ Rev. Statute: Title 33/Chapter 3 (§§33-301 to -381);
Title 33/Chapter 10 (§§33-1301 to -1381); Title 12/Chapter 8 (§§12-1171 to –1183)
RENT RULES: §33-1314(B),(C)
SECURITY DEPOSIT: §33-1321 NON-PAYMENT OF RENT: §33-1368(B)
BREACH OF LEASE: §33-1368(A)
RENT WITHHOLDING: §33-1365
REPAIR AND DEDUCT: §33-1363, 1364
LL ACCESS: §33-1343
LL RETALIATION: §33-1381

Other: Title 33/Chapter 9 (Condominiums); Title 33/Chapter 11 (Mobile Home Parks)

Arkansas

AK Code: Title 18, Chapter 16 (§§18-16-101 to –306); Title 20, Chapter 27 (§§20-27-601 to –608)
RENT RULES: —
SECURITY DEPOSIT: §§18-16-301 to -306
NONPAYMENT OF RENT: §§18-16-101, -201
BREACH OF LEASE: —
RENT WITHHOLDING: —
REPAIR AND DEDUCT: —
LL ACCESS: —
LL RETALIATION: §20-27-608

California

CA Civil Code: Division 3/Part 4/Title 5/Chapters 1–7 (§§1925-1997.270)
RENT RULES: §1942
SECURITY DEPOSIT: §1950.5
NONPAYMENT OF RENT: §§1161, 1162
BREACH OF LEASE: §1161
RENT WITHHOLDING: Green v. Sup. Ct: 10 Cal. 3d 616 (1974)
REPAIR AND DEDUCT: Civ. Code §1942
LL ACCESS: §1954
LL RETALIATION: §§1942.5

Other: Division 2/Part 2/Title 2/Chapter 2.5 (Mobile Home), Chapter 2.6 (Recreational Vehicle Park) and 2.7 (Floating Home)

Colorado

CO Rev. Statute (§§38-12-101 to -104; 38-12-301; 13-40-101 to –13-80-104)
RENT RULES: —
SECURITY DEPOSIT: §§ 38-12-102, -103, -104
NONPAYMENT OF RENT: §13-40-104
BREACH OF LEASE: §13-40-104(1)(e)
RENT WITHHOLDING: —
REPAIR AND DEDUCT: Shanahan v. Collins, 539 P.2d 1261 (Colo. 1975).
LL ACCESS: —
LL RETALIATION: —

Connecticut

CT Gen. Statute: Title 47a/Chapter 830 (§§47a-1 to –74)
RENT RULES: §§47a-3a, -15a, -4a(8)
SECURITY DEPOSIT: §47a-21, -22a
NONPAYMENT OF RENT: §§47a-15a, -23
BREACH OF LEASE: §47a-15
RENT WITHHOLDING: §§47a-14a, -14h
REPAIR AND DEDUCT: §47a-13
LL ACCESS: §§47a-16 to -16a
LL RETALIATION: §§47a-20, 47a-33

Delaware

DE Code: Title 25/Chapters 53 and 55 (§§5101-7114)
RENT RULES: §§5501
SECURITY DEPOSIT: §5114
NONPAYMENT OF RENT: §5502
BREACH OF LEASE: §5513
RENT WITHHOLDING: §5308
REPAIR AND DEDUCT: §5307
LL ACCESS: §§5509, 5510
LL RETALIATION: §5516

Other: Title 25/Chapter 70 (Manufactured Homes); Title 25/Chapter 71
(Conversion of Manufactured Homes to Condo or Co-op)

Washington, D.C.

D.C. Code §§45-1401 to -1597, -2501 to -2593
RENT RULES: §45-2514 to -2519
SECURITY DEPOSIT: §45-2527; Mun. Regs. Title 14 §§308-311i
NONPAYMENT OF RENT: §45-2551
BREACH OF LEASE: §45-2551
RENT WITHHOLDING: Javins v. First Nat'l Realty: 428 F.2d 1071 (DC circ.
1970)
REPAIR AND DEDUCT: —-
LL ACCESS: —-
LL RETALIATION: §45-2552

Florida

FL Statute §§83.40 to .681
RENT RULES: §83.46
SECURITY DEPOSIT: §83.49
NONPAYMENT OF RENT: §83.20, 83.56(3)
BREACH OF LEASE: §83.56
RENT WITHHOLDING: §§83.60, .201, .232
REPAIR AND DEDUCT: —
LL ACCESS: §83.53
LL RETALIATION: §83.64

Georgia

GA Code §§44-7-1 to -81
RENT RULES: §§44-7-1 to -16
SECURITY DEPOSIT: §44-7-30 to -36
NONPAYMENT OF RENT: §44-7-52
BREACH OF LEASE: —
RENT WITHHOLDING: §44-7-54
REPAIR AND DEDUCT: —
LL ACCESS: —
LL RETALIATION: —

Hawaii

HI Rev. Statute §§521-1 to -78
RENT RULES: §521-21(b)
SECURITY DEPOSIT: §521-44
NONPAYMENT OF RENT: §§521-68(a),(b)
BREACH OF LEASE: §§521-69, -51
RENT WITHHOLDING: §521-78
REPAIR AND DEDUCT: §521-64
LL ACCESS: §521-53 LL RETALIATION: HI §521.74

Idaho

ID Code §§6-301 to –324; 55-201 to -313
RENT RULES: §§55-301 to -313
SECURITY DEPOSIT: —
NONPAYMENT OF RENT: §6-303
BREACH OF LEASE: §6-303
RENT WITHHOLDING: —
REPAIR AND DEDUCT: —
LL ACCESS: —
LL RETALIATION: §§55-2015; Wright v. Brandy, 126 Idaho 671, 889 P.2d 105 (Ct. App. 1995)

Illinois

IL Rev. Statute Chap. 765 para. 705/0.01-740/5
RENT RULES: —
SECURITY DEPOSIT: Ch. 765 para. 710, 715
NONPAYMENT OF RENT: Ch. 735 para. 5/9-209
BREACH OF LEASE: —
RENT WITHHOLDING: Ch. 765 para. 710/1
REPAIR AND DEDUCT: —
LL ACCESS: —
LL RETALIATION: Ch. 765 para. 720/1

Indiana

IN Code §§32-7-1-1 to 37-7-19
RENT RULES: Watson v. Penn, 108 Ind. 21, 8 NE 636
SECURITY DEPOSIT: §§32-7-5-1 to -19
NONPAYMENT OF RENT: §32-7-1-5 BREACH OF LEASE: —
RENT WITHHOLDING: —
REPAIR AND DEDUCT: —
LL ACCESS: —
LL RETALIATION: —

Iowa

IA Code §§562A.1-.37
RENT RULES: §562A.9
SECURITY DEPOSIT: §562A.12
NONPAYMENT OF RENT: §562A.27
BREACH OF LEASE: §562A.27, .27A
RENT WITHHOLDING: §562A.24
REPAIR AND DEDUCT: §562A.23
LL ACCESS: §§562A.19, .28, .29
LL RETALIATION: §562A.36

Kansas

KS Statute §§58-2501 to -2512; 58-2540 to -2573
RENT RULES: §58-2545
SECURITY DEPOSIT: §58-2550
NONPAYMENT OF RENT: §§58-2507, -2508, -2564
BREACH OF LEASE: §58-2559, -2564
RENT WITHHOLDING: §58-2561
REPAIR AND DEDUCT: —
LL ACCESS: §§58-2557, -2565
LL RETALIATION: §58-2572

Kentucky

KY Rev. Statute §§383.010-.715
RENT RULES: §383.565
SECURITY DEPOSIT: §383.580
NONPAYMENT OF RENT: §383.660
BREACH OF LEASE: §383.660
RENT WITHHOLDING: §383.645
REPAIR AND DEDUCT: §§383.635, .640
LL ACCESS: §§383.615, .665
LL RETALIATION: §383.705

Louisiana

LA Rev. Statute §§9:3201-:3261; Civil Code of Procedure 2668-2744
RENT RULES: —
SECURITY DEPOSIT: §9:3251
NONPAYMENT OF RENT: CCP §4701; 9:3259
BREACH OF LEASE: CCP §4701
RENT WITHHOLDING: —
REPAIR AND DEDUCT: Civil Code Ann. art. 2694
LL ACCESS: —
LL RETALIATION: —

Maine

ME Title 14 §6001 to 6045
RENT RULES: § 6028
SECURITY DEPOSIT: §§6031-6038
NONPAYMENT OF RENT: ME Title 14 §6002
BREACH OF LEASE: — RENT WITHHOLDING: §6025
REPAIR AND DEDUCT: §6026
LL ACCESS: §6025
LL RETALIATION: §6001

Maryland

MD Code §§8-101 to -501
RENT RULES: §8-208(3)
SECURITY DEPOSIT: §8-203
NONPAYMENT OF RENT: §8-401
BREACH OF LEASE: §8-402.1
RENT WITHHOLDING: §§8-118, -211, 211.1
REPAIR AND DEDUCT: —
LL ACCESS: —
LL RETALIATION: §§8-206, -208.1, -208.2

Massachusetts

MA Gen. Laws Chapter 186 §§1-21
RENT RULES: Ch. 186 §§11, 15B(1)(c)
SECURITY DEPOSIT: Ch. 186 §15B
NONPAYMENT OF RENT: Ch. 186 §§11, 11A, 12
BREACH OF LEASE: —
RENT WITHHOLDING: Ch. 239 §8A
REPAIR AND DEDUCT: Ch. 186 §14
LL ACCESS: Ch. 186 §15B1(a)
LL RETALIATION: Ch. 239 §2A; Ch. 186 §18

Michigan

MI Comp. Laws §§554.601-.640
RENT RULES: Hilsendegen v. Scheich, 55 Mich. 468
SECURITY DEPOSIT: §§554.602-.613
NONPAYMENT OF RENT: §27A.5714
BREACH OF LEASE: §27A.5714
RENT WITHHOLDING: §125.530
REPAIR AND DEDUCT: —
LL ACCESS: —
LL RETALIATION: §27A.5720

Minnesota

MN Statute §§609.5317; 504B.001 to .385; 363.02-.03; 299.67-.69; 216.095-.097
RENT RULES: —
SECURITY DEPOSIT: §504B.178
NONPAYMENT OF RENT: §504B.291
BREACH OF LEASE: §504B.281
RENT WITHHOLDING: §504B.441
REPAIR AND DEDUCT: §504B.385
LL ACCESS: §504B.211
LL RETALIATION: §504B.411

Mississippi

MS Code §§89-8-1 to -27
RENT RULES: —-
SECURITY DEPOSIT: §89-8-21
NONPAYMENT OF RENT: §89-7-27
BREACH OF LEASE: §89-8-13
RENT WITHHOLDING: —-
REPAIR AND DEDUCT: §89-8-15
LL ACCESS: —-
LL RETALIATION: —-

Missouri

MO Statute §§441.005-.880; 535.010-.300
RENT RULES: —-
SECURITY DEPOSIT: §535.300
NONPAYMENT OF RENT: —-
BREACH OF LEASE: —-
RENT WITHHOLDING: §441.580
REPAIR AND DEDUCT: §441.234
LL ACCESS: —-
LL RETALIATION: —-

Montana

MT Code §§70-24-101 to -442; 70-25-101 to -206
RENT RULES: §§70-24-201
SECURITY DEPOSIT: §§70-25-201 to -206
NONPAYMENT OF RENT: §70-24-422(2)(b)
BREACH OF LEASE: §70-24-422
RENT WITHHOLDING: §70-24-421
REPAIR AND DEDUCT: §§70-24-406, -407, -408
LL ACCESS: §70-24-312
LL RETALIATION: §70-24-431

Nebraska

NE Rev. Statute §§76-1401 to -1449; 69-2301 to -2314
RENT RULES: §76-1414(3)
SECURITY DEPOSIT: §76-1416
NONPAYMENT OF RENT: §76-1431
BREACH OF LEASE: §76-1431
RENT WITHHOLDING: §76-1428
REPAIR AND DEDUCT: §76-1427
LL ACCESS: §§76-1423, -1438
LL RETALIATION: §§76-14, -1439

Nevada

NV Rev. Statute §§118A.010-.530
RENT RULES: §§118A.210; 118A.200(3)(c)
SECURITY DEPOSIT: §§118A.240-.250
NONPAYMENT OF RENT: §§40.251, .2512, .253
BREACH OF LEASE: §40.2516
RENT WITHHOLDING: §76-1428
REPAIR AND DEDUCT: §76-1427
LL ACCESS: §118A.330
LL RETALIATION: §118A.510

New Hampshire

NH Rev. Statute §§540:1-29 to 540-A:1-8
RENT RULES: —-
SECURITY DEPOSIT: §§540-A:5 to :8
NONPAYMENT OF RENT: §§540:2, :3
BREACH OF LEASE: —-
RENT WITHHOLDING: §540:13d
REPAIR AND DEDUCT: —-
LL ACCESS: §540-A:3
LL RETALIATION: §§540:13-a, 13-b

New Jersey

NJ Statute §§46:8-1 to -49
RENT RULES: §2A-42-6.1
SECURITY DEPOSIT: §§46:8-19 to -26
NONPAYMENT OF RENT: §§2A:18-61.2; 2A:42-9
BREACH OF LEASE: Vijon v. Custodio, 598 A2.d 251 (NJ Supr. L. 1991)
RENT WITHHOLDING: §§2A: 42-85 to -96
REPAIR AND DEDUCT: —
LL ACCESS: —
LL RETALIATION: §§2A:42-10.10, -10.12

New Mexico

NM Statute §§47-8-1 to -52
RENT RULES: §47-8-15
SECURITY DEPOSIT: §47-8-18
NONPAYMENT OF RENT: §47-8-33
BREACH OF LEASE: §47-8-33
RENT WITHHOLDING: §47-8-30
REPAIR AND DEDUCT: §47-8-29
LL ACCESS: §47-8-24
LL RETALIATION: §47-8-39

New York

NY Gen. Oblig. Law §§7-101 to -109; Real Prop. Laws §§220-238; Multi-Dwelling
Laws §§1-11; Multi-Resid. Laws §§305
RENT RULES: —
SECURITY DEPOSIT: Gen. Law §§7-101 to -109
NONPAYMENT OF RENT: Real Prop. §711
BREACH OF LEASE: Real Prop. §§711(3), (6)
RENT WITHHOLDING: Multi. Res. §305-a
REPAIR AND DEDUCT: Multi. Res. §§305-c, 235-a
LL ACCESS: —
LL RETALIATION: Gen. Law §42-37.1

North Carolina

NC Gen. Statute §§42-1 to -56
RENT RULES: §42-46
SECURITY DEPOSIT: §§42-50 to -56
NONPAYMENT OF RENT: §42-3
BREACH OF LEASE: —-
RENT WITHHOLDING: —-
REPAIR AND DEDUCT: —-
LL ACCESS: —-
LL RETALIATION: §42-37.1

North Dakota

ND Code §§47-16-01 to -41
RENT RULES: §47-16-07
SECURITY DEPOSIT: §47-16-07.1
NONPAYMENT OF RENT: —-
BREACH OF LEASE: —-
RENT WITHHOLDING: —-
REPAIR AND DEDUCT: §47-16-13
LL ACCESS: §47-16-07.3
LL RETALIATION: —-

Ohio

OH Rev. Code §§5121.01-.19
RENT RULES: —-
SECURITY DEPOSIT: §5321.16
NONPAYMENT OF RENT: —-
BREACH OF LEASE: §5321.11
RENT WITHHOLDING: §5321.07
REPAIR AND DEDUCT: —-
LL ACCESS: §§5321.04(B), .05(B)
LL RETALIATION: §5321.02

Oklahoma

OK Statute, Title 41 §§1-136
RENT RULES: §§109
SECURITY DEPOSIT: §115
NONPAYMENT OF RENT: §131
BREACH OF LEASE: §132
RENT WITHHOLDING: —
REPAIR AND DEDUCT: §121
LL ACCESS: §128
LL RETALIATION: —

Oregon

OR Rev. Statute §§90.100 to .840
RENT RULES: OR §§90.240(4)(a); 90.260
SECURITY DEPOSIT: §§90.300-.302
NONPAYMENT OF RENT: §90.400(2)(a)(b)
BREACH OF LEASE: §§90.400, .405
RENT WITHHOLDING: §90.370
REPAIR AND DEDUCT: §§90.335, .360, .365, 370
LL ACCESS: §90.322 LL RETALIATION: §90.385

Pennsylvania

PA Statute, Title 68 §§250.101-.513
RENT RULES: —
SECURITY DEPOSIT: §§250.511a-.512
NONPAYMENT OF RENT: §250.501
BREACH OF LEASE: §§250.501, .505-A
RENT WITHHOLDING: §250.206
REPAIR AND DEDUCT: —
LL ACCESS: —
LL RETALIATION: —

Rhode Island

RI Gen. Law §§34-18-1 to -57
RENT RULES: §§34-18-35, -15(c)
SECURITY DEPOSIT: §34-18-19 NON-PAYMENT OF RENT: §§34-18-35, -51
BREACH OF LEASE: §34-18-36
RENT WITHHOLDING: §34-18-32
REPAIR AND DEDUCT: §§34-18-30, -31
LL ACCESS: §§34-18-26, -46 LL RETALIATION: §34-18-46

South Carolina

SC Code §§27-40-10 to -910
RENT RULES: §27-40-310
SECURITY DEPOSIT: §27-40-410
NONPAYMENT OF RENT: §27-40-710
BREACH OF LEASE: §27-40-710
RENT WITHHOLDING: §§27-40-640, -790
REPAIR AND DEDUCT: §§27-40-640, -790
LL ACCESS: §27-40-530
LL RETALIATION: §27-40-910

South Dakota

SD Real Property Laws §§43-32-1 to -29
RENT RULES: §43-32-12
SECURITY DEPOSIT: §§43-32-6.1, -24
NONPAYMENT OF RENT: §21-16-2
BREACH OF LEASE: —-
RENT WITHHOLDING: §43-32-9
REPAIR AND DEDUCT: §43-32-9
LL ACCESS: —-
LL RETALIATION: —-

Tennessee

TN Code §§66-28-101 to -517
RENT RULES: §§66-28-201(c),(d)
SECURITY DEPOSIT: §66-28-301
NONPAYMENT OF RENT: §66-28-505
BREACH OF LEASE: §§66-28-401, 505
RENT WITHHOLDING: —-
REPAIR AND DEDUCT: §66-28-502
LL ACCESS: §66-28-403
LL RETALIATION: §§66-28-514; 68-111-105

Texas

TX Prop. Code §§91.001-92.301
RENT RULES: —-
SECURITY DEPOSIT: §§92.101-.109
NONPAYMENT OF RENT: —- BREACH OF LEASE: —-
RENT WITHHOLDING: —-
REPAIR AND DEDUCT: §92.0561
LL ACCESS: —-
LL RETALIATION: §92.331

Utah

UT Code §§57-17-1 to -5, -22-1 to -6
RENT RULES: —-
SECURITY DEPOSIT: §§57-17-1 to -5
NONPAYMENT OF RENT: §78-36-3 BREACH OF LEASE: §78-36-3
RENT WITHHOLDING: —-
REPAIR AND DEDUCT: —-
LL ACCESS: §57-22-5(c) LL RETALIATION: Bldg. Monitoring Sys. v. Paxton, 905 P.2d 1215 (Utah 1995)

Vermont

VT Statute, Title 9, Chapter 137 §§4451-4468
RENT RULES: §4455
SECURITY DEPOSIT: §4461
NONPAYMENT OF RENT: §4467
BREACH OF LEASE: —-
RENT WITHHOLDING: §4458
REPAIR AND DEDUCT: §4459
LL ACCESS: §4460
LL RETALIATION: §4465

Virginia

VA Code §§55-248.1 to .40
RENT RULES: §55-248-7(c)
SECURITY DEPOSIT: §55-248.11
NONPAYMENT OF RENT: §§55-225; 55-243; 55-248.31
BREACH OF LEASE: §55-248.31
RENT WITHHOLDING: §55-248.25 to .30
REPAIR AND DEDUCT: §55-248.32
LL ACCESS: §§55-248.18, .38
LL RETALIATION: §55-248.39

Washington

WA Rev. Code §§59.04.010-.900, .18.010-.910
RENT RULES: —
SECURITY DEPOSIT: §§59.18.260 to .285
NONPAYMENT OF RENT: §59.12.030
BREACH OF LEASE: §59.12.030
RENT WITHHOLDING: §59.18.115
REPAIR AND DEDUCT: §59.18.100
LL ACCESS: §59.18.150
LL RETALIATION: §§59.18.240, .250

West Virginia

WV Code §§37-6-1 to -30; 55-3A-1
RENT RULES: —
SECURITY DEPOSIT: —
NONPAYMENT OF RENT: §55-3A-1
BREACH OF LEASE: §55-3A-1
RENT WITHHOLDING: —
REPAIR AND DEDUCT: —
LL ACCESS: —
LL RETALIATION: §§55-3A-1, -3

Wisconsin

WI Statute §§704.01-.40; ATCP 134.01-.10
RENT RULES: —
SECURITY DEPOSIT: Code ATCP §134.06
NONPAYMENT OF RENT: §§704.17, 704.17(2), 704.17(3)
BREACH OF LEASE: §704.17(3)
RENT WITHHOLDING: §254.30(1)(b)
REPAIR AND DEDUCT: —
LL ACCESS: §704.05(2)
LL RETALIATION: §704.45; ATCP 134.09(5)

Wyoming

WY Statute §§34-2-128 to -130; 1-21-1201 to -1211
RENT RULES: —-
SECURITY DEPOSIT: §1-21-1208, -1209
NONPAYMENT OF RENT: —-
BREACH OF LEASE: §1-21-1205
RENT WITHHOLDING: —-
REPAIR AND DEDUCT: —-
LL ACCESS: —-
LL RETALIATION: —-

Statutes and Notice Required for Changing or Terminating

Almost every state requires that notice must be given to change and/or terminate agreements; at least 30 days' notice for month-to-month tenancies and 7 days' notice for week-to-week tenancies. Some states do not have explicit statutes regarding how much notice is required for increasing rent, and some states have no statutes regarding rental increase notices.

Unless otherwise stated, notice required is for both the landlord and tenant. Be sure to double-check your state's laws before making any changes or terminating your rental agreements. (L=landlord, T=tenant, M-M=month-to-month, and W-W=week-to-week).

Month-to-Month and Week-to-Week Tenancies

State	Notice Required	Statute
Alabama	M-M: 10 days W-W: 10 days	AL §35-9-3, -5
Alaska	M-M: 30 days W-W: 14 days	AS §34.03.290(a)(b)
Arizona	M-M: 30 days W-W: 10 days	AZ §33.1375
Arkansas	M-M: —- W-W: —-	No statute
California	M-M: 30 days W-W: 7 days	CA §1946

State	Notice Required	Statute
Colorado	M-M: 10 days W-W: 3 days	CO §13-40-107; 38-12-202
Connecticut	M-M: — W-W: —	No statute
Delaware	M-M: 60 days W-W: not specified	Title 25 DE §5107
D.C.	M-M: 30 days W-W: —	DC §45-1402
Florida	M-M: 15 days W-W: 7 days	FL §83.57
Georgia	M-M: 60 days (L), 30 days (T) W-W: 60 days (L), 30 days (T)	GA §47-7-7
Hawaii	M-M: 45 days (L), 28 days (T) W-W: 10 days; 15 days to increase rent	HI §521-71
Idaho	M-M: 30 days W-W: not stated	ID §55-208
Illinois	M-M: 30 days W-W: 7 days	No statute
Indiana	M-M: 30 days W-W: 7 days	IN §32-7-1-3
Iowa	M-M: 30 days W-W: 10 days	IA §562A.34
Kansas	M-M: 30 days W-W: 7 days	KS §58-2570
Kentucky	M-M: 30 days W-W: 7 days	KY §383.695
Louisiana	M-M: 10 days W-W: 10 days	LA CCP 2686
Maine	M-M: 30 days W-W: —	ME Title 14 §6002
Maryland	M-M: 30 days W-W: 7 days	MD §8-402
Massachusetts	M-M: 30 days W-W: 7 days	MA Chap. 186 §12

continues

Month-to-Month and Week-to-Week Tenancies (continued)

State	Notice Required	Statute
Michigan	M-M: 30 days W-W: 30 days	MI §554.134
Minnesota	M-M: 30 days W-W: no statute	MN §504B.135
Mississippi	M-M: 30 days W-W: 7 days	MI §89-8-19
Missouri	M-M: 30 days W-W: 7 days	MO §441.060
Montana	M-M: 30 days W-W: 7 days	MT §70-24-441
Nebraska	M-M: 30 days W-W: 7 days	NE §76-1437
Nevada	M-M: — W-W: —	No statute
New Hampshire	M-M: 30 days W-W: 7 days	NH §540.3
New Jersey	M-M: 30 days W-W: —	NJ §46:8-10
New Mexico	M-M: 30 days W-W: 7 days	NM §47-8-37
New York	M-M: 30 days W-W: —	NY Gen. Law §232-b
North Carolina	M-M: 7 days W-W: —	NC §42-14
North Dakota	M-M: 30 days W-W: not specified	ND §47-16-15
Ohio	M-M: 30 days W-W: 7 days	OH §5321.17
Oklahoma	M-M: 30 days W-W: 7 days	OK Title 41 §111
Oregon	M-M: 30 days W-W: 10 days	OR §91.060
Pennsylvania	M-M: 15 days W-W: 15 days	PA Tit. 68 §250.501

State	Notice Required	Statute
Rhode Island	M-M: 30 days W-W: 10 days	RI §34-18-37
South Carolina	M-M: 30 days W-W: 7 days	SC §27-40-770
South Dakota	M-M: 30 days, T can terminate within 15 days of receiving change in lease W-W: —	SD §43-32-13
Tennessee	M-M: 30 days, 60 days to increase rent W-W: 10 days	TN §66-28-512
Texas	M-M: 30 days W-W: 7 days	TX §91.001
Utah	M-M: — W-W: —	No statute
Vermont	M-M: 30 days, 60 days to increase rent W-W: 7 days	VT Tit. 9 §4456; 4467
Virginia	M-M: 30 days W-W: 7 days	VA §55-223; 55-248.37
Washington	M-M: 30 days to change, 20 days to terminate W-W: not specified	WA §59.04.020
West Virginia	M-M & W-W: One full rental period	WV §37-6-5
Wisconsin	M-M: 28 days W-W: 7 days	WI §704.19
Wyoming	M-M: — W-W: —	No statute

A Landlord's Resource Guide

The following is a list of Rental Management software, rental-property-owner organizations, and trade associations throughout the country that rental owners may find useful. This information was compiled with help from Internet resources as well as the authors' own personal address books and research.

Rental Management Software

Software is another tool that rental investors must consider obtaining to help operate their property and track tenants, rent payments, and repairs. The authors, after careful research, listed the following software products as potential useful choices for rental owners and managers based on the features each possessed. Although the authors are not endorsing the products, they do feel that key software features are essential for proper successful property management. These are just a few of the products available; it is left to you to compare the features and prices of software to determine which, if any, is right for you.

Rent Manager XP
www.rentmanager.com
1-800-669-0871

Rent Right
www.rent-right.com
1-800-736-8065

Promas Landlord Software Center
www.promas.com
1-800-397-1499

HTC Apartment Manager 2.0
Safer Software
www.aptmgr.com
205-956-0636

The Property Manager Release 4
Just So Software
www.softwareforlandlords.com
937-322-2708

The Landlord Report
www.mdansby.com
616-219-2818

National Rental Property Organizations

The United Property Owners Association of America
PO Box 395
Vernon, CT. 06066
860-871-2121
www.upoaa.com

National Apartment Association
201 North Union St., Suite 200
Alexandria, VA 22315
703-518-6141
www.naahq.org (Several State Affiliations)

National Multi Housing Council
1850 M Street N.W. #540
Washington, DC 20036-5803
202-974-2300
www.nmhc.org (Informational Site Only)

National Association of Residential Property Managers
PO Box 140647
Austin, TX 78714-0647
1-800-782-3452
www.narpm.org (Management Agents for Owners Only)

The Small Property Owners of America
PO Box 8115
Cambridge, MA 02139-8115
617-354-5533
www.spoa.com

State and Local Rental Property Associations

The following list includes organizations that granted permission to be listed in this book. If your state or area is not listed, check with one of the national organizations listed above to find a local association.

Alabama

Apartment Association of North Alabama
2608 Arti St. #300
Huntsville, AL 3580 5
256-539-2998
www.aanaonline.org (NAA Affiliate)

Arizona

Arizona Multihousing Association
5110 N. 44th St, Suite L160
Phoenix, AZ 85018
1-800-326-6403 or 602-224-0135
www.azama.org

California

Apartment Association of Greater Los Angeles
621 S. Westmoreland Ave.
Los Angeles, CA 90005
213-384-4131
www.aagla.org

Apartment Owners Association
6445 Sepulveda Blvd. #30
Van Nuys, CA 91411
1-800-827-4262
www.aoausa.com

California Apartment Association
980 9th St., 200
Sacramento, CA 95814-2741
1-800-967-4222
www.caanet.org

San Francisco Apartment Association
265 Ivy St.
San Francisco, CA 94102
415-255-2288

Colorado

Apartment Association of Metro Denver
650 S. Cherry St., Suite 635
Denver, CO 80246
303-329-3300
www.aamdhq.org

Apartment Association of Colorado Springs
888 West Garden of Gods St. #103
Colorado Springs, CO 80907
719-264-9195
www.aacshq.org

Connecticut

The Connecticut Rental Housing Alliance
PO Box 985
Bristol, CT 06011-0985
860-585-0520
www.rhol.org/crha

The Greater Bristol Property Owners Association
PO Box 985
Bristol, CT 06011
860-585-0520

Norwich Property Owners Association
43 12th St.
Norwich, CT 06360
860-889-7190

The Tolland County Property Owners Association
PO Box 395
Vernon, CT 06066
860-871-2121
www.tollandpoa.com

District of Columbia

Apartment and Office Building Association of Metropolitan Washington
1050 17th St. NW #300
Washington, DC 20036
202-296-3390
www.aoboa-metro.org

Florida

Florida Apartment Association
1133 West Morse Blvd. #201
Winter Park, FL 32789
407-647-8839
www.fl-apartments.com

Indiana

Central Indiana Real Estate Investors Association
7931 South Franklin Rd.
Indianapolis, IN 46259
317-514-0009
www.indianapolislandlords.org

Kentucky

Greater Cincinnati & Northern Kentucky Apartment Association
525 West 5th St. #233
Covington, KY 41011
859-581-5990
www.gcnkaa.org

Louisiana

Apartment Association of Southwest Louisiana
PO Box 6534
Lake Charles, LA 70606
337-477-2951

Massachusetts

Massachusetts Rental Housing Association, Inc.
167 Milk St. #442
Boston, MA 02109
617-491-5605
www.massrha.com

Attleboro Area Rental Housing Association
PO Box 3031
North Attleboro, MA 02761
508-699-0545

Rental Housing Association of Greater Springfield
PO Box 80553
Springfield, MA 01138
413-732-9899
www.rhags.org

Montana

Helena Property Owners Association
2021 11th Ave.
Helena, MT 59601
406-443-4480

Nevada

Apartment Association of Northern Nevada
575 Forest St. #105
Reno, NV 89509
775-322-6622

New Hampshire

New Hampshire Property Owners Association
PO Box 3181
Nashua, NH 03061
603-881-3682
www.nhpoa.org

New Mexico

Apartment Association of New Mexico
6755 Academy Rd. NE #B
Albuquerque, NM 87109
505-822-1114
www.aanm.org

New York

Schenectady Rental Property Owners Association
PO Box 2222
Scotia, NY 12302
518-374-6367

Small Property Owners of New York
1681 Third Ave.
New York, NY 10128
212-410-4600
sponyinc@aol.com

North Carolina

Charlotte Apartment Association
2101 Rexford Rd. #330
Charlotte, NC 28211
704-334-9511
www.cltaa.org

Ohio

Greater Cincinnati & Northern Kentucky Apartment Association
525 West 5th St. #233
Covington, KY 41011
859-581-5990
www.gcnkaa.org

Greater Dayton Apartment Association
2555 S Dixie Dr., Suite 100
Dayton, OH 45409
937-293-1170
www.gdaa.org

Northeast Ohio Apartment Association
408 W Saint Cloud Ave. #200
Cleveland, OH 44113
1-800-506-2256
www.noaaonline.com

Oregon

Rental Housing Association of Greater Portland
10520 NE Weidler
Portland, OR 972 20
503-254-4723
www.orapt@jps.com

South Dakota

South Dakota Multi-Housing Association
808 South Minnesota Ave.
Sioux Falls, SD 57104
605-336-7756

Vermont

Vermont Rental Property Owners Association
158 North Main St.
Rutland, VT 05701
802-773-9707
www.vrpoa.org

Vermont Apartment Owners Association
PO Box 701
Shelborne, VT 05482
802-985-2764
www.vermontapartmentowners.org

Virginia

Virginia Apartment & Management Association
8611 Mayland Dr.
Richmond, VA 23294
804-273-6801
www.vamaonline.org

Washington

Rental Housing Assoc. of Puget Sound
529 Warren Ave. North
Seattle, WA 98109
206-283-0816
www.rha-ps.com

Clark County Rental Association
5620 Gher Rd. #I
Vancouver, WA 98662-6166
360-693-2272
www.clarkcountyrentalassociation.org

Wakima Valley Landlords Association
1218 West Lincoln
Wakima, WA 98908
509-457-4770
www.wakimalandlords.org

Washington Apartment Association
924 Capitol Way South, Suite 211
Olympia, WA 98501
360-534-0266

Wisconsin

Wisconsin Apartment Association
7 N Pinckney St. # 225D
Madison, WI 53703
608-227-1024
www.waaonline.org

Glossary

absentee owner A rental owner who does not reside at the property.

addendum A special section added to contract to list special terms that may apply.

application A type of form used by landlords and property managers. It is filled out by potential new tenants as a screening and information-gathering technique.

appraisal The process by which someone estimates the quantity, quality, or value of something.

appraiser A real-estate professional who specializes in appraisals.

appreciation An increase in property value.

asbestos A mineral once used in insulation and other materials; it can cause respiratory diseases.

assessment A value placed on a property for tax purposes.

assessor The town or county employee responsible for fairly assessing property.

bait and switch An illegal form of advertising and selling in which an item is offered for sale or rent but is not available for customers.

broker A person who acts as an intermediary on behalf of another for a fee or commission.

building code Regulations that set the minimum requirements for how buildings are to be constructed to protect public health and safety.

bundle of rights A legal concept of land ownership that includes ownership of all legal rights to the land such as possession, legal control, and enjoyment.

capital gain The profit earned from the sale of an asset.

capital improvement A physical improvement to a property that increases the value of property.

capitalization A mathematical process for estimating the value of a property using the proper rate of return on the investment and the annual net operating income expected to be produced by the property. The formula is expressed as

Income/Rate = Value

caveat emptor A Latin phrase meaning "Let the buyer beware."

checker An individual who secretly poses as a potential applicant in an effort to investigate fair trade practices.

common law The body of law based on custom, usage, and court decisions.

credit check A legal screening technique used to determine whether an applicant is qualified to rent.

deductible The amount of money the insured is responsible for before a claim will be paid.

demand The amount of goods people are willing and able to buy at a given price.

double damages Money equal to twice a month's rent, sometimes awarded to a victorious tenant in a lawsuit.

employee Someone who works for another person.

equity The interest or value that an owner or tenant has in a property, over and above any indebtedness.

escrow The process by which funds are set aside for certain purposes and are used only to pay certain encumbrances.

eviction The legal process to remove a person from occupation of real estate.

execution A legal order directing an official to enforce a judgment against the property of a debtor.

expense   The outflow of funds from a business used to carry out certain operations of the business.

Fair Housing Act   The federal law that prohibits discrimination in housing based on race, religion, gender, handicap, familial status, or national origin.

Fair Rent Commission   Elected panel charged with overseeing rent rates in a specific area. Typically charged with handling disputes relating to excessive rent charges.

fire code   Regulations that set the minimum requirements for fire safety.

fire insurance   A type of insurance policy obtained to protect an owner of real estate from loss of value due to fire.

fixture   An item of personal property that has been converted to real property by being permanently affixed to the property.

foreclosure   A legal procedure in which a property used as security for a debt is sold to satisfy the debt in the event of default of payment of the debt.

FMR   Abbreviation for Fair Market Rent.

health code   Regulations that set the minimum requirements for clean and sanitary conditions.

homeowners insurance   A standardized package insurance policy that covers a residential real-estate owner against financial loss from fire, theft, liability, and other common risks.

Housing Assistance Payment Contract   Often referred to as the HAP contract, this is a special contract that is used by the Federal Government when processing Section-8 subsidies for housing.

housing code   Regulations that set the minimum requirements in regards to property maintenance.

implied warranty of habitability   A theory in landlord/tenant law in which the landlord renting residential property implies that the property is habitable and fit to occupy.

income   Revenue generated or earned from working and investments.

inherited tenants   Occupants who continue to possess a rental unit after the property has been transferred to a new owner.

inspector   An individual who inspects a property for certain conditions.

investment Money directed toward the purchase, improvement, or development of an asset in expectation of income and profits.

judgment The formal decision on the respective rights and claims of the parties in a lawsuit or court action.

jury rig A slang word that describes a way of making repairs.

landlord An owner of land.

last month's rent Monies used to pay the rent for the last month of occupancy.

lease A written or oral contract between a landlord and a tenant that transfers the right of exclusive possession for a specified period of time and a specific amount of consideration.

lease assignment A transfer of a leased interest in property.

lessee A tenant, or the person to whom the property is rented.

lessor A landlord, or the person who rents the property to a lessee.

letter of understanding A notice sent to a rental owner from a tenant regarding the terms of a lease or rental agreement.

liability insurance A type of insurance that protects a property owner against losses from claims of liability such as falls or other injuries.

Limited Liability Company Sometimes referred to as an LLC, this is a legal entity that is allowed to own and operate a business without subjecting its owners to full liability.

make ready A slang term that means rental unit preparation. It is a rental unit that still needs to be prepared before renting.

manager A person who oversees the day-to-day operations of a business or property on behalf of an owner.

market rent The most probable price at which property can be rented.

mill rate The percentage of an assessment charged for property taxes. A mill is equal to $\frac{1}{10}$ of a cent.

minor An individual under the legal age of majority who does not have the legal capacity to enter a contract.

month-to-month tenancy A periodic tenancy under which the tenant rents for one month at a time.

notice of termination   A notice sent by either party in a contract regarding the party's intent to terminate the contract.

occupancy permit   A certificate given to a property owner from an inspector declaring a unit or building fit to occupy.

offer and acceptance   Two essential components of a valid contract, a "meeting of the minds."

owner occupied   When an owner of a rental property resides at the property.

Philadelphia lawyer   A genius.

professional tenant   A tenant who is well educated in the art of stealing from landlords.

profit   The money left over from the income earned on an investment after expenses are paid.

protected categories   Specific categories of people protected by federal law from acts of discrimination.

Real Estate Settlement Procedures Act (RESPA)   The federal law that requires certain disclosures to consumers about mortgage loan settlements. The law also prohibits the payment on receipt of kickbacks and certain kinds of referral fees.

receipt   A slip of paper given to a customer as proof of payment made.

reference check   A type of screening technique in which personal references are checked for an applicant.

rent   A fixed, periodic payment made by a tenant of a property to the owner for possession and use, usually by mutual prior agreement.

rent control   Regulations enacted to prevent and stabilize the increased payment of rent and place limitation on the landlord's right to evict. Sometimes referred to as rent stabilization.

rental agreement   A written or oral contract used in month-to-month agreements.

renter's insurance   A standardized package insurance policy that covers a tenant against losses due to fire, theft, and liability.

revaluation   The period and process in which property is assessed in a locality for tax purposes. Typically, the process takes place every 10 years.

Section 8   A type of rental subsidy.

security deposit   A payment made by a tenant and held by the landlord during the lease term to protect against the default or destruction of a rented property by a tenant.

stipulated agreement   A court-mediated agreement between a landlord and a tenant. If the agreement is not adhered to properly, judgment is awarded. Sometimes referred to as a "stip."

sublease   Type of lease used when lessee leases premises to a third party.

subletting   The leasing of premises by a lessee to a third party.

superintendent   An individual hired by a landlord to do light repair and maintenance at a property.

supply   The amount of goods available in a market to be sold at a given price.

tax review committee   Panel of officials who listen to and review a challenge by a property owner regarding a tax assessment.

ten percenter   A private insurance adjuster.

tenancy at will   A type of tenancy created when a landlord and tenant agree to rent for an indefinite period of time.

tenant   A person who rents a property.

title insurance   A policy insuring an owner or mortgagee against loss by reason of defects in the title to the real estate, other than encumbrances.

title search   The examination of public records in regard to a particular parcel of real estate.

two per bedroom plus   The HUD standard for determining occupancy limits.

unit   Rental space.

vacancy   Empty rental space.

zoning ordinances   An exercise of police power by a municipality to regulate and control the character and use of property.

Index

Check Out These
Best-Selling
COMPLETE IDIOT'S GUIDES®

Understanding **Catholicism** — SECOND EDITION
1-59257-085-2
$18.95

Learning **Spanish** — THIRD EDITION
0-02-864451-4
$18.95

The **Bible** — SECOND EDITION
0-02-864382-8
$18.95

Being a **Groom** — SECOND EDITION
0-02-864456-5
$9.95

Grammar and **Style** — SECOND EDITION
1-59257-115-8
$16.95

Playing the **Guitar** — SECOND EDITION
0-02-864244-9
$21.95 w/CD

Personal Finance in Your **20s & 30s** — SECOND EDITION
0-02-864374-7
$19.95

Knitting and Crocheting — SECOND EDITION — Illustrated
1-59257-089-5
$16.95

The **Perfect Resume** — THIRD EDITION
0-02-864440-9
$14.95

Buying and Selling a Home — FOURTH EDITION
1-59257-120-4
$18.95

Low-Carb Meals
1-59257-180-8
$18.95

Calculus
0-02-864365-8
$18.95

More than *450 titles* in *30 different categories*
Available at booksellers everywhere

ALPHA